Science Olympiad

Highly useful for all school students participating
in Various Olympiads & Competitions

Series Editor Keshav Mohan

Authors
Preeti Gupta (Chemistry) • *Karuna Thakur* (Physics) • *Shikha* (Biology)

Class 7

arihant

ARIHANT PRAKASHAN, MEERUT

Contents

1.	Nutrition in Plants	1-7
2.	Nutrition in Animals	8-15
3.	Heat	16-24
4.	Acids, Bases and Salts	25-33
5.	Physical and Chemical Changes	34-40
6.	Respiration in Organisms	41-48
7.	Transportation in Plants and Animals	49-54
8.	Reproduction in Plants	55-61
9.	Motion and Time	62-68
10.	Electric Current and Its Effects	69-79
11.	Light	80-86

Practice Sets (1-3) — 89-103
Answers and Explanations — 107-120

Chapter 1

Nutrition in Plants

1. Given below are some chemical changes that take place in living organisms. Which of these chemical changes is/are an exception for green plants?

    A. Glucose $\longrightarrow$ Cellulose   B. Glucose $\longrightarrow$ Glycogen
    C. Starch $\longrightarrow$ Glycogen   D. Starch $\longrightarrow$ Glucose

Choose the correct option.

  a A and B   b B and C   c Only D   d Only A

2. Some of the features of plant leaves are listed below

    I. Hair on lower surface   II. Large surface area   III. Waxy cuticle

Which features reduce water loss from the leaves?

  a I and II   b I and III   c II and III   d I, II and III

3. Observe the part of the leaf shown in the figure given alongside. Identify the part and its respective functions.

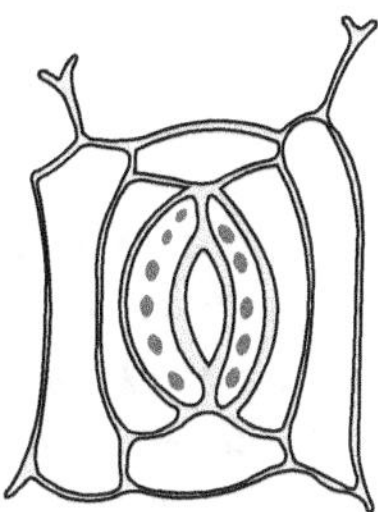

	Part of Leaf		Function
A.	Guard cells	1.	Regulate rate of respiration
B.	Stomata	2.	Regulate rate of transpiration
C.	Stoma	3.	Gaseous exchange to facilitate photosynthesis
D.	Chloroplast	4.	Contain green pigment for photosynthesis

Codes

  a B – 2   b A – 2   c B – 3   d D – 4

4. Pick out the correct name and function of part '*A*' in the figure given below from the options that follow.

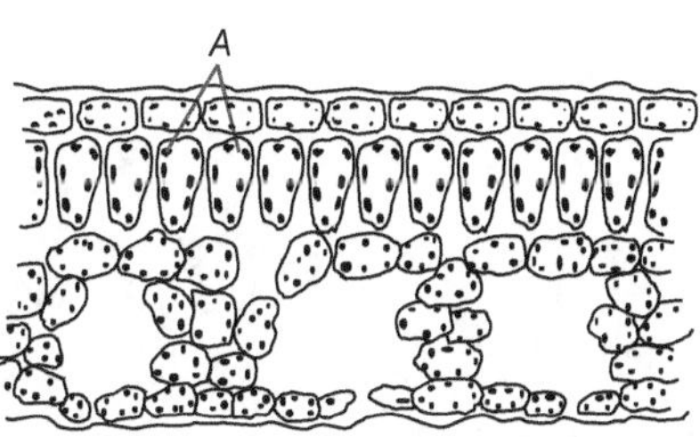

    A. Provide chemical energy   B. Allow gaseous exchange
    C. Regulate rate of transpiration   D. Conduct photosynthesis by absorbing sunlight
    I. Stoma   II. Chlorophyll
  III. Guard cells   IV. Chloroplast

Mark the correct match.

  a I–B   b II–C
  c IV–D   d III–B

5. The chemical equation for photosynthesis is as follows:

$$X + \text{Water} \xrightarrow[Y]{\text{Sunlight}} \text{Carbohydrate} + Z$$

What are the identities of X, Y and Z?

	X	Y	Z
a	Carbon dioxide	Chlorophyll	Oxygen
b	Carbon dioxide	Chloroplast	Oxygen
c	Carbon dioxide	Chloroplast	Glucose
d	Oxygen	Chlorophyll	Carbon dioxide

6. In which of the following ways are the products of photosynthesis used by plants?

I. To make vitamins.

II. To make oils (fats).

III. To build up cell wall.

Codes

a I and II   b I and III

c II and III   d I, II and III

7. The following equations represent the process in photosynthesis.

$$6CO_2 + 6H_2O \xrightarrow[\text{energy}]{\text{Sunlight}} C_6H_{12}O_6 + 6O_2$$

From your understanding of this process, if radioactive oxygen (^{18}O) was incorporated into water. Which of the following substances will contain ^{18}O?

a Oxygen   b Glucose

c Water   d Carbon dioxide

8. Which of the following substances are synthesised in plants, using mineral salts from the soil?

I. Protein

II. Chlorophyll

III. Starch

Codes

a Only II   b I and II

c I, II and III   d I and III

9. Find out A, B and C in the passage from the options that follow:

_A_ are synthesised by plants through the process of photosynthesis. 'A' are made of carbon, hydrogen and _B_. These are used to synthesise other components of food such as proteins and fats. Proteins are _C_ substances.

a A–Vitamins, B–Nitrogen, C–Nutritious

b A–Carbohydrates, B–Nitrogen, C–Nutritious

c A–Carbohydrates, B–Oxygen, C–Nitrogenous

d A –Vitamins, B–Oxygen, C–Nitrogenous

10. What does I shows in the given figure? Also mention the mode of nutrition.

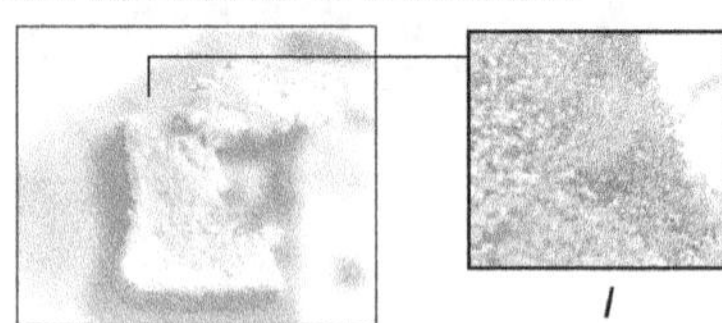

A.	Bacterial growth	i.	Parasitic
B.	Fungal growth	ii.	Autotrophic
C.	Viral growth	iii.	Symbiotic
D.	Lichen	iv.	Saprotrophic

Choose the correct option.

a A – iii   b B – iv

c C – i   d D – ii

11. Which type of nutrition is observed in the given figure? Choose the set of organisms with this type of nutrition.

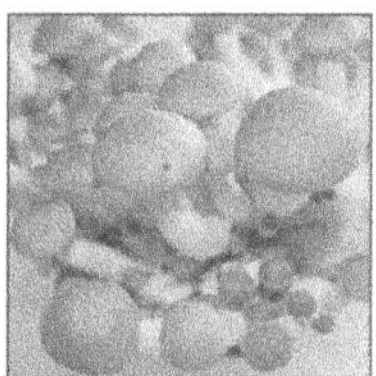

A.	Heterotrophic	i.	Pitcher and sundew
B.	Saprotrophic	ii.	Lichen and _Rhizobium_
C.	Autotrophic	iii.	Mushrooms and bread mould
D.	Both A and B	iv.	_Cuscuta_ and cornsnut

Codes

a A – iv   b D – iii

c B – i   d B – ii

12. Observe the graphical representation below and opt the option that defines the limiting factor.

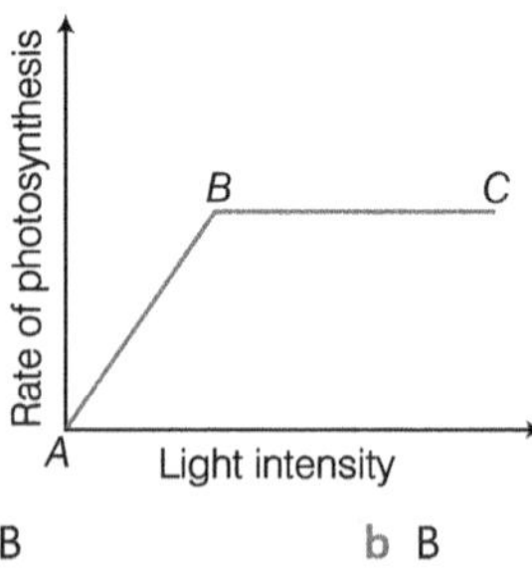

a A – B   b B

c B – C   d C

13. Preeti set-up an experiment as shown in the figure. She took a destarched plant and left it in sunlight for few hours. Then, she tested X and Y leaves for the presence of starch and observed that leaf X did not give starch test while leaf Y was tested positive for it.

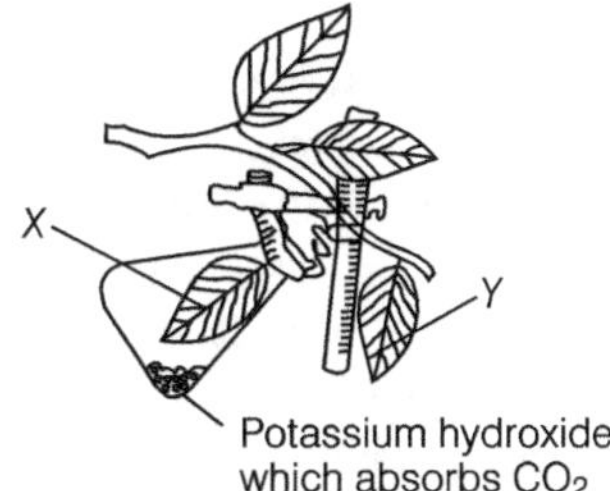

What does this experiment conclude?
a Chlorophyll is necessary for photosynthesis.
b Carbon dioxide is necessary for photosynthesis.
c Light is necessary for photosynthesis.
d Oxygen is given out during photosynthesis.

14. The most abundant gas in our atmosphere cannot be utilised by plants directly in its atmospheric form. It is therefore captured by certain organisms that live symbiotically in their roots. Identify the gas and the organism.

	Gas		Organism
A.	Hydrogen	i.	Yeast
B.	Carbon dioxide	ii.	*Rhizobium*
C.	Nitrogen	iii.	Earthworms
D.	Oxygen	iv.	Goats

Mark the correct option.
a A – iv
b B – i
c C – ii
d D – iii

15. Choose the correct pairs.
A. Green plants – Autotrophs
B. *Rhizobium* – Parasitic
C. *Cuscuta* – Insectivorous
D. Mushrooms – Saprophytes

Codes
a A and B
b B and C
c C and D
d All except B

16. The given diagram shows the arrangement of cells inside a green leaf.

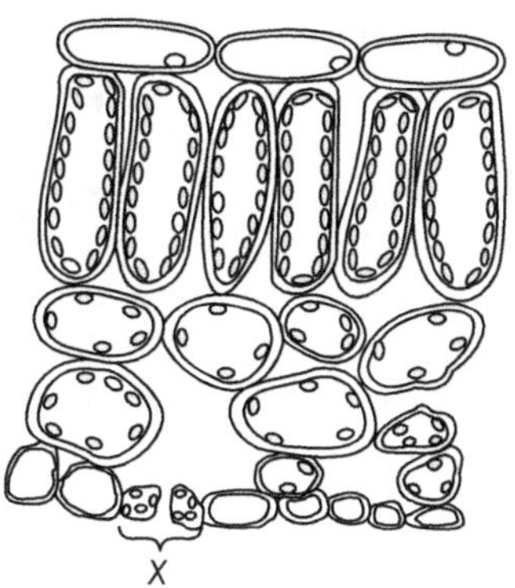

Name a substance that is carried to leaf cells $\underline{A}$ and product that moves out $\underline{B}$ from the part X.

	A	B
a	Water	Minerals
b	Carbon dioxide	Oxygen
c	Oxygen	Carbon dioxide
d	Starch	Amino acids

17. Lichen is an example of a symbiotic association. Here two different species live together and help each other in obtaining food. It can be represented by lichen $\longrightarrow A + B$. Choose appropriate term for A and B

Codes
a A – Bacteria, B – Fungi
b A – Fungi, B – Algae
c A – Bacteria, B – Algae
d A – Fungi, B – Legumes

18. Which of the following statements about photosynthesis is/are correct?
A. Energy is released during photosynthesis.
B. Photosynthesis occurs only in the presence of CO_2.
C. Glucose is a product formed during photosynthesis.
D. A plant kept in dark can photosynthesise.

Choose the correct option.
a A and B
b B and C
c C and D
d All are correct

19. Which of the following functions of the parts of a leaf is/are not correctly matched?

	Part of a leaf	Function
A.	Cuticle	Reduces the evaporation of water
B.	Stoma	To obtain CO_2 for photosynthesis
C.	Xylem	Distribution of water and mineral salts
D.	Phloem	Conduction of manufactured food

Codes
a All are correct
b A and B
c B, C and D
d Only B

20.

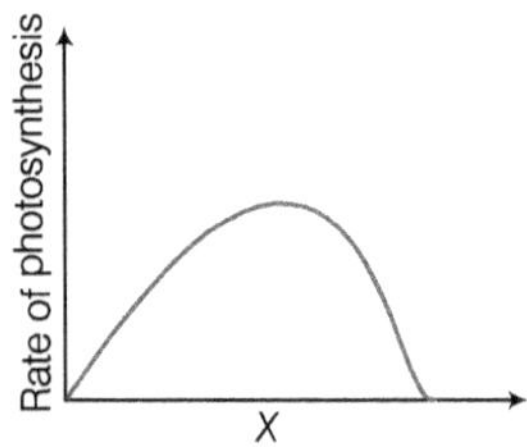

Study the graph given above carefully. Identify the factor(X) that is taken into account and the conclusion that can be drawn from it.

	Factors	Conclusion
a	Water	As the level of water increases, rate also increases
b	CO_2	Does not increase the rate beyond a certain level
c	Temperature	Photosynthesis ceases as temperature rises.
d	Light	Photosynthesis decreases beyond a point with increase in light intensity

21. The diagram below shows three green plants with identical leaf surface areas.

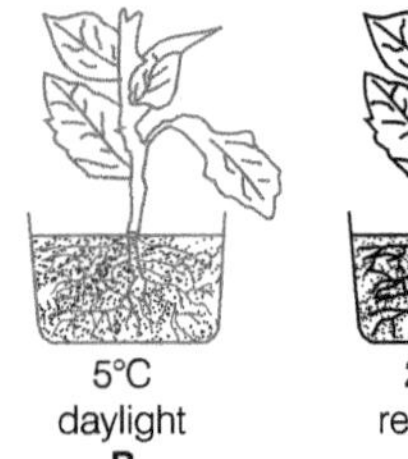

Assuming all other conditions were identical for all three plants, which of the plants would likely to photosynthesise, the slowest and the fastest?
a P is the slowest, R is the fastest.
b R is the slowest, Q is the fastest.
c P is the slowest, Q is the fastest.
d Q is the slowest, R is the fastest.

22. The teacher asked Roshan to perform an activity to test the presence of starch in leaves. Roshan wrote the steps randomly and is now confused as to how the activity is to be done.

Help him perform the activity by arranging the steps in correct sequence.
A. Pour dilute iodine solution over leaf.
B. Boil the leaf in alcohol.
C. Pluck the green leaf from plant.
D. Wash the leaf with water to remove chlorophyll.
E. Blue-black colour.

Codes
a C $\longrightarrow$ A $\longrightarrow$ E $\longrightarrow$ B $\longrightarrow$ D
b C $\longrightarrow$ B $\longrightarrow$ E $\longrightarrow$ D $\longrightarrow$ A
c C $\longrightarrow$ B $\longrightarrow$ D $\longrightarrow$ A $\longrightarrow$ E
d E $\longrightarrow$ B $\longrightarrow$ C $\longrightarrow$ D $\longrightarrow$ A

23. What is the function of the part labelled as A? Identify the plant and its mode of nutrition from the codes given below.

Codes
1. Flowering part of the plant
2. Trap insects for nutrition
3. Photosynthesise
4. Fruit of the plant
5. Sundew
6. Pitcher plant
7. Venus fly trap
8. Symbiotic
9. Insectivorous
10. Saprophytic

Choose the correct combination
a 1, 5 and 10
b 2, 6 and 9
c 3, 7 and 9
d 4, 6 and 8

24. The graph below shows the rate of oxygen uptake of a plant in 24 hours.

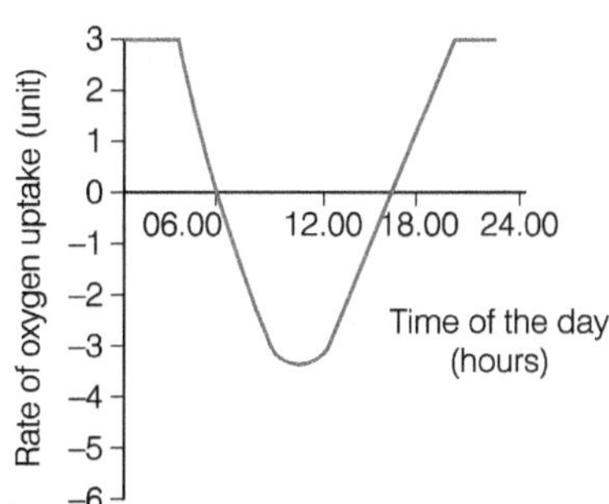

Which of the following correctly describes the plant at 1200 hour ?
a It carried out photosynthesis, but not respiration.
b It carried out photosynthesis at the maximum rate.
c The rate of photosynthesis was equal to the rate of respiration.
d The rate of photosynthesis was lower than the rate of respiration.

25. The solid arrows in the diagram below represent the direction of movement of substances P and Q when photosynthesis is taking place in a leaf.

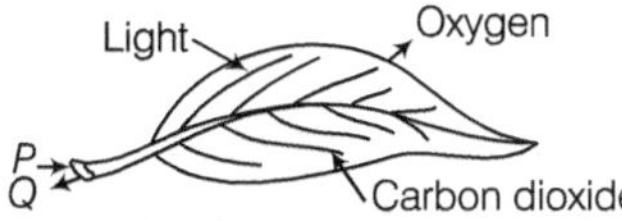

What are P and Q?

	P	Q
a	Water	Sugar
b	Starch	Sugar
c	Sugar	Starch
d	Water	Oxygen

Direction (Q. Nos.26-28) Refer to the diagram below showing an experimental set-up.

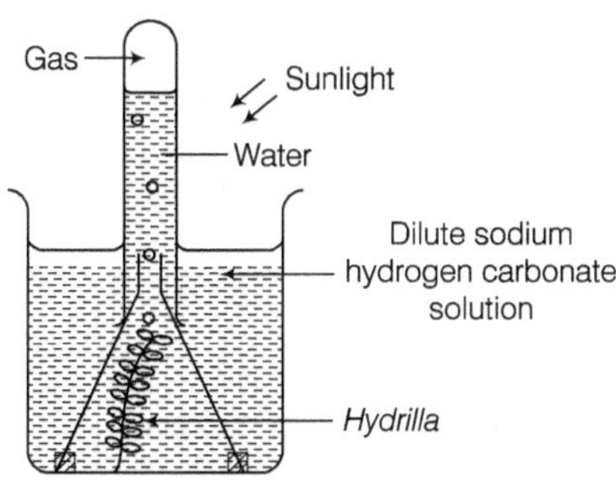

26. Which of the following represents the aim of this experiment?
a Carbon dioxide is produced as a waste product of respiration.
b Carbon dioxide is necessary for photosynthesis.
c Oxygen is evolved during photosynthesis.
d The plant can carry out anaerobic respiration.

27. After several hours, some gas is collected in the test tube which relights a glowing splint. Which of the following can be concluded from the above information?
a A suitable temperature is necessary for photosynthesis.
b Oxygen is given out during photosynthesis.
c Starch is produced in the aquatic plant.
d The gas contains carbon dioxide.

28. Which of the following is the reason for using sodium hydrogen carbonate solution in this experiment instead of water?
a It provides a suitable pH to *Hydrilla*.
b It provides more oxygen to *Hydrilla*.
c It provides more carbon dioxide to *Hydrilla*.
d It provides more minerals to *Hydrilla*.

29. Four test tubes as shown in the diagram below were left under sunlight for ten hours. Which of the test tubes contains the least amount of carbon dioxide?

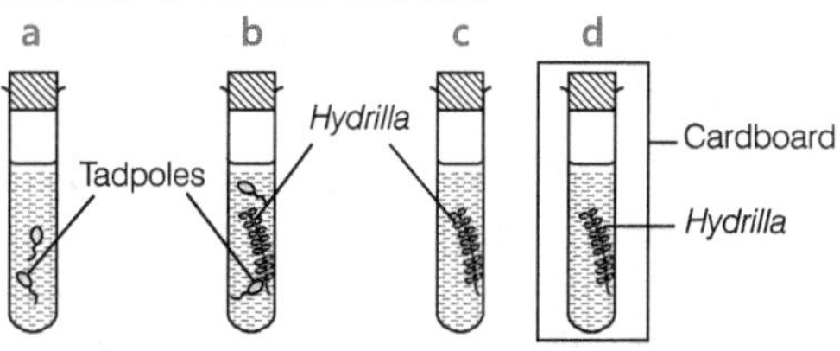

30. The graph below shows oxygen released and taken up by a tree during a 24 hour period.

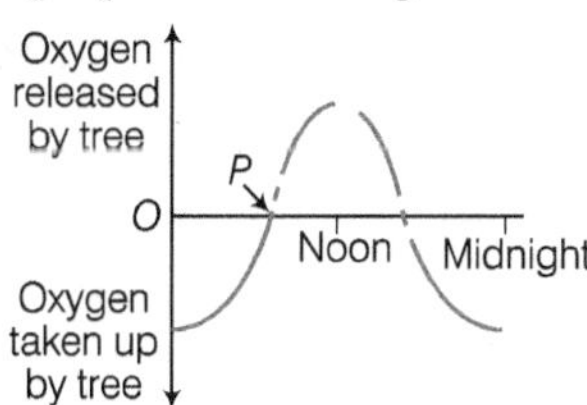

Which statement describes the situation at point P?
a Photosynthesis stops.
b Respiration begins.
c The rate of respiration is equal to the rate of photosynthesis
d The rate of respiration is greater than the rate of photosynthesis.

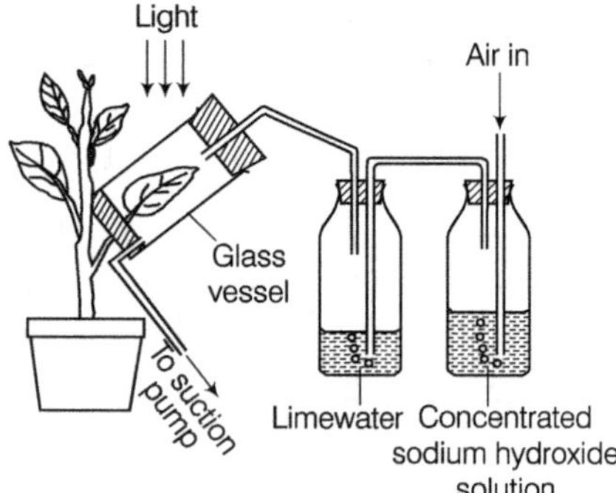

31. Which of the following is the conclusion of the above experiment?

   a Plants release carbon dioxide in respiration.

   b Plants release oxygen in photosynthesis.

   c Plants require carbon dioxide for photosynthesis.

   d Plants require oxygen for respiration.

32. If the above experiment is successful, which of the following can probably be observed when the leaf is tested?

   a A brick-red precipitate will be obtained with Benedict's test.

   b A white emulsion will be obtained with ethanol emulsion test.

   c The iodine solution will turn bluish black.

   d The iodine solution will remain brown.

33. The table below shows the main features of a dicotyledonous leaf. For each corresponding feature, contribute the adaptation of the leaf for photosynthesis. Find the incorrect combination of feature and adaptation.

	Feature		Adaptation
1.	Thin but large surface lamina	A.	To expose as large an area possible to the sunlight and air.
2.	Waxy cuticle	B.	To allow CO_2 and O_2 diffusion.
3.	Clear epidermis cells without chloroplasts	C.	To allow sunlight to penetrate to the mesophyll layer.
4.	Chloroplasts present in mesophyll cells	D.	To absorb energy from sunlight, so that CO_2 will combine with H_2O.

Codes

   a 1–A   b 2–B

   c 3–C   d 4–D

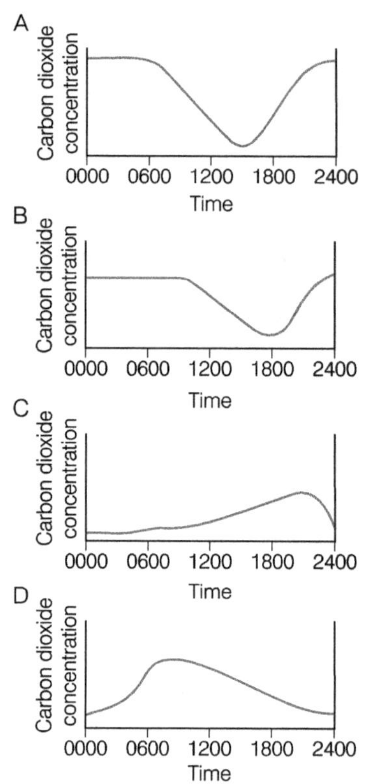

34. Which of the above graphs would best represent the change of carbon dioxide concentration in a freshwater pond on a hot, sunny day?

   a A   b C   c B   d D

35. Based on the change of carbon dioxide concentration alone, how would you describe the pH of the pond water at noon on a hot, sunny day?

   a Acidic   b Very acidic

   c Alkaline   d Neutral

36. Match the Column I with Column II and mark the correct option

	Column I		Column II
A.	Stomata	1.	Middle layer of cell that contains chloroplast
B.	Guard cells	2.	Cells nearer to the top of the leaf, arranged like fence
C.	Mesophyll cell	3.	Small openings in the lower epidermis
D.	Palisade layer	4.	Cells in epidermis that contain chloroplast

Codes

	A	B	C	D
a	4	3	1	2
b	3	4	1	2
c	4	3	2	1
d	1	2	3	4

37. Consider the given passage and opt the option that correctly fill its blanks.

Glucose may be turned into _A_ and stored in the leaf. Glucose is a _B_ sugar. It is soluble in _C_ and reactive substance. Thus, it is not a good storage molecule but it may be used to make other _D_ substances. The plant can use glucose as a starting point for making all the other substances it needs.

Codes

	A	B	C	D
a	CO_2	Complex	Water	Inorganic
b	Starch	Simple	Water	Organic
c	Cellulose	Complex	CO_2	Inorganic
d	Water	Simple	O_2	Organic

38. Consider the statements given below and opt the option that correctly declares them either true (T) or false (F).

I. Sucrose is used for fruit growth in plants.

II. Sucrose is used for shoot growth.

III. Iodine solution is used to test presence of cellulose.

IV. The chemical reactions of photosynthesis can take place very slowly at low temperature.

Codes

	I	II	III	IV
a	T	T	F	T
b	T	T	T	T
c	T	F	F	T
d	F	T	F	T

39. **Assertion** (A) If stomata are closed, then photosynthesis cannot takes place.

Reason (R) The carbon dioxide which the plant uses enters into the leaf through stomata.

a Both A and R are true and R is the correct explanation of A

b Both A and R are true, but R is not the correct explanation of A

c A is true and R is false

d Both A and R are false

40. Complete the crossword given below.

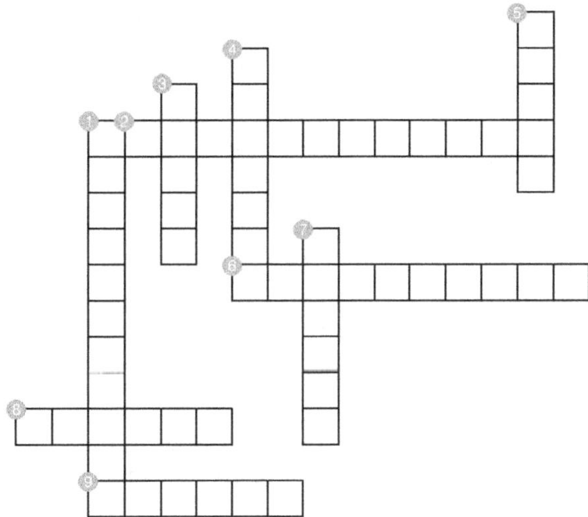

Across

1. A gas needed for photosynthesis
6. Organism that can make their own food
8. A gas released during photosynthesis
9. Part of plant where photosynthesis generally occur

Down

2. A green pigment that absorbs sunlight
3. The colour of chlorophyll
4. Small openings usually found on the underside of leaves
5. The liquid necessary for photosynthesis
7. Photosynthesis results in the production of it

Chapter 2

Nutrition in Animals

1. Given below are some structures of human body. Which of the following participates in the secretion of a component that breaks up fats. Also, name the component.

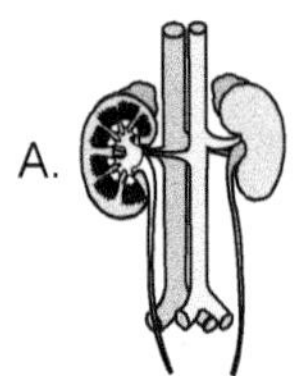
A.

B.

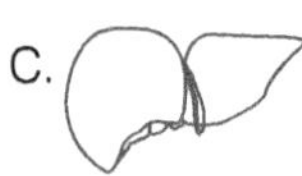
C.

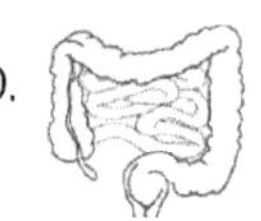
D.

(i) Bile   (ii) Ptyalin   (iii) HCl   (iv) Pepsin

Codes

a A–iv   b B–ii   c C–i   d D–iv

2. The figure given below shows protein rich food. The digestion of these begins in which part of human digestive system? Also, name the secretions of this part.

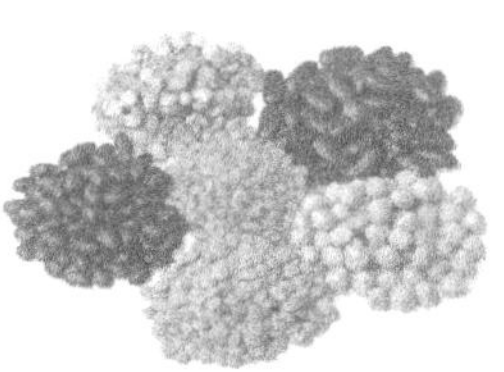

A. Small intestine   B. Mouth   C. Stomach   D. Large intestine
(i) Mucus   (ii) Bile   (iii) HCl   (iv) Ptyalin

Codes

a A–ii, iii   b B–iv, i   c C–i, iii   d D–ii, iv

3. Absorption of digested food takes place in the ....

I. stomach   II. small intestine
III. large intestine   IV. liver

Codes

a I and II   b II and III   c III and IV   d All of these

4. Which of the following occur in the liver?
A. Sugars are converted to glycogen and stored
B. Production of insulin
C. Production of enzymes
D. Fat oxidisation

Codes

a A and B   b B and C   c C and D   d All except B

5. Which of the following are the possible locations in man, where the three enzymes can be found?

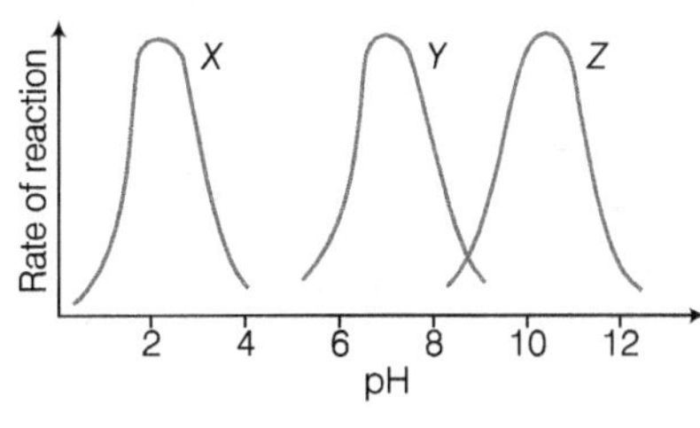

	X	Y	Z
a	Duodenum	Mouth	Stomach
b	Mouth	Stomach	Duodenum
c	Stomach	Duodenum	Mouth
d	Stomach	Mouth	Duodenum

6. The diagram shows a section through a villus.

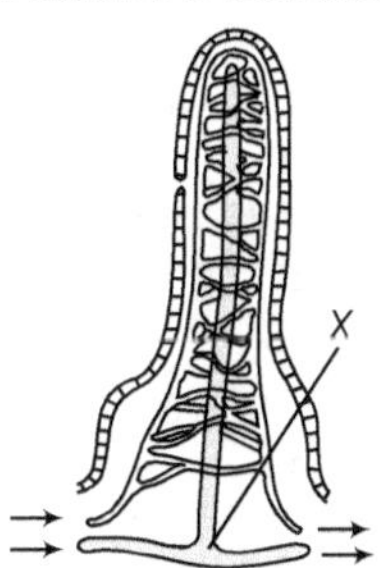

What substance does structure *X* transport?

  a Amino acids   b Blood
  c Fats   d Starch

7. Match the column I with column II.

	Column I		Column II
A.	Stomach	1.	Storage of undigested food
B.	Large intestine	2.	Release of faeces
C.	Rectum	3.	Acid release
D.	Small intestine	4.	Digestion completion

Codes

	A	B	C	D			A	B	C	D
a	3	2	1	4		b	4	2	1	3
c	4	1	2	3		d	3	1	2	4

8. Which type of teeth is used for tearing food?

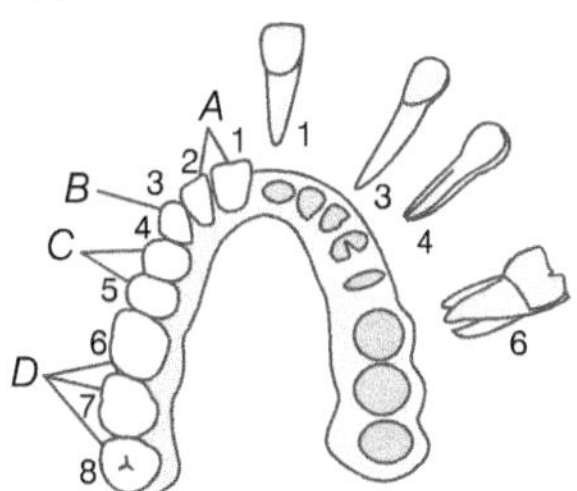

Codes

  a A   b B
  c C   d D

9. From the list of enzymes given below; identify the ones that aid in digestion of proteins

   I. Amylase   II. Pepsin
  III. Lipase   IV. Trypsin
   V. Sucrase   VI. Peptidase

Codes

  a I, V and VI   b II, IV and VI
  c III and IV   d None of these

10. Observe the figure given below and identify the structure *Y*?

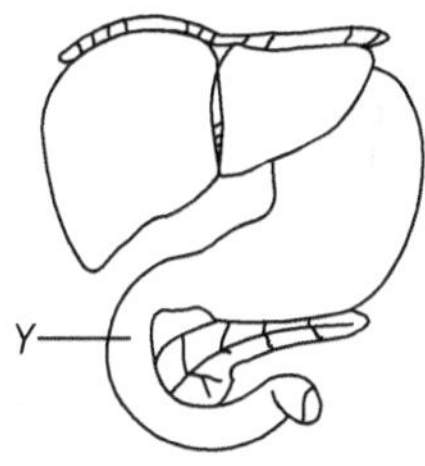

  a Duodenum   b Ileum
  c Gall bladder   d Pyloric sphincter

11. Salivary glands in mouth secrete *A* into the oral cavity that starts the digestion of *B*.

Identify *A* and *B*.

	A	B
a	Bile	Fats
b	Amylase	Starch
c	Lipase	Lipids
d	Trypsinogen	Carbohydrate

12. The diagram below shows part of the digestive system, liver, pancreas and associated blood vessels. Which labelled structure carries the highest concentration of dissolved amino acids?

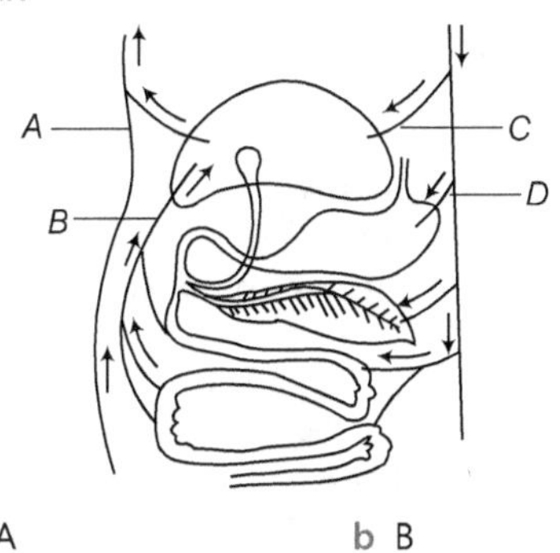

  a A   b B
  c C   d D

13. Which of the following actions take place in a mammalian stomach?

   I. Curdling of proteins in milk.

   II. Killing bacteria in food.

   III. Churning food into small pieces.

   IV. Converting amino acids into urea.

Codes

a II and IV	b III and IV
c I, II and III	d I, II, III and IV

14. Humans develop two sets of teeth in their lifetime. The figures below show different types of teeth. Which of these is/are used for chewing and grinding of food?

a Only R	b Only Q
c Both R and S	d Both P and Q

Direction (Q. Nos.15-16) Refer to the given diagram showing part of alimentary canal in human and select the correct option for the questions that follow.

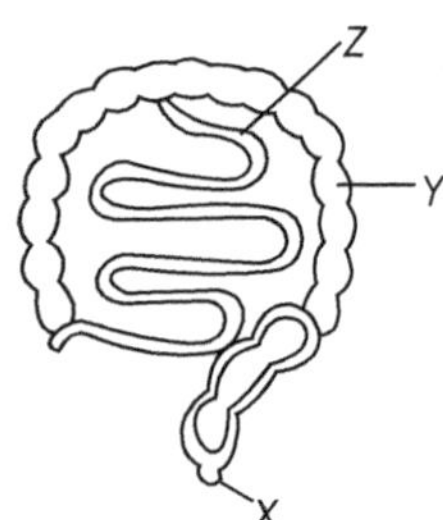

15. Which of the labelled structures absorb water from the undigestible food matter?

a Only X

b Only Y

c Only Z

d Both X and Y

16. Which of the following is correct for the structure labelled Z ?

a Food contents are completely absorbed into the stomach.

b All its content is passed out to the structure Y and release through X.

c It has very large surface area due to the presence of numerous villi.

d Both a and c.

17. In the figure, given below cow is eating grass, which component of the grass is digestible to cow but not to humans? What are such animals called?

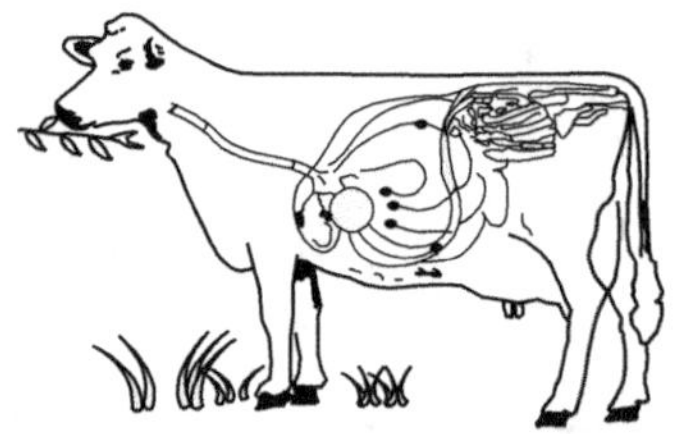

A. Protein	B. Cellulose
C. Starch	D. Glycogen
E. Menogastric	F. Abomasum
G. Pseudoruminant	H. Ruminants

Codes

a A–E	b B–H
c C–F	d D–G

18. Ruminants have a large sac-like structure called A between the oesophagus and B. What are A and B ?

a Reticulum, stomach

b Omasum, stomach

c Rumen, small intestine

d Abomasum, large intestine

19. Given below are few enzymes of the human digestive system. Which of the following combination is incorrect?

a Amylase – Starch

b Trypsin – Protein

c Lipase – Fats

d Rennin – HCl

20. What is A in the figure given below of *Amoeba*? It digests its food in the B.

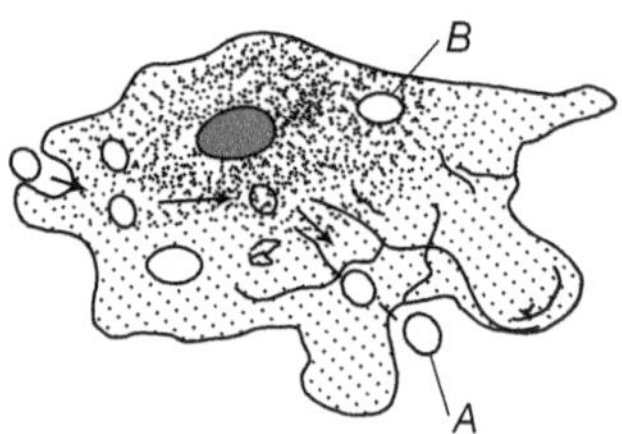

	A	B
a	Nucleus	Cytoplasm
b	Food vacuole	Stomach
c	Ingested food	Nucleus
d	Egested waste	Food vacuole

21. Match the column I with column II.

	Column I		Column II
A.	Villi	1.	Large intestine
B.	Hydrochloric acid	2.	Liver
C.	Bile	3.	Mouth
D.	Absorption of water	4.	Stomach
E.	Mastication	5.	Small intestine

Codes

```
    A  B  C  D  E          A  B  C  D  E
a   1  2  3  4  5      b   5  4  3  2  1
c   5  4  2  1  3      d   5  4  1  2  3
```

22. Consider the given statements.
  I. Small intestine is the longest part of the digestive system.
  II. Minerals and vitamins do not need to be changed, they can be absorbed as such by our cells.
  III. Large intestine absorbs most of water from food material.
  IV. The food from duodenum goes to the lower part of the intestine, jejunum.

Which of the above statements are incorrect?
  a I and III
  b II and IV
  c I and II
  d None of these

23. The given figure shows the movement of food through the oesophagus. There is a involuntary movement performed by the oesophagus. What is this movement called?

Also, name the process in which this movement is reversed.

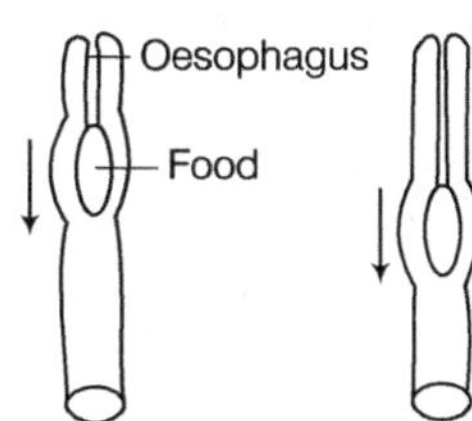

A.	Diapedesis	i.	Digestion
B.	Peristalsis	ii.	Egestion
C.	Rumination	iii.	Vomiting
D.	Muscularisation	iv.	Hiccups

Mark the correct options.
  a A–i
  b B–iii
  c C–iv
  d D–ii

24. The steps of the digestive process are given below in an incorrect manner.
  I. Water and vitamin absorption beings.
  II. Food is moistened, breakdown of proteins begins.
  III. Food mixes with amylase.
  IV. Proteins, carbohydrates and fats breakdown and nutrients are absorbed into the bloodstream.

Select the option that gives the correct order of these events as food passes through the human digestive tract.
  a II, IV, I, III
  b IV, II, III, I
  c I, III, II, IV
  d III, II, IV, I

25. Arrange the parts of digestive system below in correct order as food travels through them.

(i) Gullet	(ii) Stomach
(iii) Mouth	(iv) Ileum
(v) Duodenum	(vi) Rectum
(vii) Colon	(viii) Anus

Codes
  a (iii) → (ii) → (i) → (iv) → (v) → (vi) → (viii) → (vii)
  b (ii) → (i) → (iii) → (vi) → (v) → (iv) → (vii) → (viii)
  c (iii) → (i) → (ii) → (v) → (iv) → (vii) → (vi) → (viii)
  d (i) → (iii) → (ii) → (v) → (iv) → (vii) → (viii) → (vi)

Direction (Q. Nos.26-27) Refer to the diagram below which shows a section of the intestinal villus.

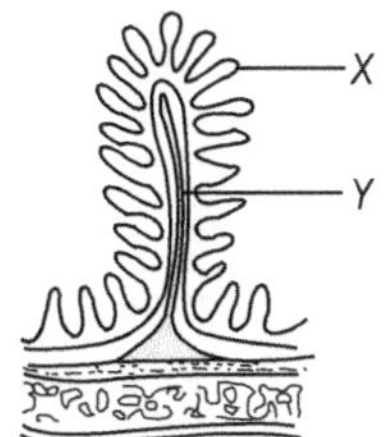

26. Which of the following description of the cells of X is correct?
  a They have thin walls to facilitate efficient absorption.
  b They secrete amylase to help digestion of starch.
  c They secrete hydrochloric acid to kill bacteria.
  d They secrete protease to help digestion of proteins.

27. Which of the following substances is absorbed into structure Y ?
  a Fats
  b Fatty acids
  c Glucose
  d Vitamin-C

 Direction (Q. Nos.28-29) Refer to the diagram below which shows part of human alimentary canal.

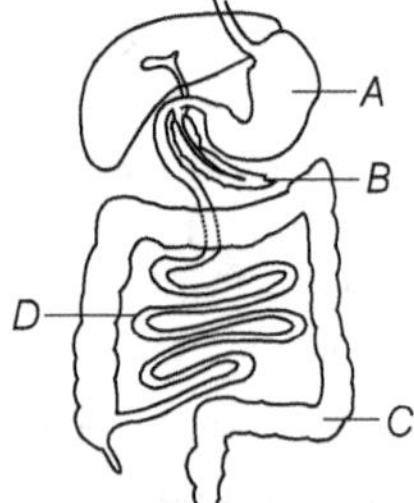

28. In which labelled region does the digestion of protein begin?

a A
b B
c C
d D

29. Various digestive juices were collected from the alimentary canal of man.

Small drops of these juices were put on a strip of film coated with protein as shown below:

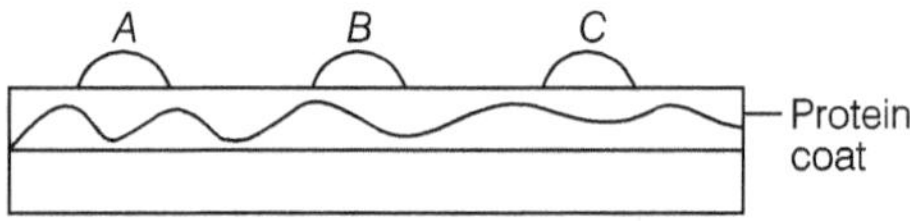

After some time, the protein coat was digested by *B* and *C*.

Referring to the human digestive system, choose the option that correctly describes the location from which the digestive juices were taken.

	A	*B*	*C*
a	Stomach	Liver	Mouth
b	Mouth	Large intestine	Stomach
c	Small intestine	Mouth	Liver
d	Mouth	Small intestine	Stomach

30. The experimental apparatus shows the action of saliva on starch.

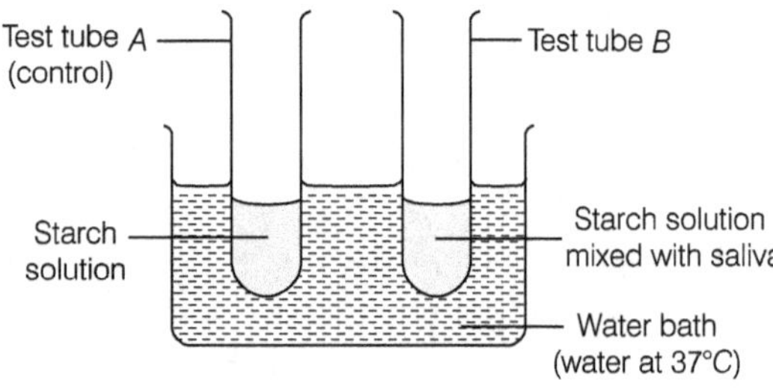

The temperature of the water bath kept at 37°C and not at room temperature because

a the human body temperature is 37°C.
b enzyme work fastly at 37°C.
c starch dissolve properly at 37°C.
d it is difficult to maintain water temperature at room temperature with enzyme.

31. Refer to the given figure showing human digestive system. What is *X* here and what is its function?

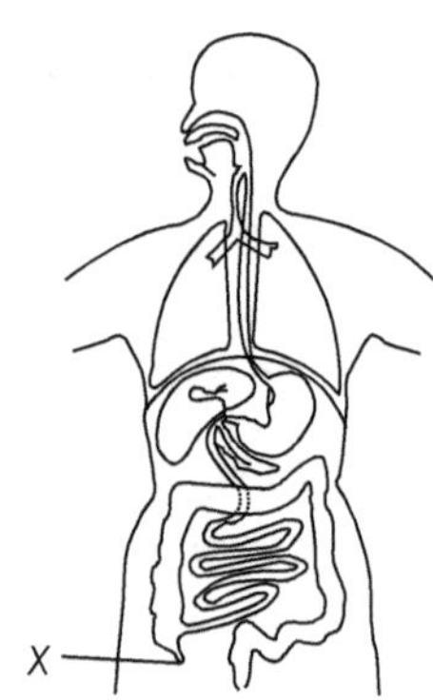

a Small intestine – Absorbs nutrients from digested food
b Stomach – Breaks down food using acts and enzymes
c Appendix – Attached to large intestine and has no function in the human body
d Appendix – Attached to rectum and breaks down food using acids and enzymes

32. Match the column I with column II.

	Column I		Column II
A.	Energy value of food is measured in calories	1.	True
B.	The semi-digested food is called chyle	2.	False
C.	Cellulose (a derivative of carbohydrate) can be digested in our digestive system		
D.	In the absence of peristalsis, food cannot travel down the oesophagus		

Codes

	A	B	C	D
a	1	2	2	1
b	2	1	2	1
c	1	1	2	2
d	2	1	1	2

33. Read the given paragraph and select the option that correctly fill the blanks.

The liver secretes ...(i)..., which plays an important role in the digestion of ...(ii)... . It is stored in an organ called ...(iii)... before being released in the ...(iv).....

Codes

	(i)	(ii)	(iii)	(iv)
a	HCl	proteins	pancreas	stomach
b	HCl	fats	pancreas	small intestine
c	bile	fats	gall bladder	small intestine
d	bile	protein	gall bladder	small intestine

34. The diagram shows the human alimentary canal.

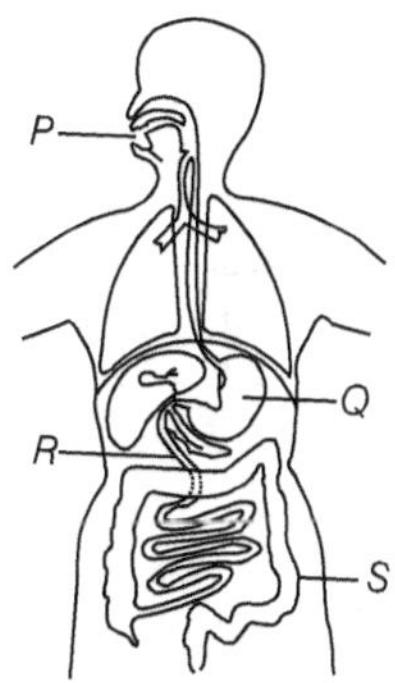

In which parts, food is digested by the action of protease?

a P and Q
b Q and R
c Q and S
d R and S

35. The table below shows the nutrients present in some food items.

	Carbohydrates	Fats	Protein
A.	✓	✗	✓
B.	✓	✓	✗
C.	✗	✓	✗
D.	✗	✗	✓

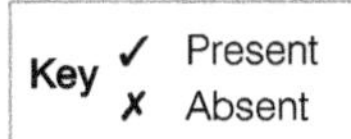

Which foods would be partly digested in the stomach?

a A and B
b B and C
c C and D
d D and A

36. The diagrams below represent molecules of starch, protein and fat.

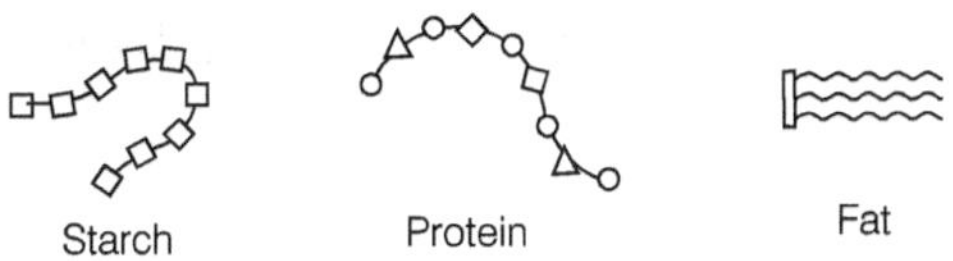

Which of the following mix of molecules will be found in the stomach?

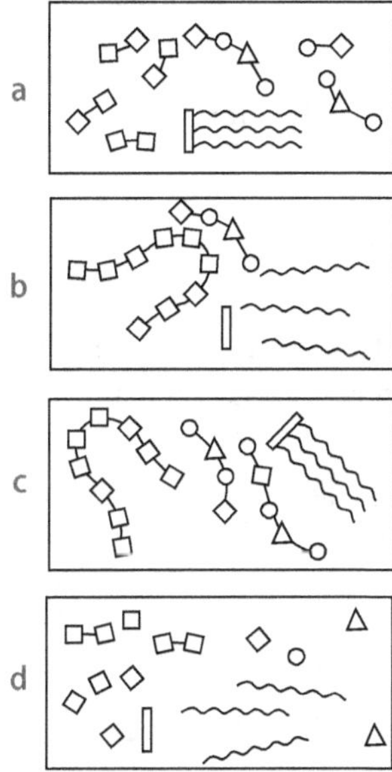

37. A scientist investigates 4 species of insects. He knows that one feeds on human blood and the others feed on plants. As the insects look similar, he investigates the digestive enzymes present in their guts. Which insect feeds only on blood?

Insect	Enzyme present in insect guts			
	Amylase	Lipase	Protease	Sucrase
a	✓	✗	✓	✓
b	✓	✗	✗	✓
c	✗	✓	✓	✗
d	✗	✓	✗	✗

38. Which of the following will be formed by excess amino acids in the liver?

I. Carbohydrate
II. Protein
III. Urea

Codes

a I and II
b Only III
c II and III
d I, II and III

39. The table below shows the composition of a can of baked beans.

Substance	Content (g/100 g)
Protein	5.2
Carbohydrate	9.0
Fat	0.4
Dietary fibre	7.3
Added sugar	2.0
Added salt	0.8

Which substance in the can helps food pass quickly through the alimentary canal?

    a Added sugar
    b Dietary fibre
    c Carbohydrate
    d Protein

Direction (Q. Nos.40-41)   Refer to the table below which shows the composition of 150 g each of four kinds of food.

Food	Protein (g)	Carbohyd-rate (g)	Fat (g)	Calcium (mg)	Iron (mg)	Vit- A (mg)	Vit-C (mg)
W	40	30	30	324	18	0.03	4.3
X	50	10	40	974	6	0.01	1.9
Y	30	10	60	226	3	0.09	1.5
Z	20	60	20	181	1	0.16	0.2

40. Which food has the highest energy value?

    a W   b X
    c Y   d Z

41. The haemoglobin content of a person's blood is found to be lower than normal. Which food would be most effective in helping the person improve the condition?

    a W   b X
    c Y   d Z

42. The figure below shows where carbohydrates, proteins and fats are digested as food moves along the part of alimentary canal J to O.

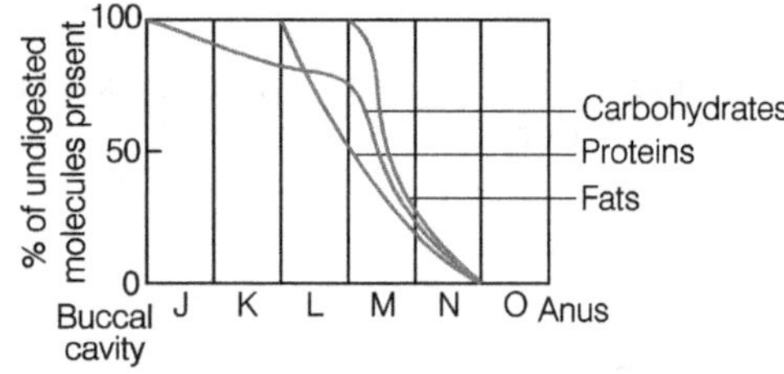

Which of the following correctly identifies K, L, M and N?

	K	L	M	N
a	Large intestine	Small intestine	Stomach	Oesophagus
b	Oesophagus	Small intestine	Large intestine	Rectum
c	Oesophagus	Stomach	Small intestine	Large intestine
d	Stomach	Oesophagus	Small intestine	Large intestine

Direction (Q. Nos.44-45)   Refer to the diagram below which shows a section of the human digestive tract.

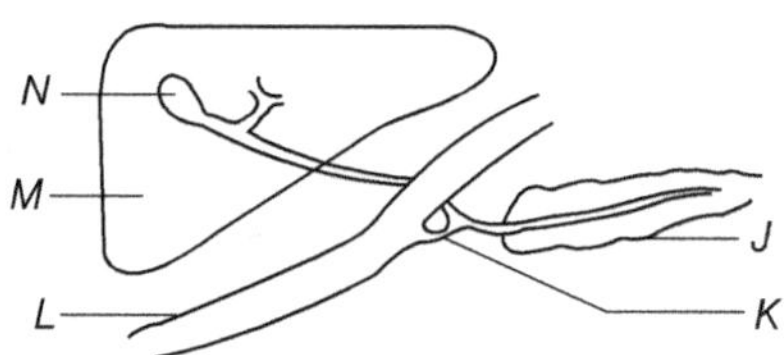

43. Which of the labelled structure secretes bile into the small intestine?

    a J   b L
    c M   d N

44. Which of the following structures is/are involved in the enzymatic digestion of fats?

    a Only N   b M and N
    c J and N   d J and L

45. State 'T' for true or 'F' for false.

   I. Fat is completely digested in small intestine.
   II. Our small intestine is approximately 20-25 inches long.
   III. Nutrients are removed from the undigested food when it is in the large intestine.
   IV. Digestion process beings in the stomach part of the human digestive system.
   V. The gall bladder temporarily stores bile.

   Codes

	A	B	C	D	E
a	T	T	T	F	T
b	T	T	F	T	T
c	T	F	T	T	T
d	T	F	F	T	F

46. Read the given statements and select the correct option.

Statement I Chewing breaks down the food into small pieces and aids in digestion.

Statement II Chewing increases the surface area of food for the saliva to act upon.

- a Both statements I and II are true and statement II is the correct explanation of statement I
- b Both statements I and II are true, but statement II is not the correct explanation of statement I
- c Statement I is true, but statement II is false
- d Both statements I and II are false

47. Solve the crossword with the help of clues given

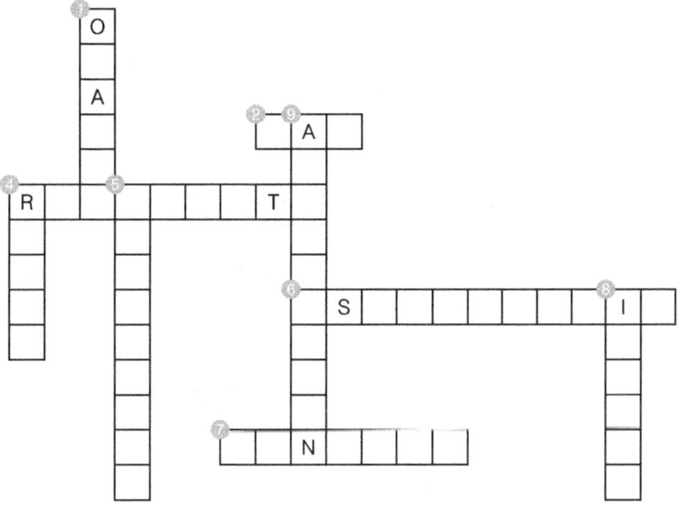

Across

2. Liver secrete bile to digest them.
3. The plant eating animals that brings back swallowed food into mouth.
6. Finger-like projections formed by *Amoeba*.
7. Tearing teeth of human is

Down

1. Third chamber of the digestive system of ruminant.
4. The first and largest part of ruminant stomach.
5. The intake of food into the body
8. Biting teeth of human is
9. The main job of small intestine is

Chapter 3

Heat

A Heat, Temperature and Types of Thermometers

1. What is the direction of heat flow in the diagram below?

   a From the flask to the ice
   b From the ice to the flask
   c From the surroundings to the air trapped inside
   d From the ice to the surroundings

2. Elin wanted to have a drink of milk but found it too hot to drink. She then placed it in a container of cold water.

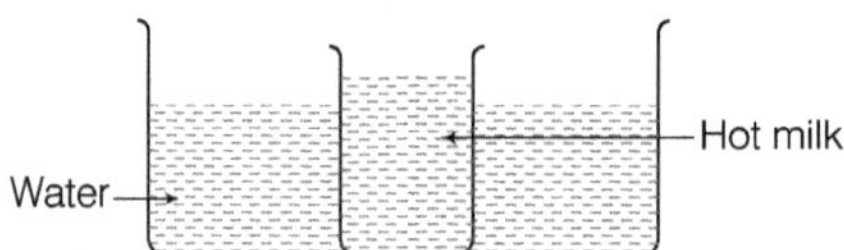

After a while ....
   a the hot milk gained coldness from the cold water and became cooler
   b the temperature of the hot milk decreases to become lower than the cold water
   c the temperature of the cold water decreases as it loses heat to the hot milk
   d the temperature of the cold water rises as it gains heat from the hot milk

3. Gemma set-up an experiment. She put a warm metal spoon into a glass of water with ice cubes.

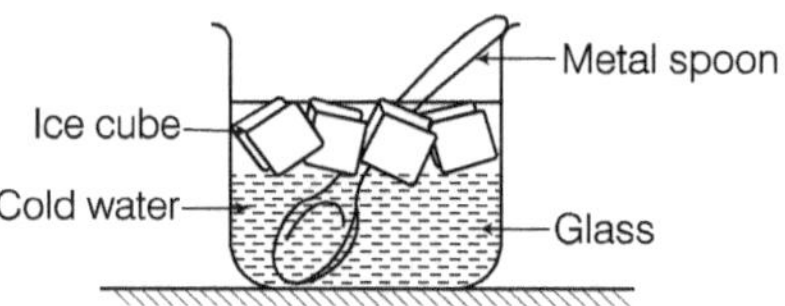

After a few minutes, she observed that the metal spoon had become colder. Which of the following statements best explains what had happened to the spoon?
   a Heat flowed from the warm metal spoon to the cold water and ice cubes
   b The coldness from the ice flowed to the warm metal spoon
   c The surrounding air temperature caused the metal spoon to lose heat
   d The coldness from the ice cubes and water travelled to the warm metal spoon

4. Boojho has three thermometers as shown in the given figure. He wants to measure the temperature of his body and that of boiling water. Which thermometer(s) should he choose?

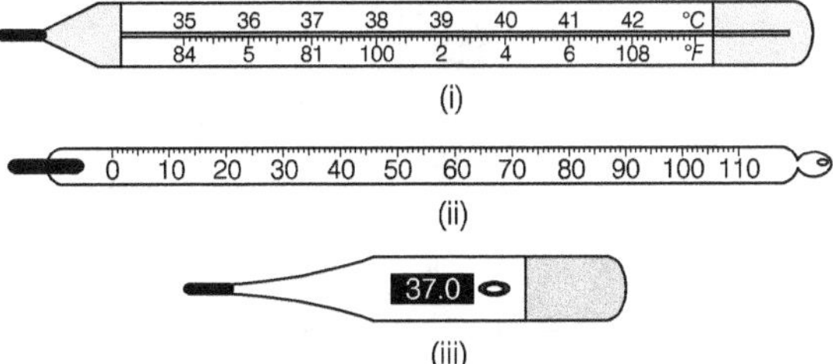

a Thermometer (i) or (iii) for measuring the temperature of body and (ii) for measuring the temperature of boiling water

b Thermometer (i) for measuring temperature of both

c Thermometer (ii) for measuring temperature of both

d Thermometer (iii) for measuring temperature of both

5. A clinical thermometer is designed to respond quickly to a change in temperature and to have a high sensitivity.

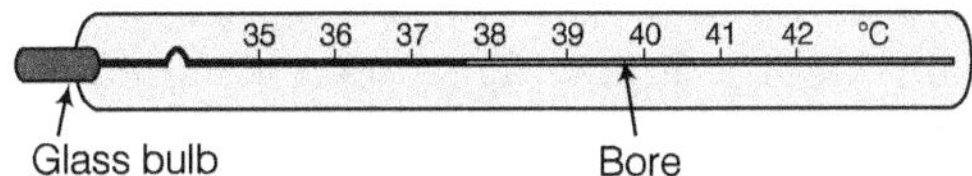

Which design feature should the clinical thermometer have?

	Bulb	Bore
a	Thick glass	narrow
b	Thick glass	wide
c	Thin glass	narrow
d	Thin glass	wide

6. Figures show a student reading a doctor's thermometer. Which of the figure indicates the correct method of reading temperature?

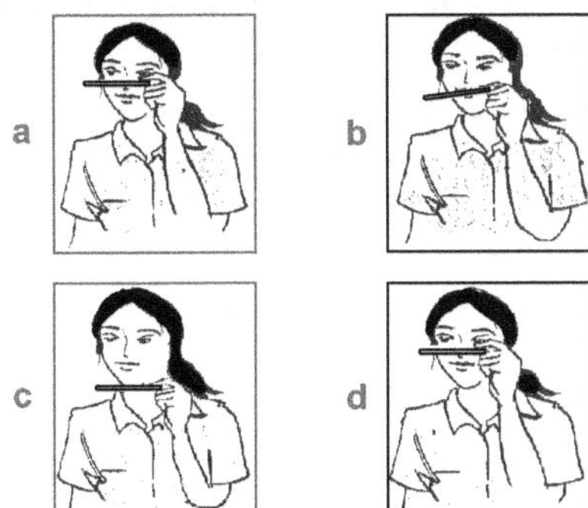

7. Four arrangements to measure temperature of ice in beaker with laboratory thermometer are shown in figures given below. Which one of them shows the correct arrangement for accurate measurement of temperature?

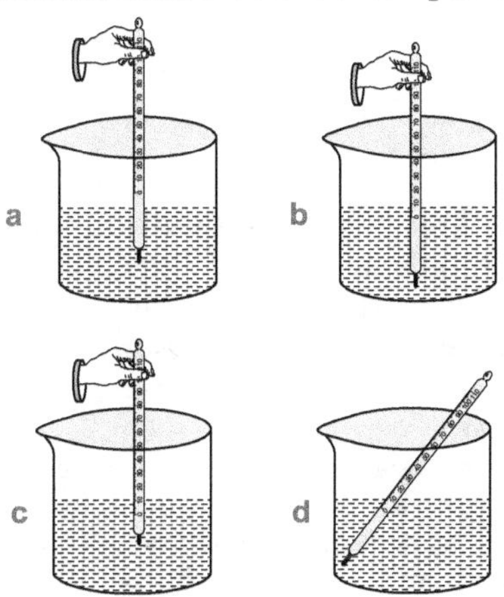

8. Mindy has three tubs of water A, B and C. Tub A contains warm water, tub B contains iced water and tub C contains tap water. She places her left hand in tub A and her right hand in tub B for 15 s. Then, she lifts both hands out of the tubs and puts them both into tub C.

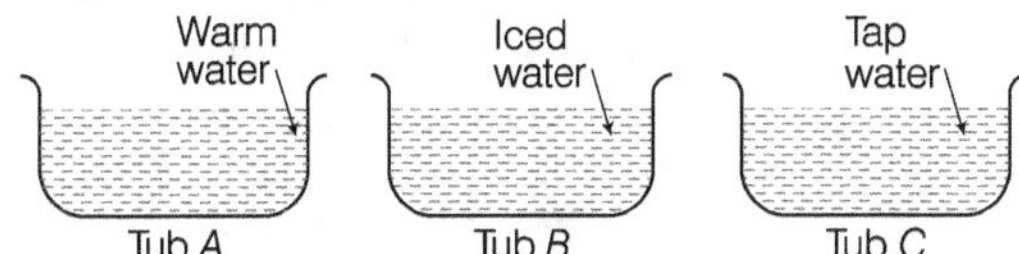

What will she feel?

a Her left hand feels that the water is warmer than in tub A and her right hand feels that the water is colder than in tub B

b Her left hand feels that the water is cold and her right hand feels that the water is warm

c Both hands feel the same temperature

d Both her hands feel numb so she cannot tell the temperature of the water

9. Tina ordered a plate of fish and chips. When her meal arrived, it was piping hot. She cut it into small bite-sized pieces and after a while, she found that she was able to eat them without burning her tongue. Why was this so?

a Heat from the food is lost to the surroundings

b The air from the surroundings cools the food down

c The temperature of the food falls because there was wind

d The food gained heat from the surroundings causing the temperature to rise

10. Two thermometers *A* and *B* are placed in sunshine for equal time. The bulb of *A* is coated with lamp black while the bulb of *B* is coated with silver. Which of them will show a higher rise in thermometer?

   a *A*
   b *B*
   c Both (a) and (b) will rise equally
   d Neither of them will rise

11. Radha bakes cake in the oven and then keeps it in the refrigerator for sometime. What happens to the baked cake when she takes it out from the refrigerator?

   a It gains heat from the surroundings and cools down
   b It loses heat to the surroundings and cools down
   c It gains heat from the surroundings and maintains its temperature
   d It loses heat to the surroundings and maintains its temperature

12. Ram goes to a doctor and observes him while taking temperature of his patients. Which of the following statements are correct?

   I. The doctor dips the thermometer in a liquid before use to disinfect it.
   II. The thermometer is kept above the tongue of the patient because this part of body gives accurate body temperature.
   III. The temperature can also be measured by keeping the thermometer in the armpit of the patient.
   IV. The temperature of different parts of the body is exactly same.

Codes
   a I and II
   b I and III
   c II and IV
   d III and IV

13. Arpita and Shristi measured their body temperature. Arpita found her's to be 98.6°F and Shristi recorded 37°C. Which of the following statements is true?

   a Arpita has a higher body temperature than Shristi
   b Arpita has a lower body temperature than Shristi
   c Both have normal body temperature
   d Both are suffering from fever

14. Ashley carried out an experiment to find out if the amount of heat used will affect the time taken for the ice cubes to melt.

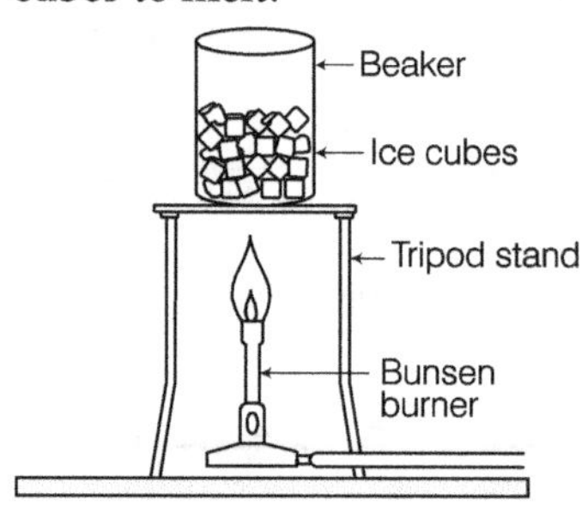

Number of Bunsen burners	1	2	3	4
Time taken for the ice cubes to melt (min)	7	5	3	1

Which of the following statements about the experiment is correct?

   a The number of Bunsen burners should not be changed
   b The time taken for the ice cubes to melt when there were 3 Bunsen burners should be 9 min
   c When more Bunsen burners were used, the ice cubes melted quickly
   d When more Bunsen burners were used, the ice cubes took a longer time to melt

15. Consider the following statements and choose the correct ones.

   I. The level of expansion of mercury is used to measure the temperature of a substance using a thermometer.
   II. The normal temperature of a human is the average body temperature of a large number of healthy persons.
   III. Clinical thermometer measures temperature more accurately than laboratory thermometer.

Codes
   a I and II   b II and III
   c I and III   d All are correct

16. Consider the following statements and choose the correct ones.

   I. The kink present in laboratory thermometer helps to measure the temperature of a room.
   II. The kink is a sharp bent in the capillary of a thermometer.
   III. The range of laboratory thermometer is −10°C to 110°C.

Codes
   a I and II   b II and III
   c I and III   d All are correct

17. Fill in the blanks with the help of options given in the box.

(i) wave	(ii) above
(iii) energy	(iv) 37°F
(v) thermometer	(vi) below
(vii) 37°C	(viii) clinical thermometer
(ix) kink	(x) temperature

I. Heat is a form of ....

II. The hotness of an object is determined by its ....

III. The .... in clinical thermometers prevent the back flow of mercury.

IV. The normal human body temperature is ....

V. Before using clinical thermometer, one should ensure that mercury level in its tube is .... 35°C mark.

Codes

	I	II	III	IV	V
a	(i)	(iv)	(vii)	(viii)	(ii)
b	(iii)	(x)	(ix)	(vii)	(vi)
c	(ii)	(iii)	(iv)	(v)	(vii)
d	(iv)	(viii)	(vi)	(vii)	(ix)

18. State 'T' for true and 'F' for false.

I. Heat is the degree of hotness of a body.

II. The temperature is expressed in degree celsius.

III. The range of clinical thermometer is 32°C-45°C.

IV. Laboratory thermometer is more accurate than clinical thermometer.

V. Laboratory thermometer cannot be used to measure human body temperature.

Codes

	I	II	III	IV	V
a	T	F	T	F	T
b	F	T	F	T	F
c	F	T	T	F	T
d	F	F	T	T	F

19. Match the given matrix.

1.	Temperature	p.	35°C to 42°C
2.	Clinical thermometer	q.	No mercury
3.	Laboratory thermometer	r.	Weather forecasting
4.	Digital thermometer	s.	Degree of hotness
5.	Maximum-minimum thermometer	t.	−10°C to 110°C

Codes

	1	2	3	4	5
a	s	t	p	q	r
b	s	p	t	q	r
c	s	t	p	r	q
d	r	p	t	q	s

20. Assertion (A) Clinical thermometer cannot be used to measure the temperature of ice.

Reason (R) The range of clinical thermometer is from 35°C to 43°C.

a Both A and R are true and R is the correct explanation of A

b Both A and R are true, but R is not the correct explanation of A

c A is true, but R is false

d A is false, but R is true

Direction (Q. Nos.21-22) Read the following information and answer the questions that follow.

A thermometer is a device which measures the temperature or degree of hotness. The operating principles of thermometers include the thermal expansion of solids or liquids with temperature or change in pressure of a gas on heating or cooling. Thermometers are widely used in industry to control and regulate the processes, in the study of weather, in medical field and scientific research.

21. Which of the following is not a measuring unit of temperature?

a Kelvin

b Joule

c Celsius

d Fahrenheit

22. A clinical thermometer shows a patient's body temperature even after it has been taken out from his mouth. This is because

a the capillary tube has a very narrow bore

b it has a constriction near the bulb

c the density of mercury is very high

d the stem of the thermometer contracts

23. Vanessa heated up a bowl of soup to 60°C and left it in an environment that has a temperature of 40°C. She noticed some 'white mist' on top of the soup as shown below:

Which of the following will she observe if she left a similar bowl of soup heated to 60°C in an environment that has a surrounding temperature of 20°C, 60°C and 80°C?

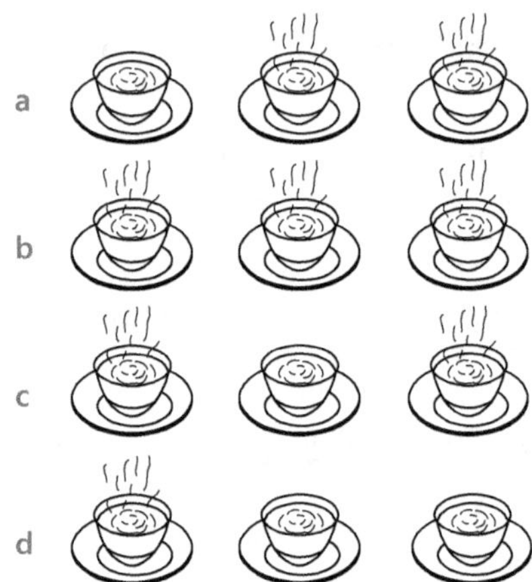

B Transfer of Heat, Conduction, Convection and Radiation

1. A beggar wrapped himself with a few layers of newspaper on a cold winter night. This helped him to keep himself warm because
   a friction between the layers of newspaper produces heat
   b air trapped between the layers of newspaper is a bad conductor of heat
   c newspaper is a conductor of heat
   d newspaper is at a higher temperature than the temperature of the surroundings

2. The body of thermos is usually made of metal to keep the beverages hot for longer period of time. Why do the outer cover and lid of thermos is made of plastic?
   a To prevent loss of heat by conduction
   b To prevent loss of heat by convection
   c To increase the durability of thermos
   d To prevent loss of heat by radiation

3. Paheli after pouring hot tea in a cup covers it with a plate. How does covering a cup of hot tea reduce the heat loss by the tea?
   a The cover is a poor radiator of heat
   b The cover greatly reduces heat loss by radiation
   c The cover greatly reduces heat loss by conduction
   d The cover minimizes the formation of convection currents above the tea

4. Convection is the mode of heat transfer in which molecules of a fluid actually move after taking heat. Why does convection only occur in liquids and gases?
   a The particles in solids heat up quickly
   b The particles in solids can flow
   c The particles in liquids and gases can flow
   d Solids are poor conductors of heat

5. When a kettle of water is boiled, what mode(s) of heat transmission is/are in action?
   I. Radiation   II. Conduction
   III. Convection   IV. Absorption

   Codes
   a Only III   b II and III
   c III and IV   d I, II and III

6. In liquids, thermal energy is transferred mainly by convection. What is the cause of convection?
   a Change in temperature
   b Change in density
   c Infrared radiation
   d Expansion

7. A student wanted to set up a convection current in water. He used a large beaker of water.

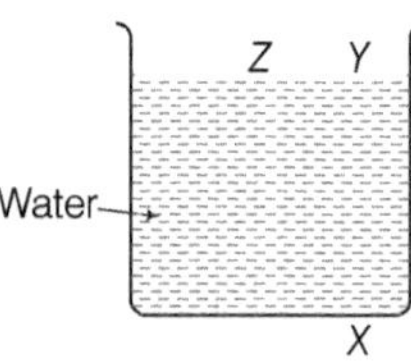

Which of the following arrangements would do this?
   a Cooling at X b Cooling at Y
   c Heating at Y d Heating at Z

8. Fuel is usually transported in tanks with shiny or white surfaces. Which of the following gives the best explanation for the above?
   a To increase visibility and prevent accidents
   b To reflect the heat from the sun and prevent ignition of the fuel
   c To allow the tank to lose heat quickly
   d To keep the fuel in the tank warm

9. Some drops of wax are stuck to the wooden rod as shown in the figure below

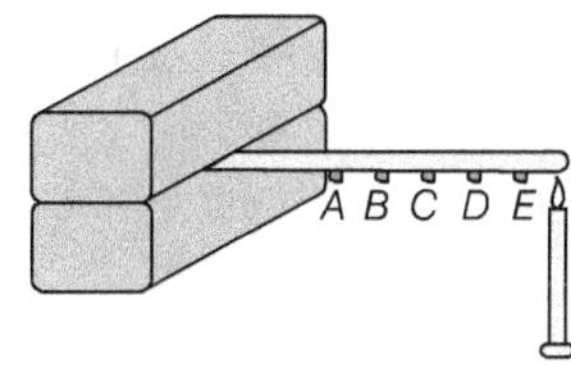

   Which of them will melt first?
   a *E*
   b *A*
   c *C*
   d None of these

10. Which of the following diagrams shows correctly the convection currents of air in a closed beaker when heated?

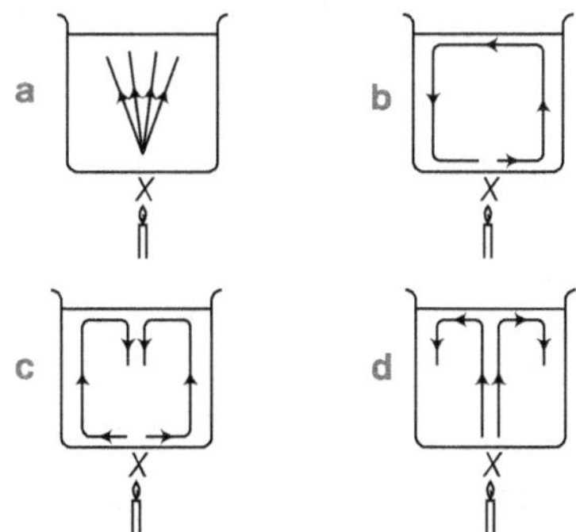

11. An experiment is carried out as shown below:

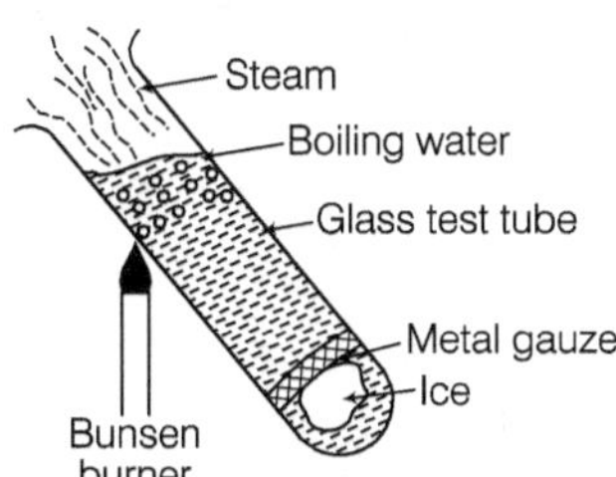

Why does the ice take a long time to melt, even though the water at the top of the test tube is boiling?
   a Convection cannot occur in water
   b Ice is a poor radiator of heat
   c The metal gauze prevents energy reaching the ice
   d Water is a poor conductor of heat

12. While cooking, closing the cooking pan with a lid allows the food to cook faster. Which of the following statements explains this correctly?
   a The lid reduces the loss of heat energy through convection to the surroundings
   b The lid reduces the loss of heat energy through radiation to the surroundings
   c The lid reduces the loss of heat energy through conduction to the surroundings
   d The lid prevents a convection current from being set up

13. Diane set up the experiment as shown below:

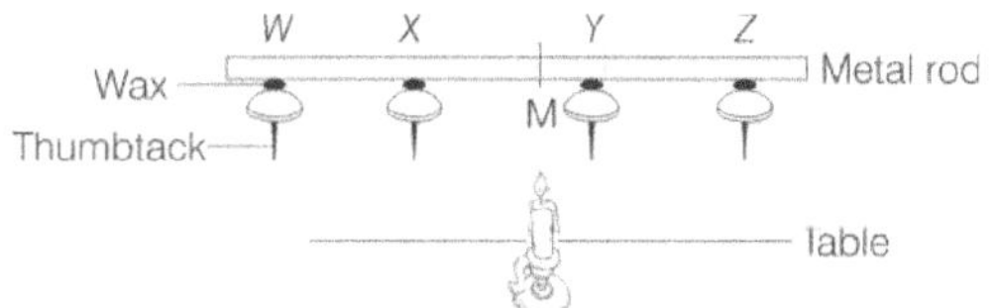

She placed the lighted candle below the metal rod at position *M*. She used the same amount of wax to hold all the thumbtacks at *W*, *X*, *Y* and *Z* on the rod. Arrange the thumbtacks according to the time each of them takes to drop from the rod, from the first to the last.
   a *Y, X, W, Z*
   b *X, Y, W, Z*
   c *Y, X, Z, W*
   d *W, Z, Y, X*

14. A hard boiled egg in a bottle could not be removed as shown below.

What can be done so that the egg can be easily taken out of the bottle without the egg or the bottle breaking?
   a Pour hot water inside the bottle
   b Put the bottle into a basin of cold water and ice
   c Pour hot water over the exterior of the bottle
   d Add cold water into the bottle

15. Yuvraj and Rohit are on a camping trip and they are sleeping outdoors without a tent. Yuvraj covered himself with one thick blanket whereas Rohit used two thin blankets. In the middle of the night, Yuvraj had trouble sleeping as he was feeling cold but Rohit managed to stay warm and slept well. Which of the following statements explains why two thin blankets are better than one thick blanket for warmth?

    a The thick blanket trapped more air than the thin blankets causing the air to move freely around Yuvraj making him cold

    b Air trapped in between the two thin blankets prevented the heat from Rohit's body from escaping and kept him warm

    c Thick materials conduct heat more than thin materials

    d Thin materials are better insulators than thick materials

16. During her science laboratory session, Janet and her classmates were asked to stick a piece of paper in the middle of a metal rod and place the metal rod over the Bunsen flame. The set up of their experiment is shown as below:

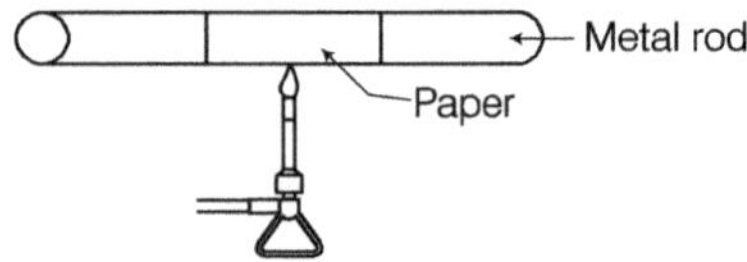

Janet noticed that the paper did not catch fire so easily although the metal rod was placed over the fire. Which of the following best explains the observation made?

    a Paper is a poor conductor of heat and therefore does not catch fire easily

    b The metal rod is a good reflector of heat and therefore did not get hot enough to burn the paper

    c The flame was not intense enough for the paper to catch fire

    d Heat was conducted away from the centre of the metal rod rapidly, so the paper did not get hot enough to catch fire

17. In the options given below, at least one line in each box is correct. Identify the option in which both the lines are correct.

    a Conduction is the process → by which heat is transferred from hotter end to colder end of object
        → which involves transfer of heat energy through liquids.

    b Radiation is the process → of transfer of heat in which no medium is required
        → by which we get heat from sun

    c Sea breeze → is flow of cool air from sea towards land to replace hot air on land
        → happens during night

    d Land breeze → is the current of air from cooler land towards warmer sea
        → happens during day

18. The diagram shows a crystal being heated in a beaker of water. The crystal releases a dye which shows how the water circulates around the beaker.

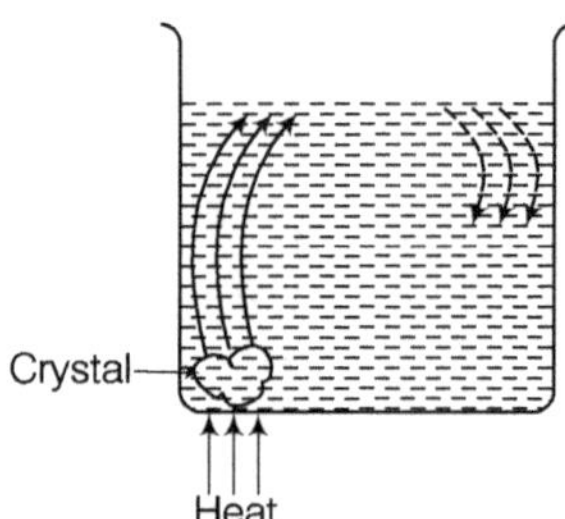

What is happening to cause the water above the crystal to rise?

    a The water contracts and its density decreases

    b The water contracts and its density increases

    c The water expands and its density decreases

    d The water expands and its density increases

19. The diagrams below show a metal strip made up of two different metals, A and B before and after it had been heated.

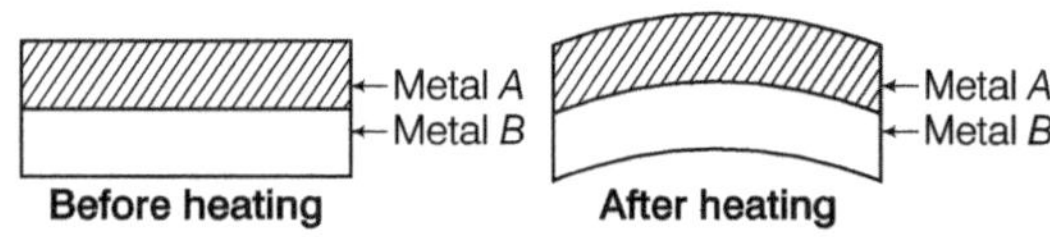

What can we conclude from this experiment?

    a Both metals do not expand

    b Metal A expands more than metal B

    c Metal B expands more than metal A

    d Both metals expand by the same amount

20. The diagram below shows two thermometers, *P* and *Q* placed near a Bunsen flame.

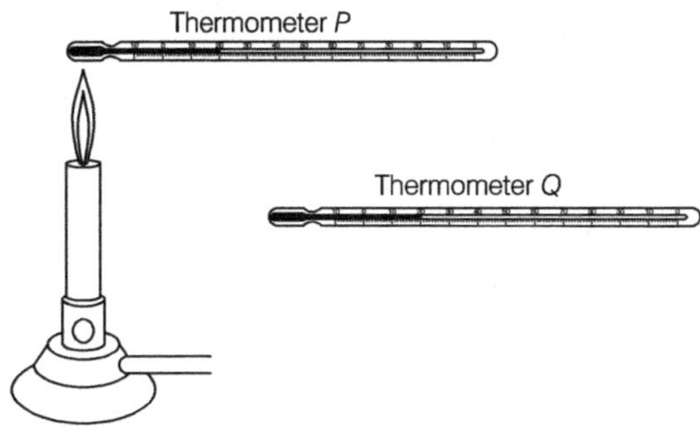

Which of the following pairs of processes correctly describe how the two thermometers got heated up by the Bunsen flame?

	Thermometer *P*	Thermometer *Q*
a	Radiation	Radiation
b	Radiation, conduction	Convection
c	Convection	Radiation
d	Radiation, convection	Radiation

21. What is the reason behind having some space between the successive lines of railway tracks?

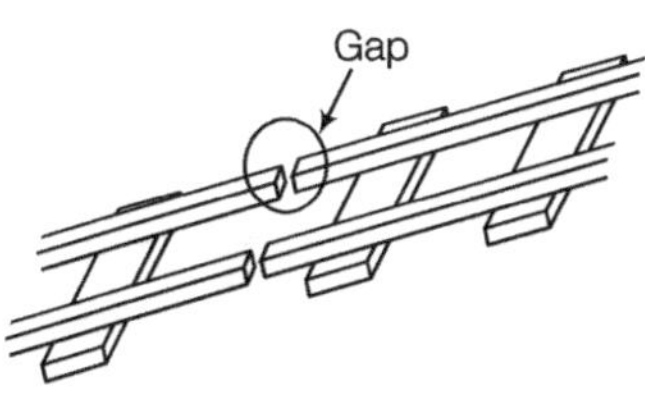

a To allow trains to go smoothly
b To allow the flow of electricity
c To allow expansion of tracks in summer and contraction in winters
d To allow contraction of tracks in summer and expansion in winters

22. Consider the following statements and choose the incorrect one.

I. Conduction needs a material medium for transmission of heat.
II. Conduction and convection need a material medium for transmission of heat.
III. Conduction, convection and radiation need a material medium for transmission of heat.

Codes

a Both I and III   b Only I
c Only II   d Only III

23. Consider the following statements and choose the correct one.

I. Wool is a good conductor of heat due to which it allows outside heat to enter into our body and keep us warm.
II. The air trapped in fibres of woollen clothes, stops the flow of heat from our body to cold surroundings.
III. Water transfers heat by the process of conduction.

Codes

a Only I   b Only II
c Only III   d All are incorrect

24. Fill in the blanks with the help of options given in the box.

(i) good	(ii) medium	(iii) infrared rays
(iv) cold	(v) vacuum	(vi) ultraviolet rays
(vii) hot	(viii) bad	(ix) convection
(x) conduction		

I. Heat flows from ...... object to .... object.
II. Heat is transferred by .... in solids.
III. Heat cannot be transferred by conduction or convection in ....
IV. Air is a .... conductor of heat.
V. The invisible heat rays which transfer heat are ....

Codes

	I	II	III	IV	V
a	(i), (ii)	(iv)	(vi)	(ix)	(x)
b	(ii), (iv)	(v)	(iv)	(x)	(ix)
c	(vii), iv)	(x)	(v)	(viii)	(iii)
d	(ii), (i)	(iii)	(iv	(vi)	(vii)

25. State 'T' for true and 'F' for false.

I. Feathers and furs keep birds and animals warm during winters because they have air trapped in them.
II. No medium is required for the transfer of heat using radiation.
III. The SI unit of temperature is degree celsius.
IV. Sea breeze blows from sea to land.
V. Heat of a body can be felt from a distance due to convection.

Codes

	I	II	III	IV	V
a	T	T	F	T	F
b	F	F	T	F	T
c	F	T	F	F	T
d	T	T	F	F	T

26. Mark where the heat is being transferred by conduction, convection and radiation.

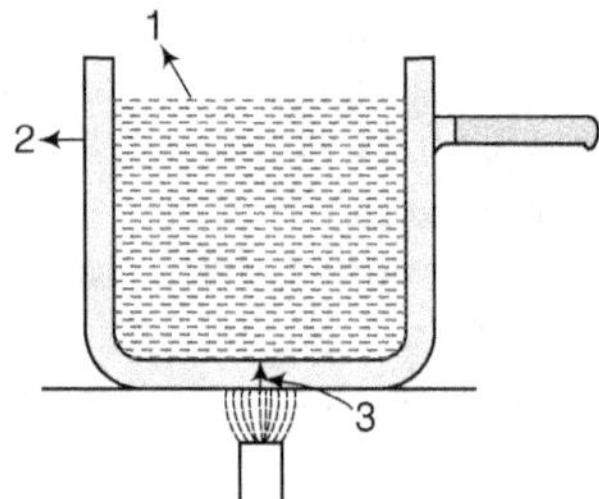

   a 1-conduction, 2-convection, 3-radiation
   b 1-convection, 2-radiation, 3-conduction
   c 1-radiation, 2-conduction, 3-convection
   d 1-radiation, 2-convection, 3-conduction

27. **Assertion** (A) The fastest mode of transfer of heat is radiation process.

Reason (R) Conduction and convection require a medium to transfer heat whereas radiations of heat can even travel through vacuum.

   a Both (A) and (R) are true and (R) is the correct explanation of (A)
   b Both (A) and (R) are true, but (R) is not the correct explanation of (A)
   c (A) is true, but (R) is false
   d (A) is false, but (R) is true

28. **Assertion** (A) Land breeze blows only at night.

Reason (R) At night, the hot land cools much faster than seawater.

   a Both (A) and (R) are true and (R) is the correct explanation of (A)
   b Both (A) and (R) are true, but (R) is not the correct explanation of (A)
   c (A) is true, but (R) is false
   d (A) is false, but (R) is true

Direction (Q. Nos.29-31) Read the following information and answer the questions that follow.

Heat transfer describes the exchange of thermal energy between physical systems depending on the temperature and pressure by dissipating heat.

The fundamental modes of heat transfer are conduction or diffusion, convection and radiation. Thermal equilibrium is reached when all involved bodies and the surroundings reach the same temperature.

29. Which mode of heat transfer comes into play to transfer heat from pan to water?
   a Conduction   b Convection
   c Radiation   d Expansion

30. Which mode of transfer of heat does not require any medium?
   a Conduction   b Convection
   c Radiation   d Expansion

31. The term thermal equilibrium refers to the stage when
   a two liquids are at same temperature
   b all the liquids are at same temperature
   c all the objects involved and the surroundings are at same temperature
   d conduction, convection and radiation all occur simultaneously

32. Solve the following crossword using the hints given below:

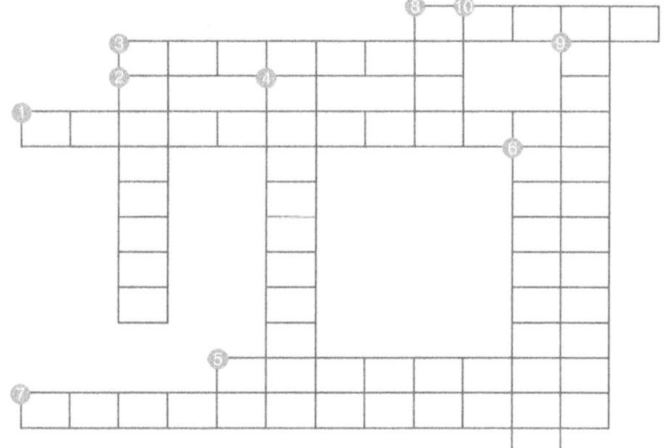

Across

1. Device used to measure temperature
3. SI unit of temperature
5. Convection in air causes
7. Heat is transferred in water using the process of
10. Clinical thermometer is different from laboratory thermometer because of the presence of

Down

2. The metal which is used in thermometers
4. Materials which allow the heat to pass through them
6. Materials which do not allow the heat to pass through them
8. One word used for transmission of hotness from a hot body
9. Degree of hotness or coldness

Chapter 4

Acids, Bases and Salts

 **A** Acids and Bases

1. Acids present in spinach, amla and unripe grapes respectively are
   a tartaric acid, oxalic acid, citric acid
   b oxalic acid, ascorbic acid, tartaric acid
   c tartaric acid, citric acid, oxalic acid
   d ascorbic acid, oxalic acid, tartaric acid

2. The dilute solutions of which of the following are not harmful to drink?
   I. Magnesium hydroxide
   II. Potassium hydroxide
   III. Sodium hydrogen carbonate
   IV. Sodium carbonate

   Codes
   a I and II   b II and III   c I and III   d II and IV

3. Rama has a drink and want to decide its nature. For this, she do the following experiments.

	Experiment	Observation
1.	She taste a few drops of it	Bitter taste
2.	She takes a few drops of it on her palm and rub	Soapy feeling

   On the basis of these observations, she predicted that the nature of drink is
   a acidic   b basic   c amphoteric   d unable to predict

4. Some bases along with their sources are given below. Which of these matchings is incorrect?

	Base	Source
a	Calcium hydroxide	Lime water
b	Ammonium hydroxide	Window cleaner
c	Magnesium hydroxide	Whitewash
d	Potassium hydroxide	Soap

5. Match the acids given in Column I with their sources given in Column II and choose the correct answer using the codes given below.

	Column I		Column II
A.	Formic acid	1.	Spinach
B.	Oxalic acid	2.	Amla
C.	Ascorbic acid	3.	Grapes
D.	Tartaric acid	4.	Ant's sting

	A	B	C	D
a	4	2	1	3
b	4	2	3	1
c	4	1	2	3
d	4	1	3	2

6. Shikha classified some of the household items present around her into acids and bases.

	Acids		Bases
1.	Orange	4.	Washing soda
2.	Antacid	5.	Baking soda
3.	Tea	6.	Curd

Which of them is/are placed under the wrong category?

a 1 and 6   b 2 and 5
c 2 and 6   d 3 and 4

7. "Bases are known to turn red litmus paper blue, taste sweet and feel oily. A common example of a base is washing soda used for washing purposes."

The above statement is

a true
b false
c sometimes true or false
d incomplete information

8. Complete the following sentences by choosing appropriate set of words for (i) to (iv).

I. The sour things we eat contain ..(i).....
II. Ammonium hydroxide is ....(ii)....
III. An acid is called .... (iii)... acid if obtained from animals or plants.
IV. An antacid generally contains a ...(iv)....

Codes

	i	ii	iii	iv
a	acid	acid	strong	base
b	acid	base	weak	alkali
c	acid	base	organic	base
d	base	acid	mineral	base

9. Some acids alongwith their sources are as follow:

	Acids	Sources	
		Natural	Mineral
1.	Lactic	×	✓
2.	Carbonic	✓	×
3.	Tartaric	✓	×
4.	Sulphuric	×	✓

Key: ✓ Yes
    × No

The correct match(es) is/are

a Only 1   b Only 3
c 3 and 4   d 2 and 4

10. Some of the venn diagrams are shown below:

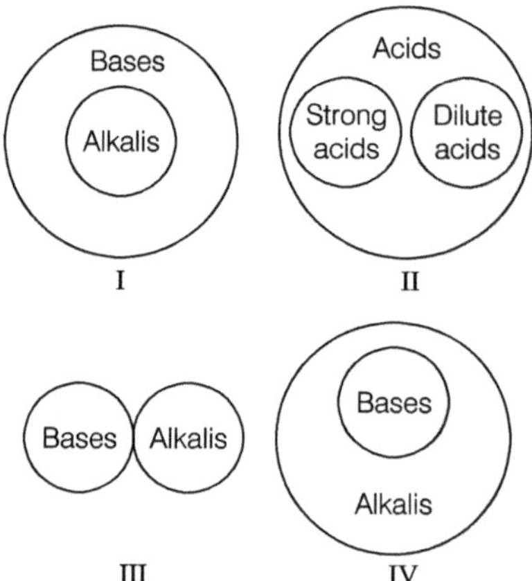

The correct diagram(s) is/are

a Only I   b I and II
c II and III   d Only IV

11. Seema, the science teacher of Class VII, in an assignment said the students to write the names of three acidic substances. The names written by some students are as follow:

Rahul	Vinegar, lime water, milk of magnesia.
Ravi	Sour milk, vinegar, tamarind.
Sonia	Soap solution, turmeric, tamarind.
Subhi	Slaked lime, soap solution, ammonia solution.

Whose answer is/are correct?

a Only Ravi   b Rahul and Ravi
c Only Subhi   d Only Sonia

12. Which of the following is/are uses of sulphuric acid?

    I. Making bleach.

    II. Making plastics and fibres.

    III. Making soaps and detergents.

    IV. Making explosives.

Codes

a Only I   b II and III

c II and IV   d II, III and IV

13. Equal length of magnesium ribbons are taken in test tubes A and B. Hydrochloric acid (HCl) is added to test tube A, while acetic acid (CH_3COOH) is added to test tube B. Amount and concentration taken for both the acids are same. In which test tube will the fizzing occur more vigorously?

a In test tube A

b In test tube B

c Fizzing in both the test tubes are same

d None of the above

14. Rama performed the following three experiments by using vinegar solution.

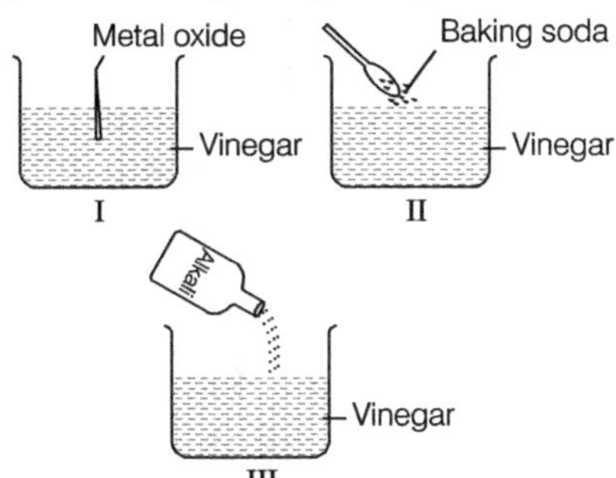

What common product she got in the above three experiments?

a Water   b Hydrogen

c Salt   d Carbon dioxide

15. Sodium hydroxide is usually used to clean blocked drains. Which of the following options gives the most suitable reason(s) for its use?

    I. It is a mild acid that will not burn the hands.

    II. It is inexpensive and easily available.

    III. It is slippery and hence, can easily enter the blocked drain and clean it.

    IV. It dissolves the grease that caused the blockage.

The correct answer is/are

a I and II   b II and IV

c Only IV   d Only III

16. Match the acids given in Column I with their applications given in Column II and choose the correct answer using the codes given below.

	Column I		Column II
A.	Hydrochloric acid	1.	In storage batteries
B.	Sulphuric acid	2.	Present in yoghurt
C.	Lactic acid	3.	In making vinegar
D.	Acetic acid	4.	As bathroom acid

	A	B	C	D
a	4	1	2	3
b	4	1	3	2
c	1	4	2	3
d	4	2	1	3

17. One day Reeta went to jeweller's shop with her mother. Her mother gave an old gold jewellery to the goldsmith to polish. Next day, when they brought the jewellery back, they found that there was a slight loss in its weight. Goldsmith had dissolved the jewellery in solution 'X'. Here 'X' is

a phosphoric acid   b sulphuric acid

c nitric acid   d aqua-regia

18. Consider the following two types of containers.

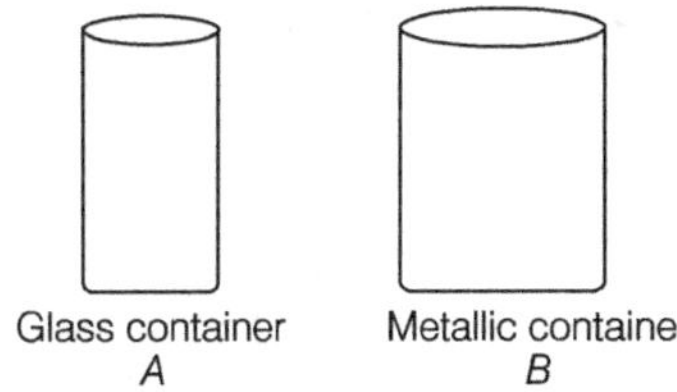

Rama preferred A for storing cut pieces of lemon. This is because

    I. A is transparent.

    II. A is cheaper.

    III. B is not easily available.

    IV. B reacts with the acid present in lemon.

The correct reason(s) is/are

a I and III   b II and IV

c I and II   d Only IV

19. Read the following statements and select the correct option.

Statement I A concentrated acid is one which has acid in larger amount and water in lesser amount.

Statement II In case of dilute acid, acid and water are present in equal amounts.

a Statements I and II both are true
b Statements I and II both are false
c Statement I is true and Statement II is false
d Statement II is true and Statement I is false

20. One day Rashmi observed that to clean the dirty bathroom tiles, her mother spilt some bathroom acid over them and wash the place. She observed the tiles become clean. She got surprised. Could you guess which acid was present in the bathroom acid?

a Formic acid   b Vinegar
c Sulphuric acid   d None of these

21. Consider the following experiment.

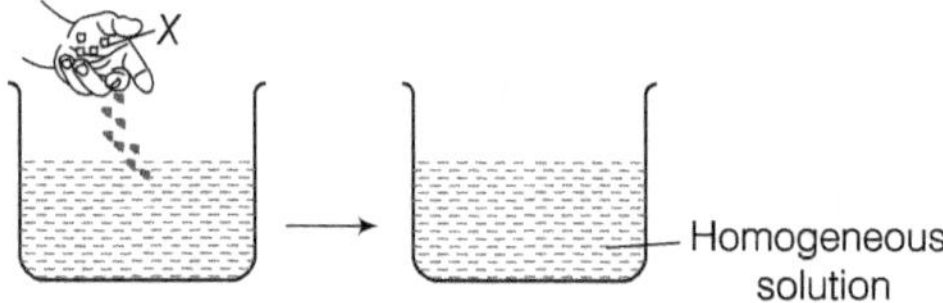

After the experiment, the performer found that his palms became slippery and smooth.

Could you guess what is the substance X which is added by the performer in the above experiment?

a Simple salt   b Sulphuric acid
c Sodium hydroxide   d Calcium hydroxide

22. Rohan takes some baking soda from his mother and pour it into a small glass vessel. He then added some lemon juice over it.

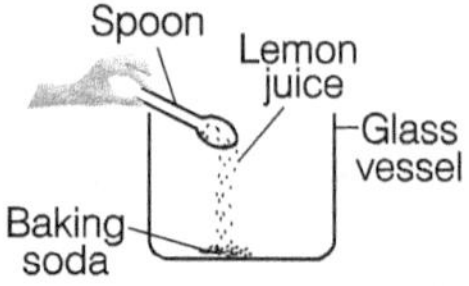

He observed some effervescence.

From this experiment, he concluded that

a lemon juice form an acidic substance when treated with baking soda
b lemon juice contains some acidic substance.
c lemon juice form a basic substance with baking soda
d lemon juice reacts with the acid present in baking soda

23. Consider the following statements.

  I. Their taste is sour.
  II. When concentrated, they are corrosive in nature.
  III. Their strength is measured in terms of hydrogen ion concentration.

Which of these is/are true for both acids and bases?

a I and II   b II and III
c II and III   d I, II and III

24. Sort out the following into Group A (i.e. strong acids) and Group B (i.e. weak acids).

  I. Vinegar   II. Carbonic acid
 III. Tartaric acid   IV. Sulphuric acid
  V. Hydrochloric acid
 VI. Lactic acid

a Group A — I, II, III, VI
   Group B — IV, V
b Group A — II, IV, V
   Group B — I, III, VI
c Group A — II, III
   Group B — IV, V, VI
d Group A — IV, V
   Group B — I, II, III, VI

25. Complete the following puzzle by appropriate words with the help of hints:

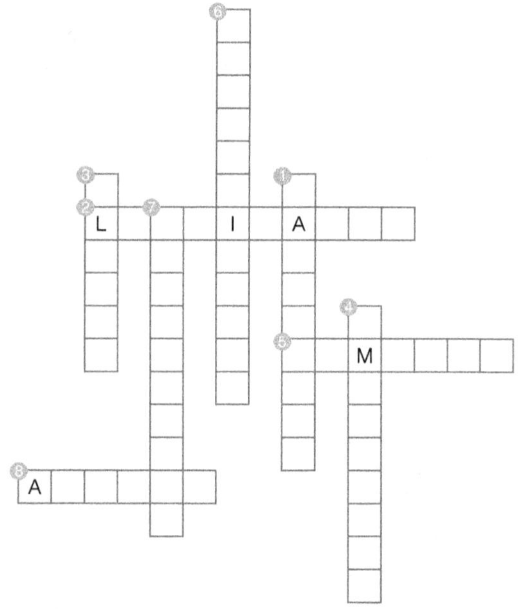

Across

  2. It is present in curd.
  5. A compound obtained from nitrogen and hydrogen.
  8. This acid is a constituent of vinegar.

Down

  1. A substance present in apples.
  3. A term used for water soluble bases.
  6. A substance found in unripe mangoes.
  4. An acid having basic amino group also.
  7. A substance present in vitamin C.

1. Complete the table about common indicators and their colour in acids and alkalis.

Indicator	Colour in acid	Colour in alkali
Litmus	Red	(i)
Methyl orange	(ii)	Yellow
(iii)	Colourless	Pink

a	Blue	Pink	Turmeric
b	Red	Pink	China rose
c	Blue	Red/Pink	Phenolphthalein
d	Blue	Red/Pink	Turmeric

2. Amy's science teacher made the class to taste small amount of a colourless liquid. It tasted sour. Now, she said to conduct litmus test on that liquid. What will the litmus test reveal?

	Red litmus paper	Blue litmus paper
a	Turns blue	Turns red
b	Remains red	Turns red
c	Turns blue	Remains blue
d	Remains red	Remains blue

3. Which of the following can be used for testing acids and alkalis?

   I. Litmus solution
  II. Universal indicator
 III. Natural indicator
 IV. pH meter

Codes
a I and III   b II and IV
c I, II and IV   d All of the given

4. Some of the substances are given below.

    I. Red cabbage   II. Turmeric
  III. Litmus paper   IV. Aspirin
   V. Phenolphthalein   VI. Vinegar
 VII. Milk of magnesia VIII. Aerated drinks

In which pair, both are the indicators?
a I and II
b III and IV
c V and VI
d VI and VIII

5. Which of the options given ranks the items below from the highest to the lowest pH value?

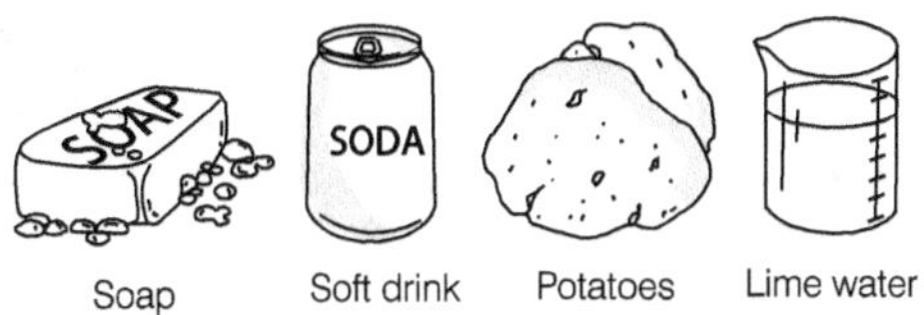

a Soap, soft drink, potatoes, lime water
b Lime water, soap, potatoes, soft drink
c Soap, lime water, soft drink, potatoes
d Soft drink, soap, potatoes, lime water

6. Rohan took three solutions *A*, *B* and *C* in three different test tubes, marked as I, II and III and added some China rose indicator in each. The change observed by him are shown below.

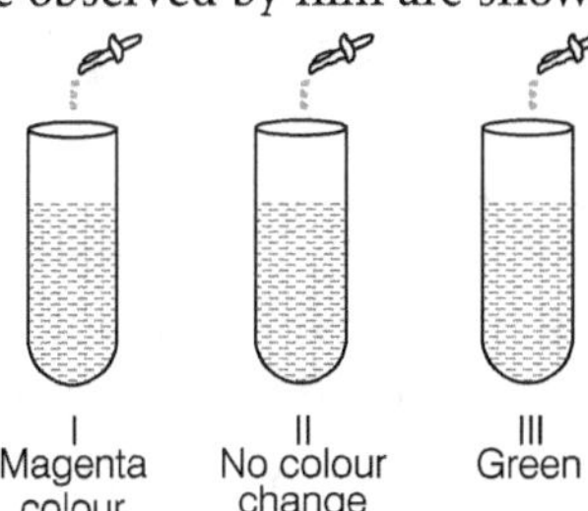

The solutions *A*, *B* and *C*, respectively are
a sugar solution, lime water, baking powder solution
b sugar solution, juice, vinegar
c lime water, sugar solution, juice
d juice, sugar solution, lime water

7. In the following table which match is correct?

S. No	Sample	Colour change with blue litmus (into red)	Colour change with red litmus (into blue)
1.	Amla juice	✓	✗
2.	Sugar solution	✗	✓
3.	Washing soda solution	✓	✗
4.	Lime water	✗	✓

Key: ✓ Yes
     ✗ No

a 1 and 4   b 2 and 3
c 1, 2 and 4   d 1, 3 and 4

8. Match the indicators with their colour in acidic and basic medium and choose the correct option.

Indicator		Colour in acidic medium	Colour in basic medium
A. Litmus	1.	Colourless	Pink
B. Red cabbage	2.	Pink	Yellow
C. Phenolphthalein	3.	Deep red	Green/yellow
D. Methyl orange	4.	Red	Blue

	A	B	C	D
a	3	4	1	2
b	2	4	3	1
c	4	2	1	3
d	4	1	2	3

9. Rohan has a paper blotted with solution 'X'. When he kept some drops of sodium hydroxide over it, it turns red or pink.

Solutions given are

   I. China rose solution   II. Turmeric

  III. Phenolphthalein   IV. Blue litmus

Choose the correct option for solution 'X'.

  a I and II   b II and III

  c III and IV   d I and IV

10. Which of the following test(s) will successfully prove that an unknown substance X is an acid? Substance X is known to have the ability to remove rust from metal surfaces.

Codes

  I. Litmus test

  II. pH meter

  III. React X with carbonates

  IV. React X with magnesium ribbon

  a Only II   b I and III

  c II, III and IV   d All of the given

11. Ravi found that the turmeric stain on her shirt turned red when his mother washed it with soap, but he was unable to understand the cause of this change. What do you think is the reason for this?

  I. Turmeric is acidic in nature.

  II. The soap solution is acidic.

  III. Turmeric is a natural indicator.

  IV. The soap solution is basic.

Codes

  a I and II   b I and III

  c II and III   d III and IV

12. Consider the following flow chart.

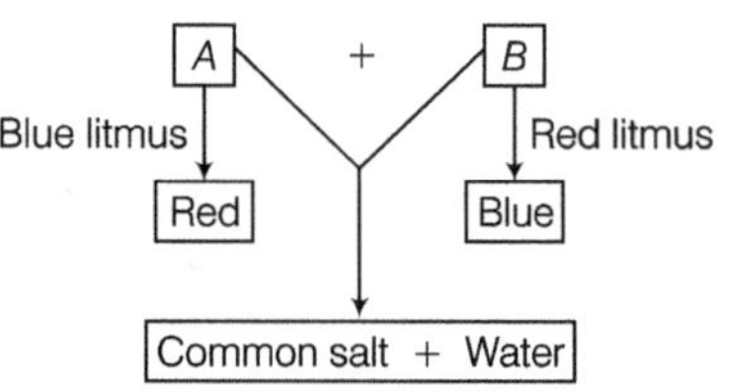

A and B are

  a $A = NaOH, B = NaCl$

  b $A = HCl, B = NaOH$

  c $A = NaOH, B = HCl$

  d $A = HCl, B = H_2O$

13. Complete the following table by choosing appropriate words for P, Q, R and S.

Name of substance	Litmus used	Colour change
Curd	Red	No change
Window cleaner	Blue	P
Sugar	Red	Q
Vinegar	R	Red
Baking soda	S	No change

	P	Q	R	S
a	No change	No change	Blue	Blue
b	Red	No change	Blue	Red
c	No change	Blue	Blue	Red
d	No change	Red	Red	Blue

14. Rama had a solution 'X'. When she added some lemon juice to it, it turns red and when she added lime water, it turns blue. This solution is obtained

  I. by diluting an acid.

  II. from a plant, called lichen.

  III. by diluting a base.

  IV. from an animal, called lichen.

The true statement(s) is/are

  a I and II   b II and IV

  c Only II   d None of these

15. Shri Krishna was a farmer. For the better yield of crops, he sprinkled a lot of sulphatic fertilisers. But after a few seasons, he found that yield of crops had decreased. Which of the following, if he used, may improve the yield of crops?

  a Calcium   b Lemon juice

  c Lime water   d Not possible

16. Sonia prepared a solution of X and dip a paper strip into it. She dried it. Now, she used it as an indicator paper and put a few drops of solution Y (in which H^+ ions are less than OH^- ions) on the paper. The colour of the paper becomes yellow. The substances X and Y, were

   a phenolphthalein, acid
   b methyl orange, acid
   c methyl orange, base
   d turmeric, base

17. **Assertion** (A) Solution of common salt is acidic.

Reason (R) Solution of common salt turns blue litmus blue.

   a Both (A) and (R) are true and (R) is the correct explanation of (A)
   b Both (A) and (R) are true but (R) is not the correct explanation of (A)
   c (A) is true but (R) is false
   d (R) is true but (A) is false

18.

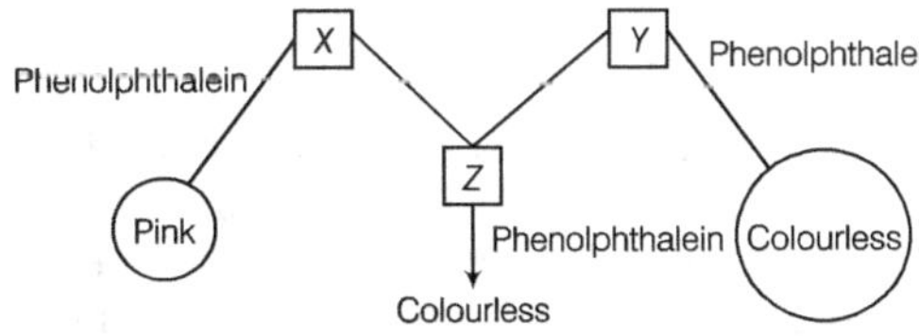

X, Y and Z are

Codes

	X	Y	Z
a	CuO	H_2SO_4	$CuSO_4$
b	NaCl	HCl	NaOH
c	H_2SO_4	CuO	$CuSO_4$
d	HCl	NaOH	NaCl

19. If a few drops of a concentrated acid accidently spill over the hand of a student, what should be done?

   a Wash the hand with saline solution
   b Wash the hand immediately with plenty of water and apply a paste of sodium hydrogen carbonate
   c After washing with plenty of water apply solution of sodium hydroxide on the hand
   d Neutralise the acid with a strong alkali

Direction (Q. Nos. 20-22) The table below shows the colour changes of indicators in acids and alkalis. Answer on the information given in the table.

Indicator	pH at which colour changes	Colour in acid	Colour in alkali
Congo red	5	Blue	Red
Methyl orange	4	Red	Yellow
Phenolphthalein	10	Colourless	Pink
Thymol blue	3	Red	Yellow
Phenol red	7	Yellow	Red

20. Which indicator would be yellow at a pH value of 2?

   a Congo red
   b Methyl orange
   c Thymol blue
   d Phenol red

21. What colour would methyl orange be at pH value of 6?

   a Blue   b Red
   c Pink   d Yellow

22. Which indicator can be used to distinguish liquids X and Y, which have pH values of 6 and 9, respectively?

   a Congo red
   b Methyl orange
   c Phenol red
   d Phenolphthalein

23. Marcus has a 25 m by 15 m plot of land. The pH of the soil was tested and it showed the soil to be slightly acidic at 5.5. He wishes to grow mint plants in the plot and for mint plant, the pH of the soil must be 7.5.

If 100 g of lime can raise the pH of $1\,m^2$ of soil by 1, how much lime would Marcus need for the whole farm?

   a 20 kg
   b 55 kg
   c 75 kg
   d 100 kg

1. Sodium chloride (common salt) is an important component of our diet and is formed by the reaction between

   a dichlorine and sodium hydride
   b hydrochloric acid and sodium hydride
   c hydrochloric acid and sodium hydroxide
   d dichlorine and sodium hydroxide

2. What happens when a solution of an acid (hydrochloric acid) is mixed with a solution of a base (sodium hydroxide). The equation given below is

Sodium hydroxide + Hydrochloric acid
$$\longrightarrow \text{Sodium chloride} + \text{Water}$$

  I. The temperature of the solution increases.
  II. The temperature of the solution decreases.
  III. The temperature of the solution remains the same.
  IV. Salt formation takes place.

Codes

   a Only I   b I and III
   c II and III   d I and IV

3. Which of the following is a neutralisation reaction?

   a $CuO + 2HNO_3 \longrightarrow Cu(NO_3)_2 + H_2O$
   b $PbCO_3 + 2HNO_3 \longrightarrow Pb(NO_3)_2 + H_2O + CO_2$
   c $Mg + H_2SO_4 \longrightarrow MgSO_4 + H_2$
   d $2K + 2HCl \longrightarrow 2KCl + H_2$

4. Complete the following paragraph by selecting appropriate words for *P*, *Q*, *R* and *S*.

P alongwith *Q* are obtained when hydrochloric acid reacts with sodium hydroxide. The process is *R* and resulting in a *S* solution.

	P	*Q*	*R*	*S*
a	Salt	water	exothermic	neutral
b	Salt	water	endothermic	acidic
c	Salt	water	endothermic	neutral
d	Salt	water	exothermic	acidic

5. Consider the following reactions.

  I. $NaOH + HCl \longrightarrow NaCl + H_2O$
  II. $CuO + 2HCl \longrightarrow CuCl_2 + H_2O$
  III. $CaCO_3 + H_2O \longrightarrow Ca(OH)_2 + CO_2$
  IV. $Na_2CO_3 + 2HCl \longrightarrow 2NaCl + H_2CO_3$

The acid-base reactions among the above are

   a I and II   b II and III
   c III and IV   d I, II and IV

6. Chemical factories added a large amount of acidic wastes to rivers and other waterbodies which may lead to a danger for the aquatic life. What do you think must be done to this waste before adding it into the river or waterbodies?

  I. Some sulphuric acid should be added to it.
  II. Salt solution should be added to neutralise it.
  III. Solution of baking soda should be added to neutralise it.
  IV. Lime water should be added to neutralise it.

Codes

   a I and II   b III and IV
   c I and IV   d II and III

7. Two farmers *A* and *B* found a sharp decrease in their crop yield. *A* observed that it is because of the sprinkling of excessive fertilisers while *B* found a supply of washing run off of clothes to his field. Could you suggest what they should added to regain high yield of crops?

   a *A* : Organic matter
      B : Quicklime
   b *A* : Quicklime
      B : Organic matter
   c *A* and *B* : Quicklime
   d *A* and *B* : Organic matter

8. Match the salts given in Column I with their formula given in Column II and choose the correct answer using the codes given below:

	Column I		Column II
A.	Limestone	1.	$CuSO_4 \cdot 5H_2O$
B.	Blue vitriol	2.	$CaSO_4 \cdot 2H_2O$
C.	Washing soda	3.	$CaCO_3$
D.	Baking soda	4.	$NaHCO_3$
		5.	$Na_2CO_3 \cdot 10H_2O$

	A	B	C	D
a	2	1	5	4
b	3	1	4	5
c	1	2	5	4
d	3	1	5	4

9. **Assertion** (A) Blue vitriol turns blue litmus red.

   Reason (R) Aqueous solution of blue vitriol is acidic.
   - a Both A and R are true and R is the correct explanation of A
   - b Both A and R are true but R is not the correct explanation of A
   - c A is true but R is false
   - d R is true but A is false

10. Consider the following statements about substance X.
    - I. Its aqueous solution is neutral.
    - II. It plays a key role in freedom movement.
    - III. It is an important source of substance Y, which is used for preparing bleaching powder.

    Substance 'X' is
    - a sodium carbonate
    - b sodium chloride
    - c soda lime
    - d sodium bicarbonate

11. Rama found that an ant bites on her hand. She immediately rubbed some baking powder over it and get relief from pain and irritation. She do so to neutralise the acid injected by ant by the base. The compound formed after neutralisation has the formula
    - a NaCl
    - b CH_3COONa
    - c HCOONa
    - d Cannot be predicted

12. 'X' has solutions of following substances.
    - I. Common salt
    - II. Vinegar
    - III. Washing soda
    - IV. Baking soda
    - V. Lime water

    Which of these resemble in nature with the floor cleaner, having ammonia as main constituent?
    - a I and III
    - b I, III and IV
    - c III, IV and V
    - d I and II

13. Which of the following representations is/are correct?

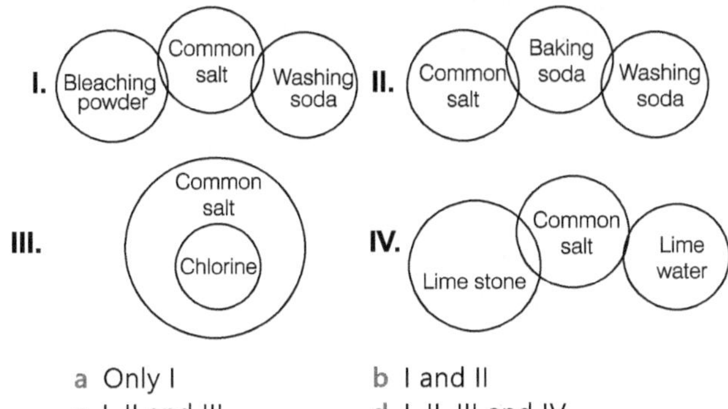

    - a Only I
    - b I and II
    - c I, II and III
    - d I, II, III and IV

14. Consider the following statements about salts.
    - I. They contain two parts, one cationic, another anionic.
    - II. During their formation, temperature of reaction mixture increases.
    - III. They get their cationic part from acids and anionic part from base.

    The true statement(s) is/are
    - a I and II
    - b II and III
    - c Only II
    - d I, II and III

15.
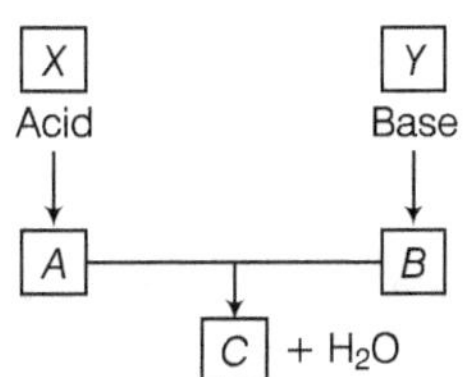

    A, B and C, respectively are
    - a cation, anion, salt
    - b anion, cation, salt
    - c cation, anion, base
    - d cation, anion, acid

16. Solve the crossword puzzle with the help of given hints.

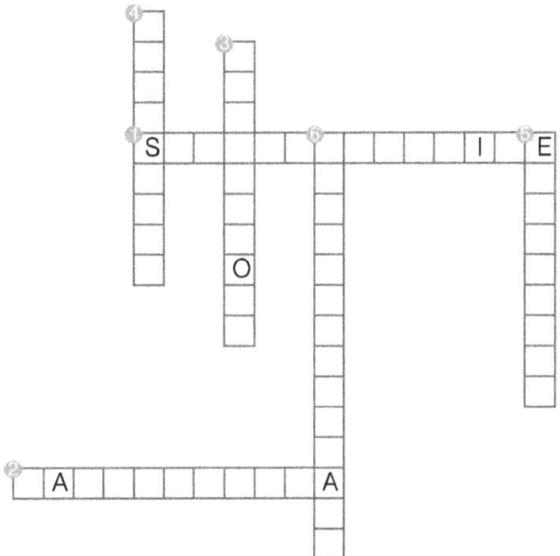

Across
1. A substance related with national movement.
2. Hydrate of sodium carbonate.

Down
3. A substance which makes cakes fluffy and soft.
4. A constituent of marble.
5. A name given to magnesium sulphate heptahydrate.
6. Chemical name of blue vitriol.

Chapter 5

Physical and Chemical Changes

A Physical Changes

1. Consider the following properties.

    I. Colour   II. Shape   III. Size

Which of these are affected during a physical change?

  a I and II   b II and III   c I and III   d I, II and III

2. Melting, boiling, freezing and P are all examples of Q. Here, P and Q, respectively are

  a electrolysis, oxidation   b photosynthesis, natural changes

  c expansion, physical changes   d precipitation, chemical changes

3. Paheli's mother made a concentrated sugar syrup by dissolving sugar in hot water. On cooling, crystals of sugar got separated.

This indicates a

  a physical change that can be reversed   b chemical change that can be reversed

  c physical change that cannot be reversed   d chemical change that cannot be reversed

4. Consider the following processes.

    I. Flammability and ability to conduct electricity.   II. Solubility and melting point.

    III. Corrosiveness and strength.   IV. Boiling point

The example(s) of physical properties is/are

  a I and II   b III and IV   c II, III and IV   d Only III

5. Which of the following sentences are true about physical changes?

    I. They are irreversible.   II. No new substance is formed.

    III. Evaporation and decomposition are examples of physical changes.

    IV. They can be caused by heat, light, electricity and mixing.

Codes

  a I and III   b II and IV   c II, III and IV   d All of these

6. Which of the following are the examples of physical change?

    I. Switching on a light bulb.   II. Making yoghurt at home.

    III. The ripening of some bananas that were left on the kitchen counter top.

    IV. Ironing a damp T-shirt.

Codes

  a I and IV   b II and III   c I, III and IV   d None of these

7. The table below shows the results when four substances were heated in the air. Which of the substances only underwent a physical change?

Substance	Appearance at start of experiment	Appearance at end of experiment	Change in mass	Effects of heating
a	White solid	White solid	Loss	Produced carbon dioxide
b	Green powder	Black residue	Loss	Produced carbon dioxide
c	White powder	Turned yellow	No change	Turned white when cooled
d	Grey metal	White ash	Gain	Burned with an intense white flame

8. Teacher wrote the following statements on the board and asked the students to wrote one word for each. The statements written by the teacher and the one word given by the students are as follows:
 I. The process in which water turns into ice when cold enough (below 0°C temperature). – Boiling
 II. The process of formation of solid crystals from solution. – Freezing
 III. Formation of a substance that differ in shape, colour, etc., from original one but not in composition. – Chemical change

The correct answers were
 a I and II   b II and III   c I and III   d None of these

9. Which of the following experiments show a physical change only?

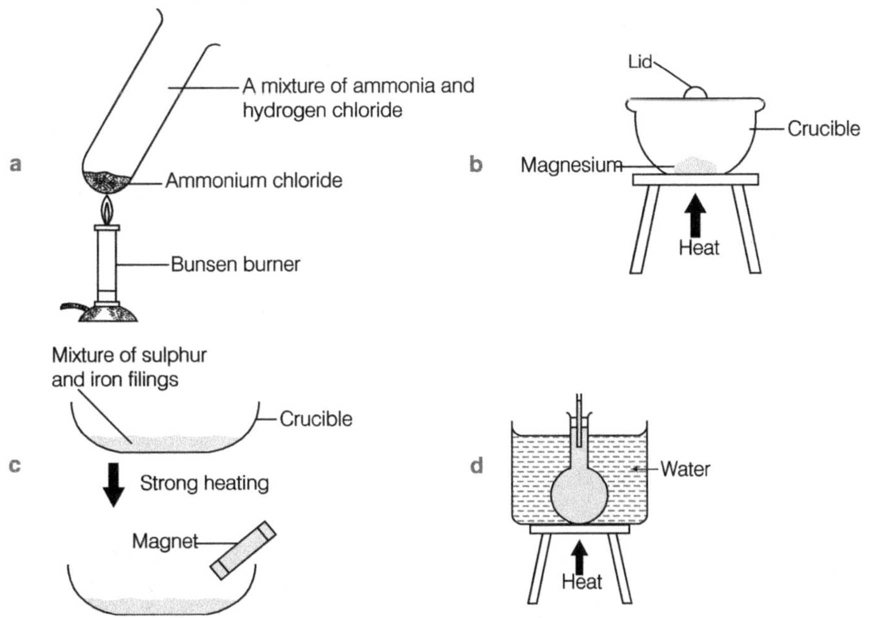

10. Richa performed the following experiment by taking some common salt.

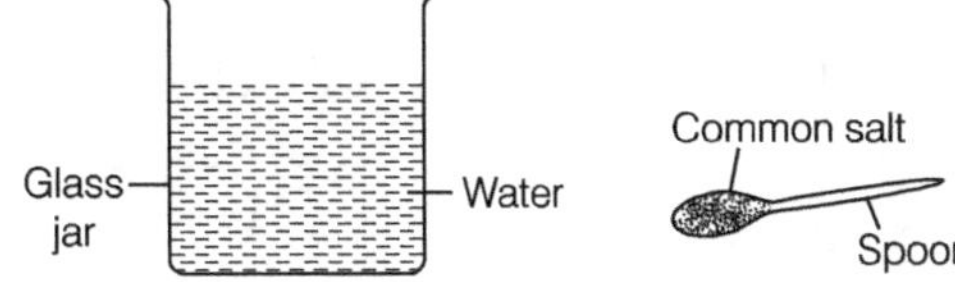

She added the common salt in water and stirs the solution. During this process,
 I. a new substance is obtained.   II. the change is temporary.
 III. salt retains its chemical properties.   IV. the change is permanent.

The true observations are
 a I and II   b I and IV   c II and III   d II and IV

11. A student took some substance X in a bowl and kept it for freezing. After the experiment, she observed the following changes.

	Initially	After freezing
Size	Not definite	Definite
Shape	Not definite	Definite
Appearance	Colourless	White
Volume	15 mL	12 mL
Composition	X_2YZ	X_2YZ

What type of change, she observed?

a Exothermic   b Endothermic
c Chemical   d Physical

12. Sohan filled an ice tray with water and kept it in the freezer for about 2 hours. The change observed by him (according to his view) are

I. A solid is obtained.
II. The movement of particles in the product decreases.
III. The force of attraction between the water molecules decreases.
IV. A new substance is formed.

The correct observations are

a I and II   b I, II and III
c I and IV   d I, II and IV

13. Consider the following processes.

I. Obtaining salt from sea water.
II. Snow flakes formation.
III. Obtaining sugar from sugar syrup.
IV. Formation of rust over iron surface.

The crystallisation processes among the above are

a I and II   b II and III
c I, II and III   d All of the above

14. Fill the following puzzle by filling appropriate words with the help of hints given.

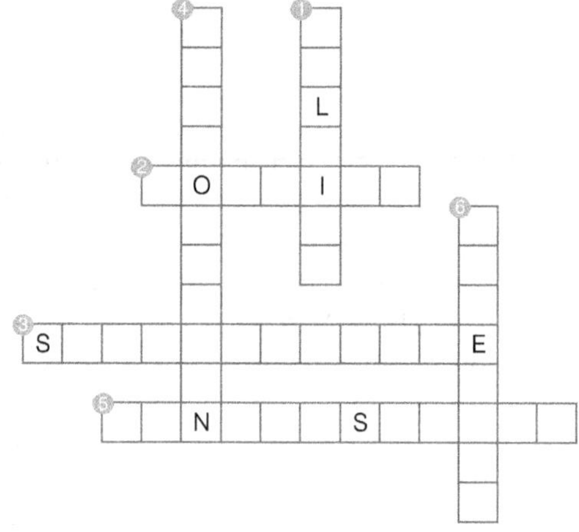

Across

2. Conversion of water into vapours.
3. A physical change occurring, when sal ammonic is heated.
5. Conversion of vapours into liquid water.

Down

1. Conversion of ice in water.
4. It produces cooling effect.
6. A process occurring when water is kept at 0°C.

B   Chemical Changes and Rusting

1. The following are generally observed during a process.

I. Heat   II. Sound   III. Gas

Which of the above can accompany a chemical change?

a I and II   b II and III
c I and III   d All of these

2. Use the table below to answer this question

Mineral	Vinegar drops produce bubble
Limestone	Yes
Sandstone	Probably not
Granite	No
Gneiss	No

Vinegar is an acid that bubbles when it interacts with calcite. Which mineral contains calcite?

a Limestone   b Sandstone
c Granite   d Gneiss

3. Choose the correct set for P, Q, R and S.

Rusting is a P process and occurs in the presence of Q and R. However, in the presence of sea water, the process of rusting becomes S.

	P	Q	R	S
a	Physical	Air	Water	Slower
b	Chemical	Water	Air	Faster
c	Physical	Water	Air	Faster
d	Chemical	Air	Water	Slower

4. Match the items of Column I with the items of Column II and choose the correct answer using the codes given below.

	Column I		Column II
A.	Depositing a layer of zinc on iron	i.	Rust
B.	Iron oxide	ii.	Chemical change
C.	Dissolving common salt in water	iii.	Galvanisation
D.	Souring of milk	iv.	Physical change

Codes

	A	B	C	D
a	iii	ii	iv	ii
b	iv	i	ii	iii
c	iii	i	iv	ii
d	iv	ii	iv	i

5. Shruti took a mixture of sulphur powder and iron turning. She could separate them with the help of magnet. Then, she heated the mixture. After heating, she tried to separate the iron turning by using magnet but she failed. This is because
   a heating results in the formation of a new substance
   b heating changes the nature of iron, so it is not attracted by magnet
   c heating results in evaporation of iron and sulphur is left behind
   d heating melts the sulphur in which iron gets dissolved

6. Which of the following children made an incorrect statement about a chemical change?
   a Anu says : It is always reversible in nature
   b Raghav says : It involves change in chemical composition
   c Meena says : Temperature shows no fixed relation with a chemical change
   d Ravi says : Combustion may be an example of chemical change

7. Seema took some pickle from the burney by using metal spoon, but she left the spoon there. After a few days, when she again take the pickle, she found the spoon but with a hole. What could be the possible reason for this?
   a Metal is dissolved by the oil present in the pickle
   b Metal is dissolved by a gas which is liberated by the oil in the presence of metal
   c Metal reacts with the acid present in the pickle to form salt and hence, gets dissolved
   d Metal reacts with the burney material (glass) to give acid which dissolves the metal

8. Which of the following statements about chemical changes is/are not correct?
   I. Mixing oil and water is an example of a chemical change.
   II. A chemical change is also known as a permanent change.
   III. New substances may or may not be formed.
   IV. Heat energy is always given out to the surroundings.

   Codes
   a Only I
   b II and III
   c I, III and IV
   d All of the given

9. Which of the following is/are the example(s) of chemical changes?
   I. Melting of candle wax when heated.
   II. Iodine crystals forming a purple vapour upon heating.
   III. Dissolving magnesium ribbon in hydrochloric acid.
   IV. Copper carbonate turns into a black powder upon heating.

   Codes
   a I and II
   b III and IV
   c II, III and IV
   d All of the given

10. A chemical change is so called because
    I. it is a permanent change.
    II. it involves the formation of a different substance.
    III. the obtained substance differ from the initial one in shape, size and colour.

    The statement which is/are not true, is/are
    a I and III
    b I and II
    c II and III
    d Only III

11. Consider the following processes.
    I. Dissolution of sugar in water
    II. Formation of clouds
    III. Cooking of food
    IV. Respiration
    V. Photosynthesis

    The processes occurring with change in composition is/are
    a I, II and III
    b III, IV and V
    c II, IV and V
    d None of the given

12. The rate of a chemical reaction depends on ....
    I. temperature   II. the presence of light
    III. electricity   IV. pressure

    Codes
    a I and II
    b III and IV
    c I, III and IV
    d All of these

13. A man painted his main gate made up of iron, to

    I. prevent it from rusting.
    II. protect it from sun.
    III. make it look beautiful.
    IV. make it dust free.

Which of the above statement(s) is/are correct?

a I and II   b II and III
c Only II   d I and III

14. Choose among the following, one that shows a correct match between chemical/physical change and energy transformation.

a Sandling wood : physical change, energy absorbed
b Burning coal : chemical change, exothermic
c Melting ice : physical change, energy released
d Digestion of food : chemical change, endothermic

15. Read the two statements given below:

Statement I Unlike photographic films which can be used only once, DVD can be used again and again.

Statement II Photography involves chemical change but DVD recording is a physical change.

a Both Statement I and Statement II are correct and Statement II is the correct explanation of Statement I
b Both Statement I and Statement II are correct but Statement II is not the correct explanation of Statement I
c Statement I is correct, Statement II is incorrect
d Both Statements I and II are incorrect

16. Consider the following two experimental set-ups.

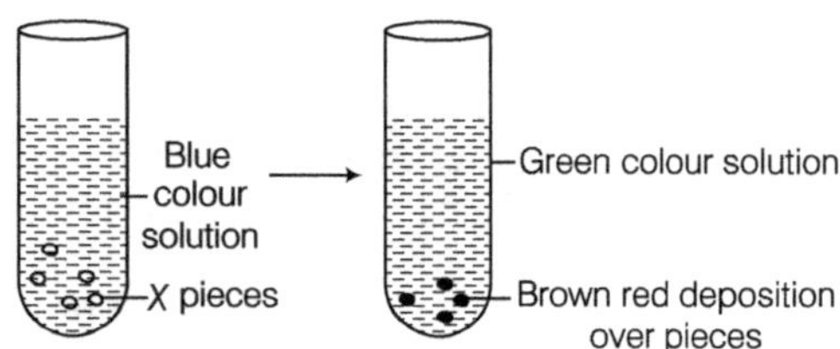

The equation correctly representing the above shown process is

a $ZnSO_4 + Cu \longrightarrow CuSO_4 + Zn$
b $CuSO_4 + Fe \longrightarrow FeSO_4 + Cu$
c $FeSO_4 + Cu \longrightarrow CuSO_4 + Fe$
d $CuSO_4 + Zn \longrightarrow ZnSO_4 + Cu$

17. Consider the following experimental set-up.

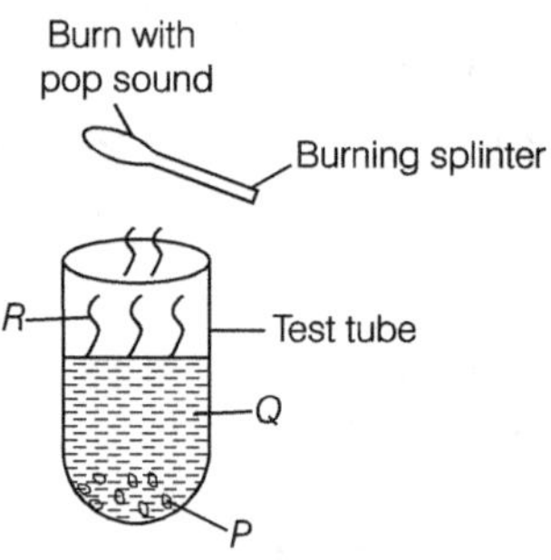

Here, P, Q and R respectively are

a zinc, hydrochloric acid, carbon dioxide
b hydrochloric acid, zinc, carbon dioxide
c zinc, hydrochloric acid, hydrogen
d hydrochloric acid, zinc, hydrogen

18. Which of these are chemical changes?

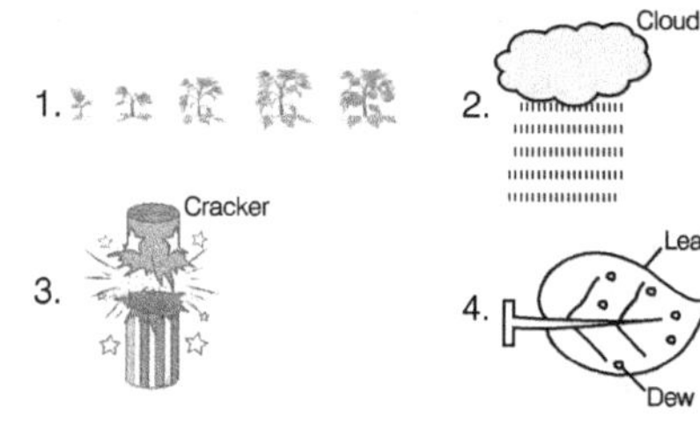

Codes
a 1 and 2   b 2 and 4
c 1, 3 and 4   d 2 and 3

19. **Assertion** (A) Plants synthesised their own food from carbon dioxide by a chemical change.

Reason (R) A chemical change may be accompanied by evolution of a gas and change in colour, shape or smell.

a Both A and R are true and R is the correct explanation of A
b Both A and R are true but R is not the correct explanation of A
c A is true but R is false
d R is true but A is false

20. Carbon dioxide $+ X \longrightarrow$ Limestone $+ Y$.
Here, X and Y are

	X	Y
a	$Ca(OH)_2$	Water
b	$CaCO_3$	Water
c	Water	$Ca(OH)_2$
d	$CaHCO_3$	$CaCO_3$

Direction (Q. Nos. 21-22) Charles burnt different quantities of magnesium ribbon in air. He plotted the following graph based on the results obtained.

21. Which point of the graph may indicate that there is still some unreacted magnesium in the crucible?
  a II
  b III
  c I
  d IV

22. Which of the following best explains the presence of unreacted magnesium?
  a Too much magnesium was added to the crucible
  b The heat supplied was not intense enough
  c Big pieces of magnesium ribbon was heated
  d Less oxygen combined with the magnesium

C) Physical as well as Chemical Changes

1. The gas we use in the kitchen is called Liquefied Petroleum Gas (LPG). In the cylinder, it exists as liquid. When it comes out from the cylinder, it becomes a gas (Change – A) then it burns (Change – B). The following statements pertain to these changes. Choose the correct one.
  a Process A is a chemical change
  b Process B is a physical change
  c Process A is a physical change but B is a chemical change
  d Process A is a chemical change but B is a physical change

2. Seema took a wooden log and try the following experiments.

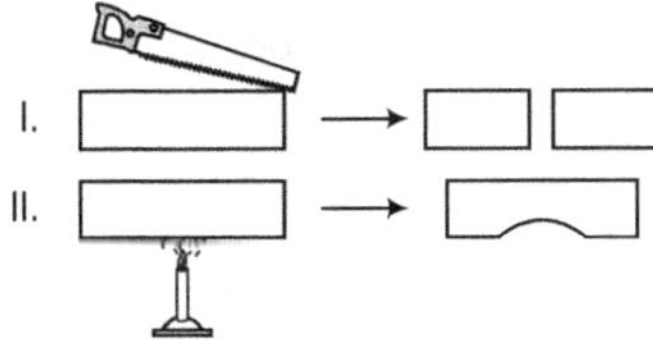

Are the above two experiments involve same type of changes and why?
  a Yes, as both are physical changes
  b No, as I is physical but II is chemical change
  c Yes, as both are chemical changes
  d No, as I is chemical but II is physical change

3. Bridges, ships, vehicles and other articles made up of iron may be rusted with passage of time, due to which their strength reduces greatly. It also harms our economy.

Some methods to overcome this problem are suggested below.
  I. Coating the articles with paint and grease.
  II. Galvanising the iron articles.
  III. Conversion of iron articles into steel.
  IV. Treatment of iron articles with salts.

The correct methods are
  a I and II
  b II and III
  c I, II and III
  d All of the above

4. The various types of changes can be represented in the form of following venn diagrams.

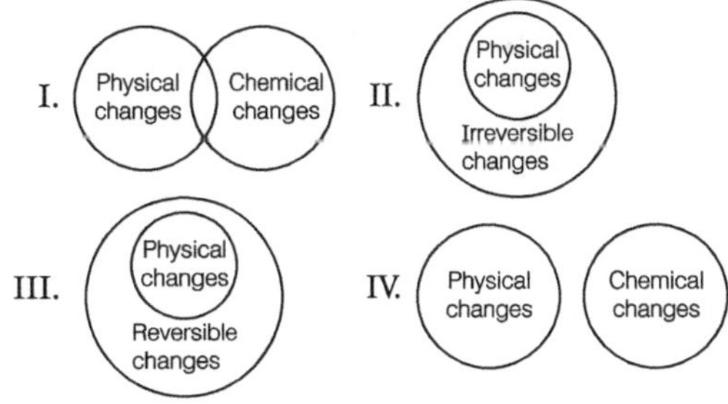

The correct diagram(s) is/are
  a Only I
  b I and II
  c I and III
  d III and IV

5. Match the processes given in Column I with their type given in Column II and choose the correct answer using the codes given below.

	Column I		Column II
A.	Heating a metal for expansion	1.	Physical change
B.	Placing a stone in sunlight	2.	Chemical change
C.	Burning of kerosene in stove	3.	Both physical and chemical change
D.	Curdling of milk	4.	Neither physical nor chemical change

Codes

	A	B	C	D		A	B	C	D
a	1	3	4	2	b	1	2	4	3
c	1	4	3	2	d	1	3	2	4

6. In a pressure kerosene stove, following processes take place.

   I. The stove is pumped to convert kerosene into vapours.

   II. The vapours are then ignited.

The true statement about the above two changes is

a I is a chemical change and II is a physical change

b I is a physical change and II is a chemical change

c I and II both are physical changes

d I and II both are chemical changes

7. Consider the following statements.

   I. Crystallisation is a permanent change.

   II. Digestion involves formation of a new substance.

   III. Burning of paper is a chemical change.

   IV. A chemical change is always reversible.

The correct statement (s) among the above is/are

a I and III   b II, III and IV

c II and III   d Only IV

8. Nidhi placed some iron nails into the solution of blue vitriol and observed that the colour of solution turns green. While, Seema heated the nail for a longer period and observed that it glows to red.

The conclusions made by them from the above experiments are

   I. Nidhi observed a physical change which is reversible.

   II. Seema observed an irreversible physical change.

   III. Nidhi observed an irreversible chemical change.

   IV. Seema observed a reversible change.

The correct conclusions are

a I and II   b II and III

c III and IV   d I and IV

9. Two drops of dilute sulphuric acid were added to 1 g of copper sulphate powder and then small amount of hot water was added to dissolve it (step I). On cooling, beautifully blue coloured crystals got separated (step II). Step I and step II are

a physical and chemical changes, respectively

b chemical and physical changes, respectively

c both physical change

d both chemical change

10. State whether the following statements are true (T) or false (F) and choose the correct option.

   I. When a candle burns, both physical and chemical changes take place.

   II. Anaerobic bacteria digest animal waste and produce biogas.

   III. Ships suffer a lot of damage though they are painted.

   IV. Stretching of rubber band is not a physical change.

	I	II	III	IV		I	II	III	IV
a	T	F	F	T	b	T	T	T	F
c	T	F	F	F	d	F	T	T	F

Chapter 6

Respiration in Organisms

1. In humans, anaerobic respiration occurs in which of the following ?

A. Bones	B. Muscles	C. Tendons	D. Lungs

Codes

a A and B b B and C c Only D d Only B

2. The air tubes of insects are also known as _______. Air enters into the body through tiny holes called _______.

A. diaphragm	B. tubes	C. bronchi	D. tracheae
E. spiracles	F. stomata	G. osculum	H. gills

Codes

a A and G b B and H c C and F d D and E

3. Study the given pie chart which shows the composition of air. Oxygen is represented by which of the following letters?

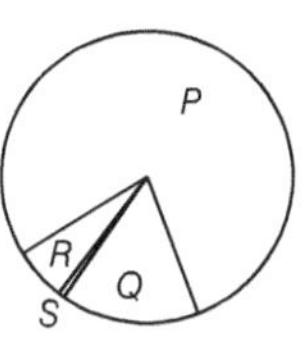

a R b Q c P d S

4. Which of the following is usually oxidised during respiration? What are the products formed?

A. Fat B. Minerals C. Carbohydrates
D. Hydrogen E. $CO_2 + H_2O + Energy$ F. $C_2H_5OH + CO_2 + Energy$
G. Hydrogen H. $CO_2 + Lactic acid + C_2H_5OH$

Codes

a A and H b C and E c D and F d B and G

5. Observe the figure given below and mark the correct option that shows the part of human respiratory system involved in exchange of gases.

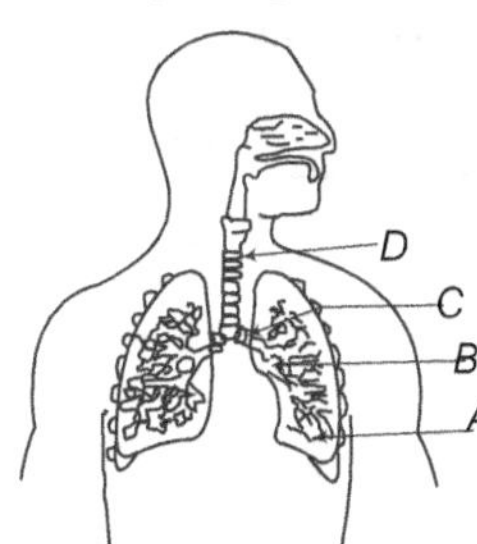

Codes

a A b C c B d D

6. During study time, three friends Kavya, Neena and Ravi wants to find out who among them had the maximum lung capacity. They decided to blow a balloon in one breath and see how big the balloon become. Which of the following factors must be kept in mind to make the test a fair one?

   I. Colour and design of the balloon
   II. Size and shape of the balloon
   III. To breathe in before blowing
   IV. Material of the balloon

Codes
a I and II
b II and III
c I, III and IV
d II, III and IV

7. Muscles in our body can respire in the presence as well as absence of oxygen.

Which substances are produced in them by aerobic respiration and by anaerobic respiration?

	Aerobic respiration	Anaerobic respiration
a	CO_2 and H_2O	Ethanol
b	CO_2 and H_2O	Lactic acid
c	Ethanol	CO_2 and H_2O
d	Ethanol	Lactic acid

Direction (Q. Nos.8-10) Refer to the table below which shows the blood flow to the skeletal muscle and an organ, X, at rest and during exercise.

Body part	Blood flow (mL/min)	
	At rest	During exercise
Skeletal muscle	1200	12500
Organ X	500	2000

8. Which of the following are reasons for increase in blood flow through the skeletal muscle during exercise?

   I. To remove more urea from the muscle.
   II. To carry more heat away from the muscle.
   III. To increase the oxygen supply to the muscle.

Codes
a I and II
b II and III
c I and III
d I, II and III

9. Which of the following is not a cause for the increase in blood flow to the skeletal muscle during exercise?

a Increase in heart rate
b Increase in blood pressure
c Increase in breathing rate
d Dilation of arterioles in the muscle

10. Which of the following may be the organ X?
a The skin
b The kidneys
c The brain
d The small intestine

11. Nitin while doing fun, is blowing air into a glass containing limewater. What will he observe?

The observation is due to.

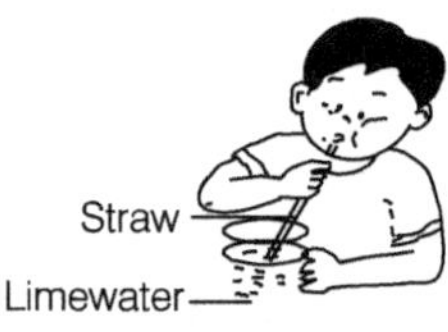

A. Limewater turns violet.
B. Limewater turns yellow.
C. Limewater turns milky.
D. No change in the colour of limewater.
E. CO_2
F. O_2
G. Ethanol
H. Glucose

Codes
a A and F
b B and G
c C and E
d D and H

12. What does the figures A and B represent?

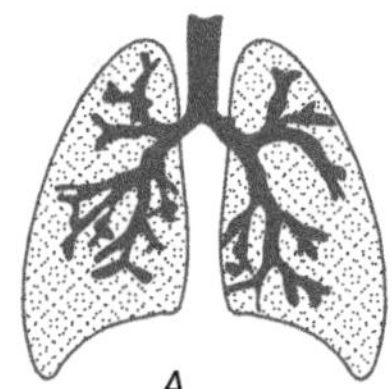
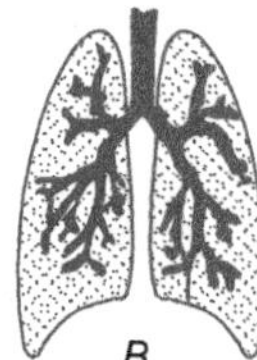

Codes
a $A \rightarrow$ Inhalation, $B \rightarrow$ Exhalation
b $A \rightarrow$ Relaxation, $B \rightarrow$ Contraction
c $A \rightarrow$ Respiration, $B \rightarrow$ Breathing
d None of the above

13. Match the column I with column II.

	Column I		Column II
A.	Yeast	I.	Gills
B.	Diaphragm	II.	Alcohol
C.	Earthworm	III.	Chest cavity
D.	Frog	IV.	Skin
E.	Fish	V.	Lungs and skin

Codes

	A	B	C	D	E
a	IV	II	III	V	I
b	III	II	IV	V	I
c	I	II	IV	V	III
d	II	III	IV	V	I

14. What happens to the diaphragm and the ribcage when a person breathes out?

	Diaphragm	**Ribcage**
a	Downwards	Downwards and upwards
b	Flattens	Outwards and upwards
c	Upwards	Downwards and inwards
d	More dome-shaped	Outwards and upwards

15. Kavi's teacher step up an experiment as shown in the figure to explain the presence of CO_2. What will Kavi observe after sometime?

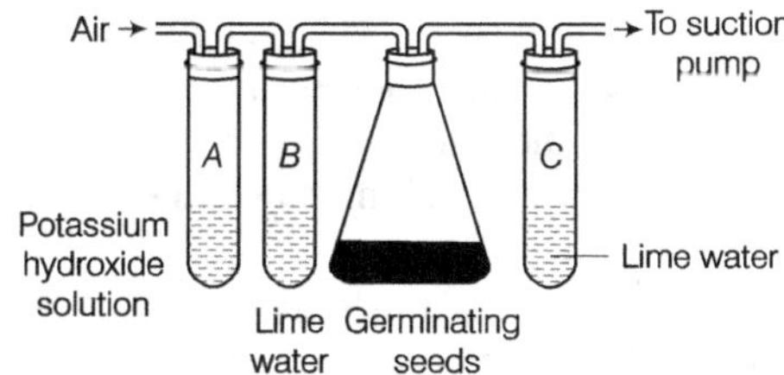

a Limewater in test tube *B* turns milky.
b Limewater in test tube *C* turns milky.
c Potassium hydroxide solution in test tube *A* turns blue.
d Temperature in the flask will go down.

16. The table shows the ventilation rates of an adult man while resting and during exercise.

Adult man	Volume of air inhaled per breath/cm³	Number of breaths per minute
Resting	400	10
Exercising	1000	40

Compared with resting, the volume of air exchanged per minute was increased during exercise by

a 2.5 times
b 4 times
c 10 times
d 100 times

17. The figure below shows the structures involved in oxygen uptake in the lungs.

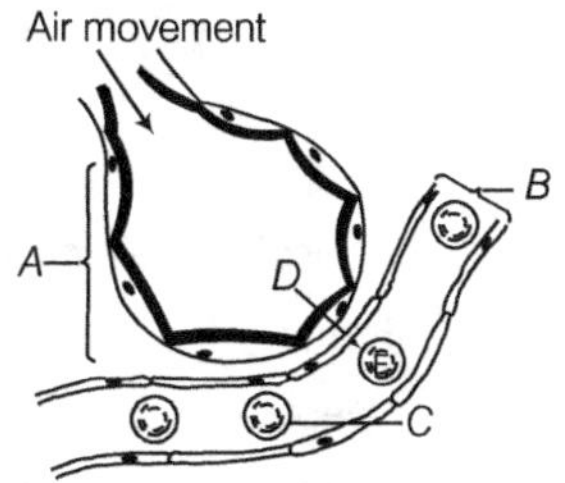

Identify structure *B*.

Codes

a Alveolus   b Capillary
c Red blood cells   d Bronchi

18. Match Column I with Column II and select the correct option from the codes given below.

	Column I		Column II
A.	Earthworms	I.	Pulmonary respiration
B.	Humans	II.	Branchial respiration
C.	Fishes	III.	Tracheal respiration
D.	Insects	IV.	Cutaneous respiration

Codes

	A	B	C	D			A	B	C	D
a	I	II	III	IV		b	IV	I	II	III
c	III	II	IV	I		d	IV	II	I	III

19. The organ used by a frog for breathing under water is

A. lungs   B. skin
C. gills   D. trachea

Codes

a Only A   b B and C
c Only B   d B, C and D

20. Consider the following equations.

I. Carbohydrate + Oxygen $\longrightarrow$ Carbon dioxide + Water + Energy.

II. Glucose $\xrightarrow{\text{Oxygen}}$ Carbon dioxide + Water + Energy.

III. Glucose $\xrightarrow{\text{Absence of oxygen}}$ Alcohol + Carbon dioxide + Energy.

IV. Glucose $\xrightarrow{\text{Absence of oxygen}}$ Lactic acid + Energy.

Which of these equations follow anaerobic respiration?

a II, III   b III, IV
c I, IV   d I, II

21. Complete the way of air, by opting the correct option.

Nose → Nasal cavity → A → B → C → D

Codes

	A	B	C	D
a	Bronchi	Bronchiole	Trachea	Alveoli
b	Alveoli	Bronchi	Bronchiole	Trachea
c	Trachea	Alveoli	Bronchiole	Bronchi
d	Trachea	Bronchi	Bronchiole	Alveoli

22. Oxygen rich air rushes through P into the Q, diffuses into R and reaches every cell of the body.

Codes

a $P →$ Spiracles, $Q →$ Tracheal tubes, $R →$ Body tissue

b $P →$ Tracheal tubes, $P →$ Spiracles, $R →$ Body cells

c $P →$ Body tissue, $Q →$ Trachea, $P →$ Spiracles

d None of the above

23. State 'T' for true and 'F' for false.

I. Cellular respiration takes place in all the cells of an animal.

II. Food can also be broken down, without using oxygen. This is called anaerobic respiration.

III. Gills are projections of the skin.

IV. During inhalation, our lungs expand and then come back to the original state as the air moves out during exhalation.

V. The breakdown of glucose in plant cells is similar to that in other living beings.

Codes

	I	II	III	IV	V
a	T	F	T	F	T
b	T	T	T	T	F
c	F	T	F	F	T
d	F	F	T	T	F

24. A person's nose was clipped and was asked to breathe in and out in a plastic bag as shown in the diagram below.

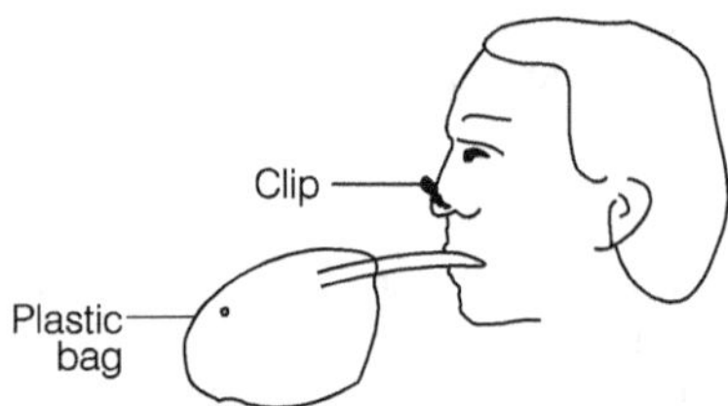

Which of the following changes in the blood of the person could be the reason for the change in his breathing rate and deep breathing?

a The carbon dioxide concentration had increased.

b The lactic acid concentration had increased.

c The oxygen concentration had increased.

d The temperature of his blood had increased.

25. The respiration of a molecule of glucose can be either aerobic or anaerobic. Which of the following correctly describes anaerobic respiration?

	Amount of energy released	Carbon dioxide produced	Lactic acid produced	Water produced
a	High	Yes	No	No
b	High	Yes	Yes	No
c	Low	Yes	No	Yes
d	Low	Yes	Yes	No

26. An experiment was set-up as shown below. It has indicators which changes from red to yellow when exposed to increased levels of carbon dioxide. At the start of the experiment, the indicator in each test tube was red.

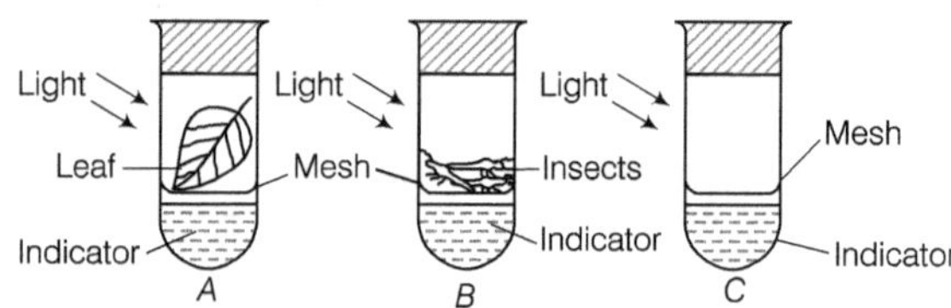

What will be the colour of the indicator in each test tube after two hours?

Codes

	A	B	C
a	Yellow	Yellow	Red
b	Red	Yellow	Red
c	Red	Red	Red
d	Red	Yellow	Yellow

27. Kripa soaked some bean seeds in water overnight. Next day, she drained the water and kept the seeds in moist for germination. She boiled half of the seeds and then kept the germinating seeds in one thermos flask (A) and the boiled seeds in another thermos flask (B).

She covered the mouths of both flasks with moist cotton wool. Then she inserted thermometers in both flasks and kept the flasks as shown in the figure. What would she must have observed?

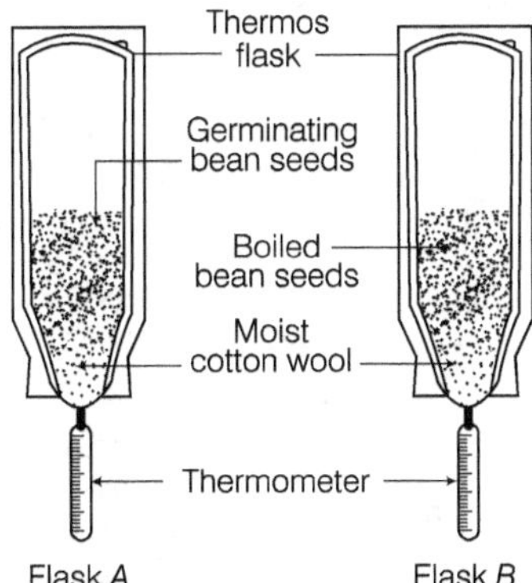

a Temperature of flask *A* increases because it has photosynthesising seeds.

b Temperature of flask *A* increases because it has respiring seeds.

c Temperature of flask *B* increases because it has boiled seeds.

d Both b and c

28. It is sometimes said that "A person breathes faster when running because the muscles need more oxygen". Which of the following is are the reason(s) that proves the above statement wrong?

A. The muscles do not use more oxygen during running.

B. It is not only when during running that muscles need more oxygen.

C. More oxygen is supplied to the muscles by more rapid circulation of the blood whether one breathes faster or not.

D. The strongest stimulus for breathing is increased concentration of carbon dioxide in the blood rather than lack of oxygen.

Choose the correct option is/are

a A and B

b C and D

c Only D

d B, C and D

29. In a traffic accident, an accident victim was found struggling for breath. His chest cavity was moving but his lungs were not inflating. Which part of his body in the diagram given alongside could possibly have been injured in this case?

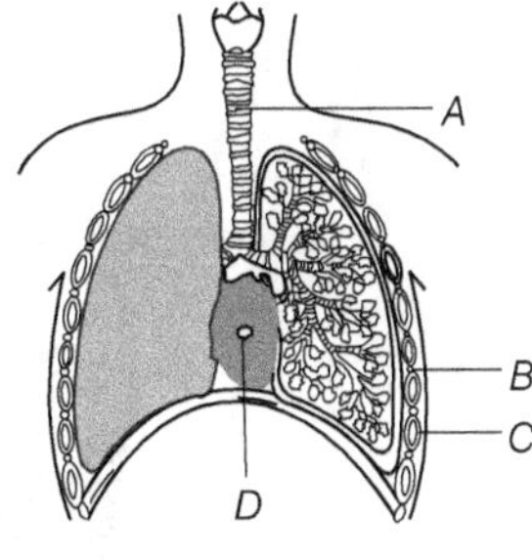

Codes

a *B*　　b *C*　　c *A*　　d *D*

30. The diagram shows organs associated with breathing in humans.

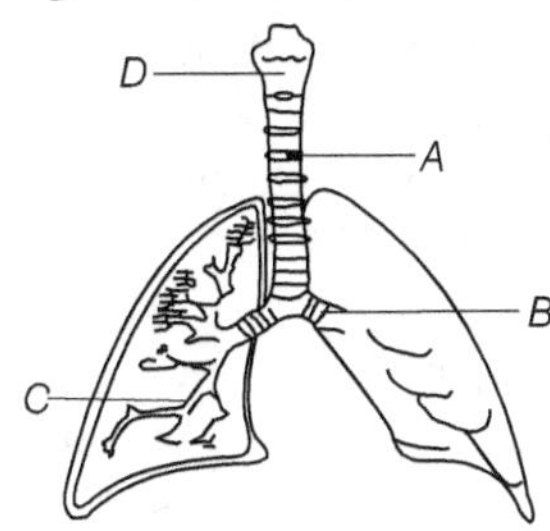

Identify the numbered structures correctly.

	A	B	C	D
a	Bronchus	Bronchiole	Larynx	Trachea
b	Bronchiole	Bronchus	Larynx	Trachea
c	Larynx	Trachea	Bronchus	Bronchiole
d	Trachea	Bronchus	Bronchiole	Larynx

31. The following represents the composition of five samples of air. Which of the following could be a sample of air breathed out by a person after vigorous outdoor exercise?

	Carbon dioxide	Oxygen	Nitrogen	Inert gases	Water vapour
a	0	24	75	1	Saturated
b	21	0	78	1	Trace
c	7	14	78	1	Saturated
d	Trace	17	82	1	Saturated

32. Read the given statements and select the correct option.

I. Glucose contains a lot of heat energy.

II. Humans follow anaerobic respiration.

III. Our contracting muscles need energy to move parts of body.

IV. Animals get sugar from carbohydrates, they eat.

V. The lungs are supplied with air through the capillary.

VI. Larynx in epiglottis contains the vocal cords.

Codes

a I, II and V are incorrect, while III, IV and VI are correct

b I, II and III are incorrect, while IV, V and VI are correct

c II an IV are incorrect, while I, III, V and VI are correct

d II and VI are incorrect, while I, III, IV and V are correct

33. When bacteria enters into the respiratory tract with the air, they are mainly

   I. destroyed by antibodies.

   II. engulfed by white blood cells.

   III. removed with the mucus film by the beating of cilia.

Codes

a I, II and III
b I and III
c Only III
d Only II

34. The structure shows how the element carbon, present in carbon dioxide and carbohydrates is passed on to the environment.

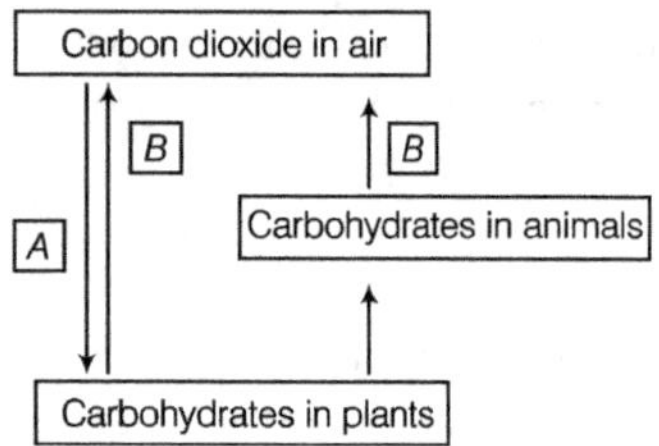

Identify processes *A* and *B*.

	A	*B*
a	Respiration	Photosynthesis
b	Photosynthesis	Respiration
c	Aerobic respiration	Photosynthesis
d	Transpiration	Aerobic respiration

35. Riti sets up an experiment. She used hydrogen carbonate as an indicator in the experiment which turns yellow in the presence of carbon dioxide.

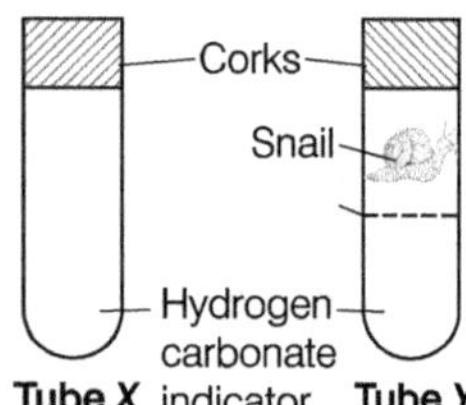

Which of the given below observations is observed by her after an hour?

	Tube *X*	Tube *Y*
a	Indicator turns yellow	No change in the colour of indicator
b	No change in the colour of indicator	Indicator turns yellow
c	No change in the colour of indicator	No change in the colour of indicator
d	Indicator turns yellow	Indicator turns yellow

36. Observe the figure given below and identify *P*, *Q*, *R* and *S* by analysing the options that follow.

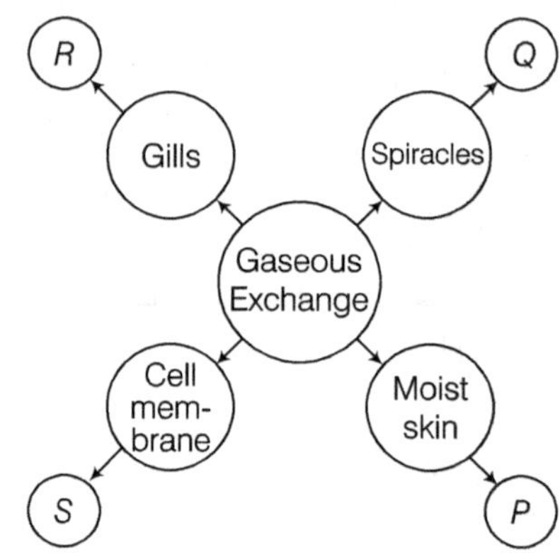

Codes

	P	Q	R	S
a	Pigeon	Cockroach	Tadpole	Earthworm
b	Frog	Grasshopper	Fish	*Amoeba*
c	Crab	Spider	Frog	*Paramecium*
d	Penguin	Mynah	Snake	Leech

37. Which of the following changes will occur when a person is doing vigorous exercise?

	Depth of breathing	Rate of breathing	% O_2 in inhaled air
a	Increases	Increases	Increases
b	Decreases	Constant	Increases
c	Increases	Increases	Constant
d	Decreases	Constant	Constant

38. The diagram below shows a section through the human thorax. Two sets of muscles are labelled *P* and *Q* and the thoracic cavity is labelled *R*.

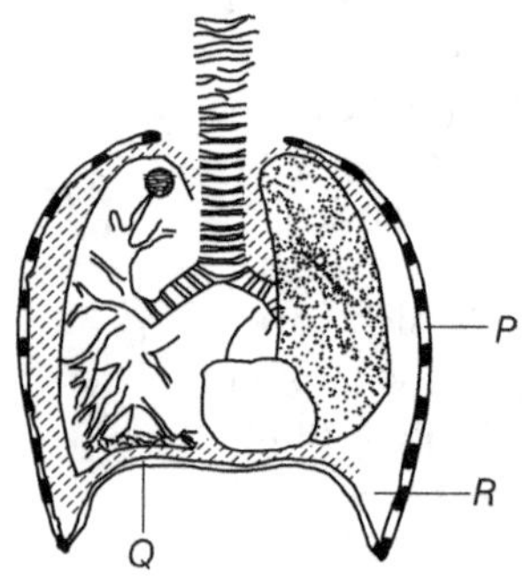

Which of the following occurs in them for air to enter the lungs?

	Muscles *P*	Muscles *Q*	Volume of *R*
a	Relax	Contract	Increased
b	Contract	Contract	Increased
c	Contract	Relax	Reduced
d	Relax	Relax	Increase

39. The diagram below shows the set-up of the apparatus used in experiments with respiring plants.

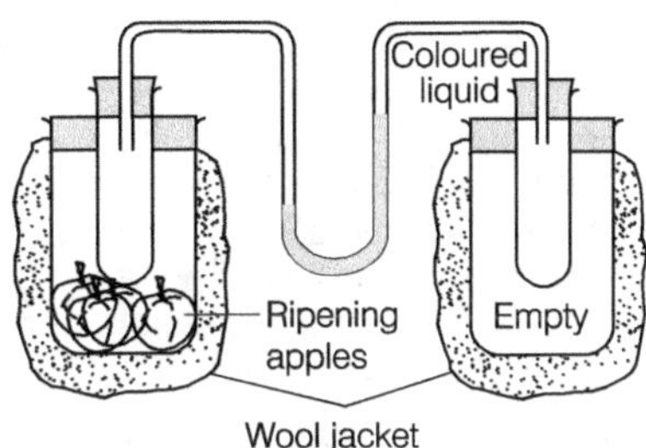

Which of the following represents the conclusion of this experiment?

a Respiring plants produce oxygen.

b Respiring plants produce carbon dioxide.

c Respiring plants give off heat.

d Respiring plants take in heat.

40. The graph below shows how the rate of breathing of a test subject changes under different conditions. At the beginning of each experiment, the subject is breathing in atmospheric air.

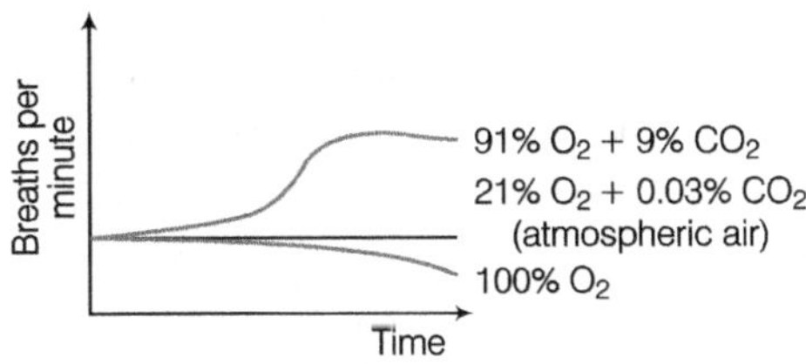

What conclusion may be derived from the graph?

a High levels of oxygen in the air cause breathing rate to drop, regardless of carbon dioxide levels.

b Increase in breathing rate causes carbon dioxide levels to increase.

c Oxygen content in the air at 21% gives the greatest stability in breathing rate.

d Increase in carbon dioxide causes breathing rate to increase.

41. In an experiment, the volume of air taken in with each breath and the number of breaths per minute were measured whilst a young person was performing a different activities. The results are shown below.

	Activity	Volume of air per breath (cm^3)	Breaths per minute
1.	Sleeping	500	20
2.	Standing	550	22
3.	Walking	700	28
4.	Running	1000	40

What volume of air is breathed in each minute whilst the person is sleeping? Also, states during which activity is the volume of air breathed in within a minute is maximum?

A 10000 cm^3 B 100 cm^3

C 1000 cm^3 d 500 cm^3

Codes

a B and 1   b C and 2

c A and 4   d D and 3

42. The diagram shows an experiment to study respiration in growing barley seeds.

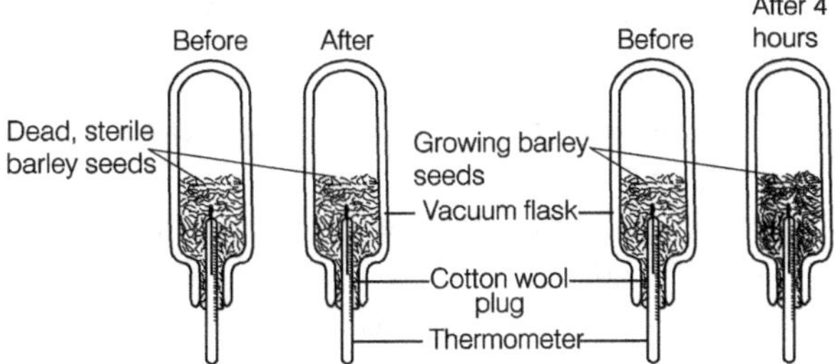

Which of the following is demonstrated by the results of this experiment?

a Respiration produces carbon dioxide.

b Respiration releases heat.

c Respiration requires glucose.

d Respiration uses oxygen.

43. Consider the given paragraph and complete it by opting the correct option.

In humans, gaseous exchange is very important for normal body activities. The most important parts involved are two lungs. Each lung is filled with __*A*__ . It is here that oxygen diffuses into the __*B*__ . The lungs are supplied with air through the __*C*__ . __*D*__ is the piece of cartilage that avoids the food from moving into the wind pipe.

Codes

	A	B	C	D
a	Bronchioles	Alveoli	Trachea	Goblet cells
b	Alveoli	Blood	Trachea	Epiglottis
c	Trachea	Bronchioles	Trachea	Palate
d	Bronchus	Alveoli	Trachea	Vocal cords

44. The diagram shows a device used to measure oxygen uptake by woodlice.

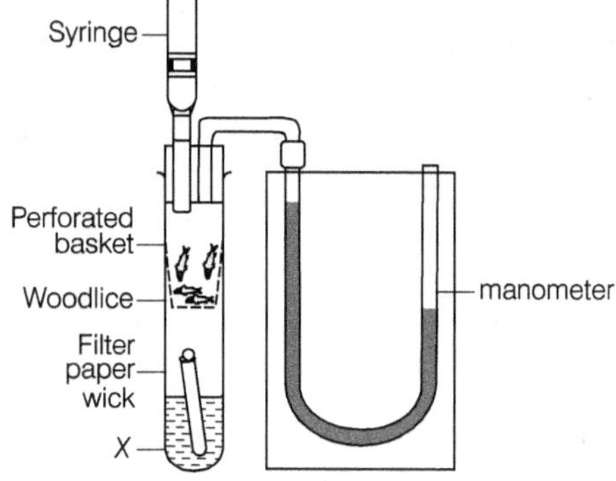

What is X?

  a Buffer solution to control the pH

  b Limewater to indicate the presence of carbon dioxide

  c Potassium hydroxide to absorb carbon dioxide

  d Water to control humidity

45. Consider the table given below and identify the conditions in the muscles when lactic acid is produced?

	Concentration of carbon dioxide	Supply of oxygen
a	High	Less than the demand
b	High	More than the demand
c	Low	Less than the demand
d	Low	More than the demand

46. The model shown in the diagram imitates the action of lungs that takes place in the human thorax.

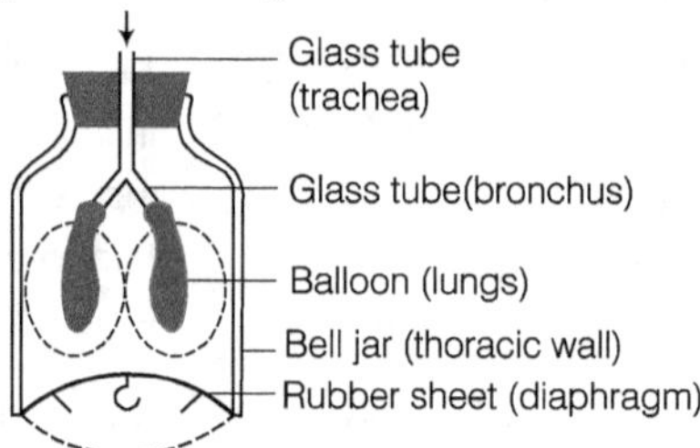

Which of the following explains the entry of air in the bell jar during inspiration?

  a Entry of air is due to decrease in volume of bell jar and increase in air pressure of bell jar.

  b Entry of air is due to increase in volume of bell jar and increase in air pressure of bell jar.

  c Entry of air is due to decrease in volume of bell jar and decrease in air pressure of bell jar.

  d Entry of air is due to increase in volume of bell jar and decrease in air pressure of bell jar.

47. Solve the following crossword using the hints given below.

Across

  3. Gas exhaled during respiration.

  5. Respiration performed in the presence of oxygen.

  7. Respiratory organ that can receive oxygen dissolved in water.

  9. Funnel-shaped tube acting as a passage way for air and food.

  10. The product of anaerobic respiration.

Down

  1. Epiglottis is the voice box or.

  2. Hair-like projections on cell that trap dust particles.

  4. The end of bronchiole has

  6. Organ called as the gate of respiratory system.

  8. Sacs of membrane that line pleural cavity.

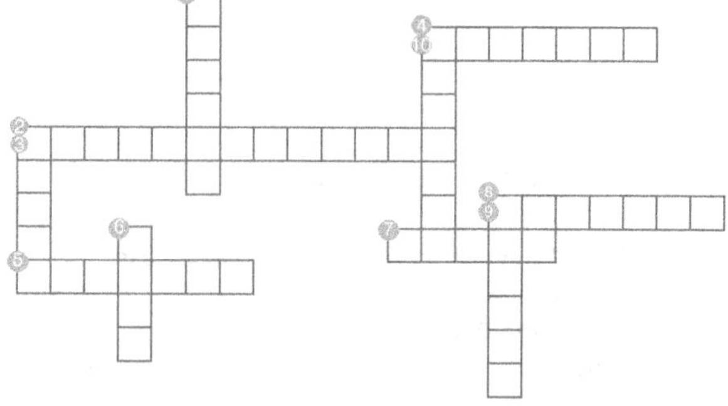

Chapter 7

Transportation in Plants and Animals

1. In human body, which part helps in eliminating wastes?

A. Kidney B. Heart C. Skin D. Stomach

Codes

a A and B b A and C c B and D d C and D

2. The figure given below shows two types of blood vessels, labelled as X and Y. Which of the following from the codes is an incorrect statement about them?

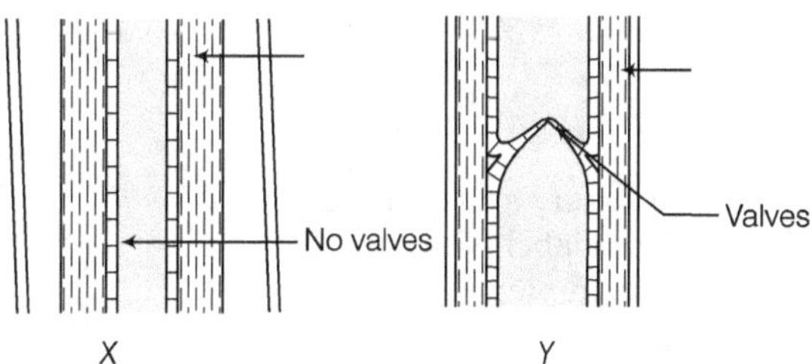

Codes

	X	Y
a	They carry blood away from the heart	They carry blood to the heart
b	They have thin walls	They have thick walls
c	They are deeply placed under the skin	They are superficially placed
d	They are arteries	They are veins

3. Observe the given pie chart that shows the concentration of oxygen in blood samples at four sites in the circulatory system of a man. Which sample was taken from the pulmonary artery?

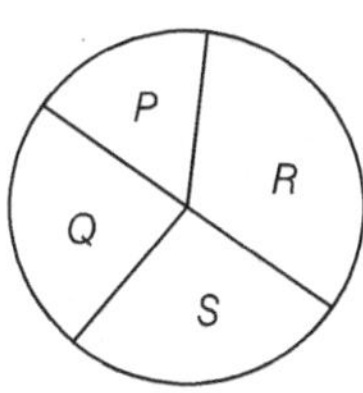

Concentration of oxygen in blood

a P b Q c R d S

4. I belong to an aquatic animal groups such as crustaceans, fishes, etc. I produce a highly soluble waste as a result of catabolism of proteins. What do I excrete?

a Ammonia b Urea c Uric acid d May be a or c

5. Observe the table given below and identify A, B and C correctly

	Function	Structure of wall	Width of lumen
A.	Carry blood away from the heart	Thick and strong, containing muscles and elastic tissues	Relatively narrow; it varies with heartbeat, as it can stretch and recoil
B.	Supply all cells with their requirements and take away waste products	Very thin, only one layer thick	Very narrow, just wide enough for a red blood cell to pass through
C.	Return blood to the heart	Quite thin, containing less muscle and elastic tissue than A.	Wide, contain valves

Codes

	A	B	C
a	Arteries	Capillaries	Veins
b	RBCs	WBCs	Lymph
c	Pulmonary vein	Aorta	Pulmonary artery
d	Capillaries	Arteries	Veins

6. The figure shows, the pulmonary and systemic circulation. Identify the parts labelled as *A*, *B*, *C* and *D* in the diagrammatic representation and select the correct option.

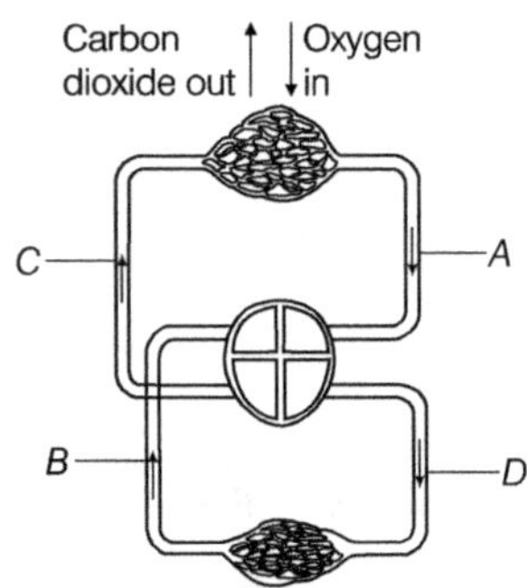

	A	B	C	D
a	Pulmonary artery	Pulmonary vein	Aorta	Vein
b	Pulmonary vein	Inferior vena cava	Pulmonary artery	Aorta
c	Pulmonary vein	Aorta	Vein	Pulmonary vein
d	Aorta	Inferior vena cava	Pulmonary vein	Pulmonary artery

7. In the figure below, which of the labelled portion carries deoxygenated blood to lungs.

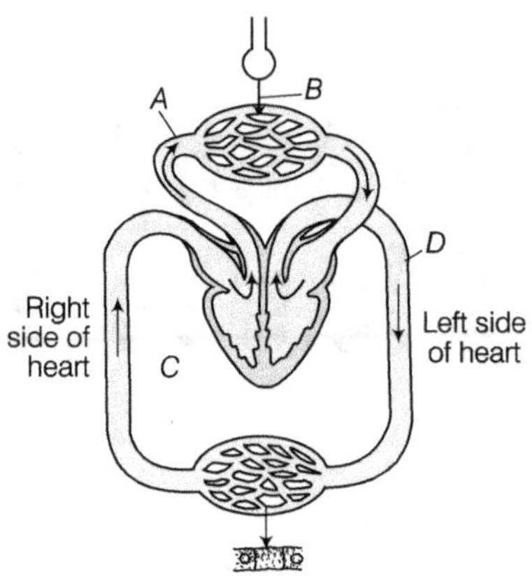

a	A and B	b	B and C
c	C and A	d	D and B

8. Which of the following statements are correct?
   A. Urea is removed from the blood by kidney.
   B. The kidney maintains the water level of our body.
   C. Ureter carry urine from the revel pelvis of the kidneys to the urethera.
   D. Nephrons are the functional unit of a kidney.

Codes
a A and B
b B and D
c C and D
d Both a and b

9. Match the column I with column II

	Column I		Column II
A.	Glomerulus	1.	Hair pin-like tubule
B.	Bowman's capsule	2.	It leads away from renal tubule to form PCT
C.	Nephron	3.	Consists of corpuscle and a renal tubule
D.	Loop of Henle	4.	Part of filtration unit composed of tiny blood capillaries

Codes

	A	B	C	D
a	1	3	2	4
b	4	3	2	1
c	4	2	3	1
d	1	2	3	4

10. Refer the given experimental set-up prepared by a group of students and select the correct option for the following question

Why do we notice tiny droplets of water on the inner surface of the glass cover?
   a Due to photolysis
   b Due to transpiration
   c Due to photorespiration
   d Due to photosynthesis

11. Observe the given figure, which shows different parts of the heart. Select the option that correctly matches the labels P, Q, R and S in the figure with the given list $(A-D)$

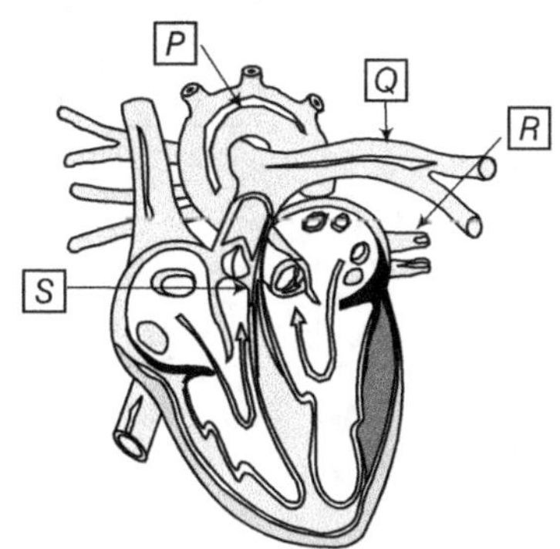

   A. It carries blood to different parts of the body
   B. It brings back oxygen rich blood from the lungs
   C. They allow the blood to flow only in one direction.
   D. It takes blood to the lungs for oxygenation.

   Codes
   a P – B, Q – D, R – A, S – C
   b P – A, Q – B, R – C, S – D
   c P – D, Q – A, R – B, S – C
   d P – A, Q – D, R – B, S – C

12. Manu fills the jam jar three-fourths with water. He adds a few drops of red ink colouring to the water. He placed the twig in this water, and record observations over a period of five days. He took a section of the stem on a slide, and observed it under microscope. The activity is given below. Choose the correct conclusion made by Manu at the end of fifth day from this activity.

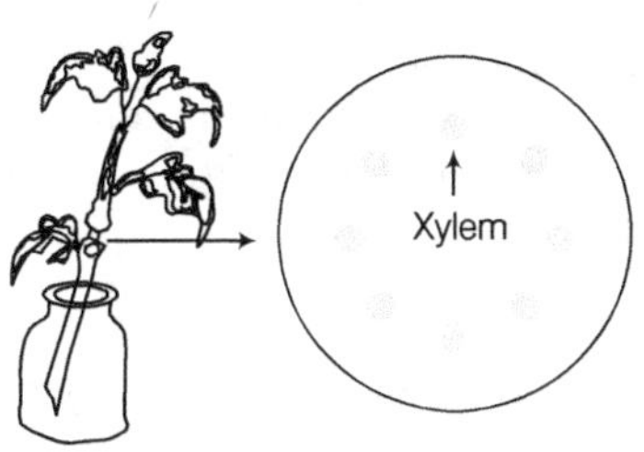

   a Transport of water takes place through xylem.
   b Transport of water takes place through phloem.
   c Translocation of water does not take place.
   d Transpiration was observed clearly.

13. The cells shown in figure can be found in the blood.

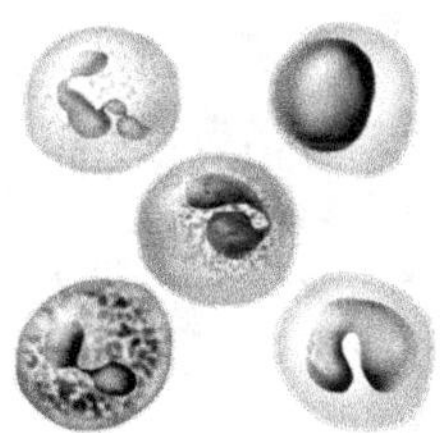

Which of the following statement(s) is/are correct regarding these cells?
   I. They do not have nucleus.
   II. They help the body to fight against infections.
   III. They help the blood to clot.
   IV. They help to transport oxygen.

   Codes
   a Only II   b I and II
   c I, II and III   d I, III and IV

14. The part labelled X in the given diagram helps plants to _______ .

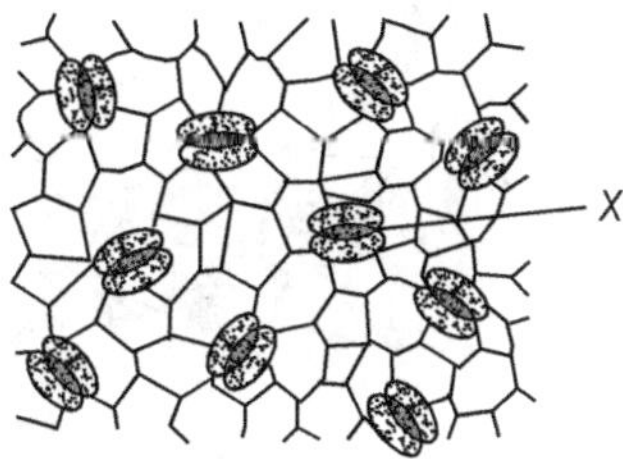

   I. take in oxygen
   II. take in water vapour
   III. give out oxygen
   IV. give out water vapour

   Codes
   a I and II   b I and IV
   c II and III   d I, III and IV

15. Urine is an excretory product formed inside our body. What could be its composition? Opt the correct composition from the given options.

Codes

	Urea	Ammonia	Uric acid	Water	Other waste salts
a	2.5%	2.5%	–	94%	1%
b	2.5%	–	–	95%	2.5%
c	–	2.5%	–	95%	2.5%
d	–	–	2.5%	95%	2.5%

16. The diagram shows blood as seen under a microscope.

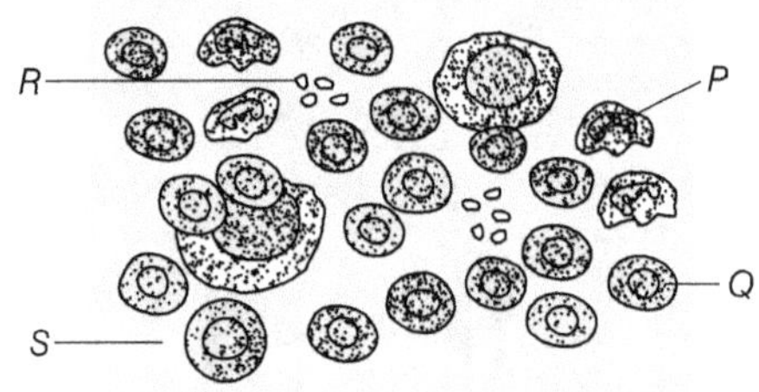

Identify parts *P*, *Q*, *R* and *S* of the blood.

	Plasma	Platelet	Red blood cell	White blood cell
a	P	Q	S	R
b	Q	P	R	S
c	R	S	P	Q
d	S	R	Q	P

17. There is a capillary network shown below. The arrows in the figure shows the blood flow. observe and identify the labelled parts in network.

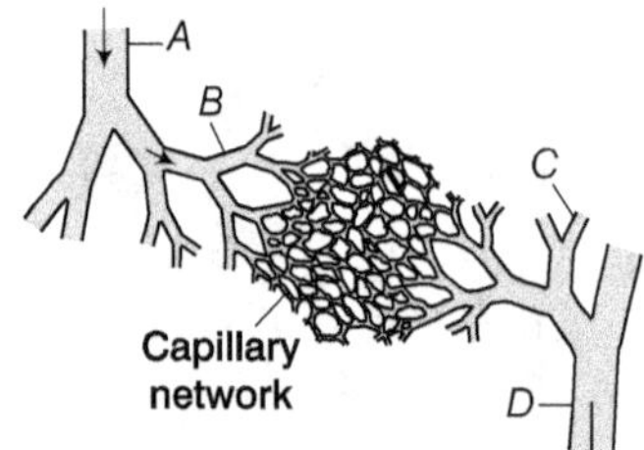

Codes

	A	B	C	D
a	Artery	Arteriole	Venule	Vein
b	Arteriole	Artery	Venule	Vein
c	Venule	Artery	Arteriole	Vein
d	Artery	Vein	Arteriole	Venule

18. Look at the picture given below carefully. Choose the correct match that identifies the name of the instrument used on the woman and the purpose for which it is used.

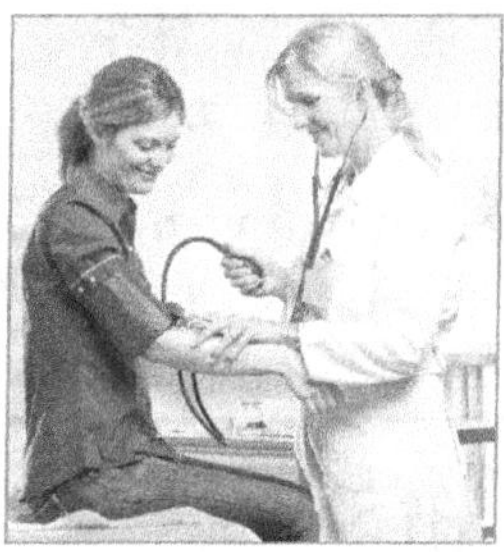

	Instrument		Purpose
A	Pacemaker	(i)	For measuring pulse
B	Stethoscope	(ii)	For determining blood pressure
C	Sphygmomanometer	(iii)	For noting the temperature of body
D	Thermometer	(iv)	For hearing heart sounds

Codes

a A – iv	b B – i
c C – ii	d D – iii

19. I : RBCs

II : WBCs

Consider the above cells and opt the correct statement regarding them.

A. I are enucleated, whereas II are nucleated.

B. I carries oxygen.

C. II fight infections.

D. I is involved in clotting process but II is not.

Choose the correct option.

a A and B	b B and C
c C and D	d Both a and b

20. Which of the following combination are correct?

	Part of plant	Function
A	Stomata	Transpiration
B	Xylem	Transport of oxygen
C	Phloem	Transport of food
D	Root hair	Gaseous exchange

Codes

a A and B	b B and C
c A and C	d A, B and D

21. Look at the set-up given below carefully. The set-up is allowed to stand for about two hours.

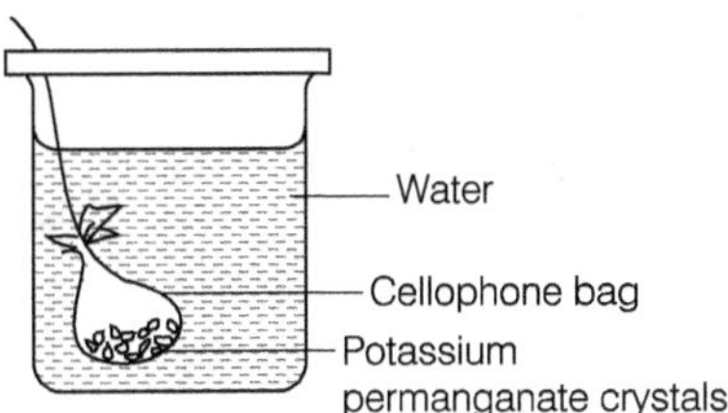

Which of the following is the correct observation of this experiment?
   a Water has diffused into the cellophone bag which acts as a semipermeable membrane
   b Water has diffused out of the cellophone bag
   c Potassium permanganate crystals degrade the bag
   d Both b and c

22. Which of the following transport are conducted by blood plasma?

	Oxygen	CO$_2$	Heat	Hormones
a	✓	✓	✗	✓
b	✗	✓	✓	✓
c	✗	✓	✗	✓
d	✓	✓	✓	✓

23. Opt the correct combination
   A. Urethra: Duct leading from the urinary bladder to outside the body.
   B. Ureter: Tube that carries urine from urethra to urinary bladder
   C. Urinary bladder: Hollow muscular sac located in pelvis
   D. Nephron: filtering unit of kidney

Codes
   a A and B
   b A, C and D
   c C and D
   d All the correct

24. Given below is the sequence of excretion in kidney.
   1. Ureter
   2. Urethra
   3. Renal pyramid
   4. Blood
   5. Urinary bladder
   6. Pelvis
   7. Renal artery
   8. Nephron

Codes
   a $1 \rightarrow 2 \rightarrow 3 \rightarrow 7 \rightarrow 8 \rightarrow 4 \rightarrow 5 \rightarrow 6$
   b $2 \rightarrow 5 \rightarrow 1 \rightarrow 3 \rightarrow 6 \rightarrow 8 \rightarrow 7 \rightarrow 4$
   c $2 \rightarrow 5 \rightarrow 1 \rightarrow 6 \rightarrow 3 \rightarrow 8 \rightarrow 7 \rightarrow 4$
   d $4 \rightarrow 5 \rightarrow 2 \rightarrow 1 \rightarrow 6 \rightarrow 8 \rightarrow 7 \rightarrow 3$

25. Observe the diagram given below and opt the option that correctly declares the waste product at the end of the flow chart.

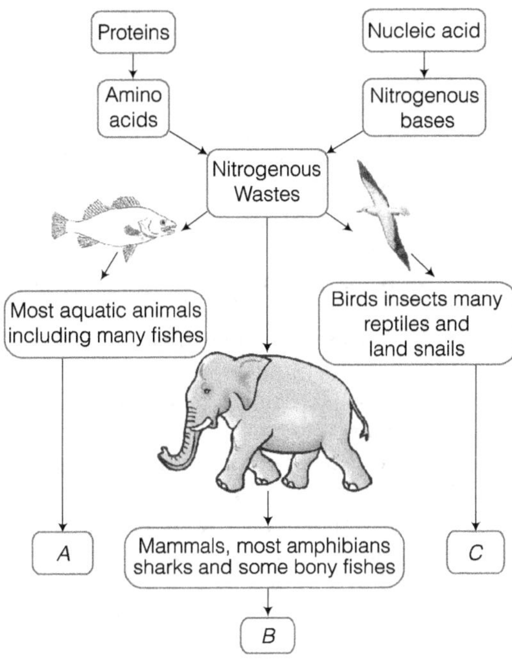

Codes

	A	B	C
a	Ammonia	Urea	Uric acid
b	Urea	Ammonia	Uric acid
c	Uric acid	Urea	Ammonia
d	Ammonia	Uric acid	Urea

26. Given alongside is a pictorial representation of human excretory system. Which of the labelled part function to filter the blood for removing urea? The urine formed is stored in part labelled as________.

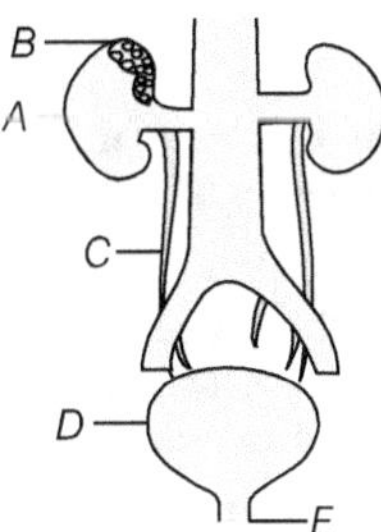

Codes
   a B, C
   b A, D
   c C, B
   d D, E

27. Which of the following is a correct match of xylem and phloem with the letters?

	Xylem	Phloem
a	P	R
b	R	S
c	S	R
d	Q	R

28. Which of the following statement(s) is/are incorrect?

   I. Plants produce excretory product like resins, gums, etc.

   II. Water evaporates through the stomata by the process of transpiration.

   III. Gaseous exchange in plants take place through stomata.

   IV. Transpiration is a process in plants that allow it to grow.

   V. CO_2 passes out through the stomata during photosynthesis.

   VI. A suction pull is needed to pass the food through phloem.

Codes

a	I, II and III	b	IV, V and VI
c	I, III and V	d	II, IV and VI

29. State 'T' for true and 'F' for false statements.

   I. Homeostasis is the tendency of higher animals to maintain internal temperature stability of the body.

   II. Kidney controls the balance of water and mineral ions in the body.

   III. Haemodialysis is the process of separating wastes from the blood by passing it through a semipermeable membrane.

Codes

	I	II	III			I	II	III
a	T	T	F		b	T	T	T
c	F	T	T		d	F	T	T

30. The steps of urine formation are given below with some blanks, fill the blanks by opting the correct option.

   I. __A__ is the process in which nephrons filter minerals, waste and water but retain __B__, and large molecules.

   II. Selective reabsorption involves reabsorption of substances like __C__ amino acids, salts and a major amount of water.

   III. __D__ involves secretion of substances not required by the body into the filtrate by the cells of DCT before it leaves the kidney.

Codes

	A	B	C	D
a	Tubular secretion	RBCs	Glucose	Ultra filtration
b	Ultra filtration	RBCs	Glucose	Tubular filtration
c	Ultra filtration	Proteins	Glucose	Tubular secretion
d	Tubular secretion	Glucose	RBCs	Ultra filtration

31. Assertion (A) A uricotelic organism excretes uric acid.

Reason (R) Uricotelic organism undergo deamination

   a (A) and (R) are true and (R) is the correct explanation of (A).

   b (A) and (R) are true, but (R) is not the correct explanation of (A)

   c (A) is correct, but (R) is false

   d (A) and (R) are false

32. Solve the crossword with the help of given clues.

Down

   1. Process of removal of wastes from the cells of living organisms

   3. Pipelines that carry food in plants

   4. Waste product produced by humans which is a combination of CO_2 and NH_3

   6. Red pigment of blood

Across

   2. Loss of water vapour from the stomata is called

   5. Ventricle that pumps oxygenated blood to all parts of the body.

   7. Chamber of heart with thinner walls.

   8. Tissue that takes water and mineral in plants.

   9. Functional unit of kidney.

Chapter 8

Reproduction in Plants

1. Manisha observed that a pond with clear water was covered up with a green algae within a week. By which method of reproduction did the algae spread so rapidly? Also, give an example of such alga.

A. Budding	B. Fragmentation
C. Sexual reproduction	D. Pollination
E. Yeast	F. *Spirogyra*
G. *Rhizopus*	H. *Amoeba*

   Choose the correct combination

   a A and G   b B and F   c C and E   d D and H

2. In the given below figure, the part '*X*' resembles to which of the following option?

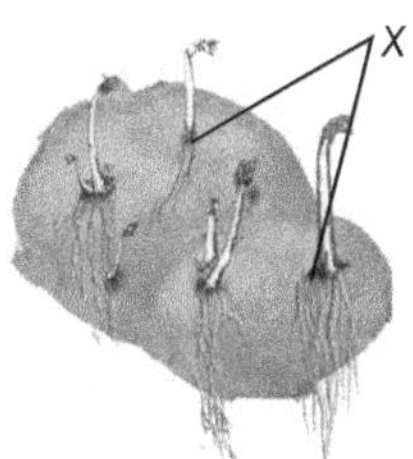

   a The root of any plant   b The bud of a flower
   c The bud of *Bryophyllum* leaf   d The anther of stamen

3. Complete the missing blank. Sepal : Calyx :: Petal : ....
   a Epicalyx   b Perianth
   c Corolla   d Carpel

4. Read the following statements made by four children.

   Kavya : A seed germinates only when there is water, warm temperature and air.
   Nishi : All flowering plants reproduce by seeds.
   Prachi : A carpel contains an ovary
   Navya : The seed leaves will continue to grow bigger as the plant grows from a young plant to an adult plant.

   Which of these children have made incorrect statements?
   a Kavya and Prachi   b Prachi and Navya
   c Nishi and Navya   d Kavya and Navya

5. Look at the classification chart carefully. Identify *X* and *Y*

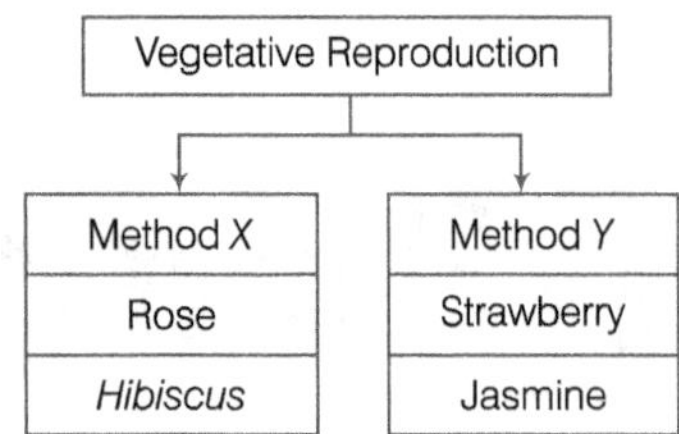

Codes

	X	*Y*
a	Cutting	Layering
b	Layering	Grafting
c	Cutting	Grafting
d	Layering	Cutting

6. To learn pollination, Priya bagged four different kinds of flowers on the potted plants as shown below and left them undisturbed. Which of these four flowers is most likely to produce fruits and seeds?

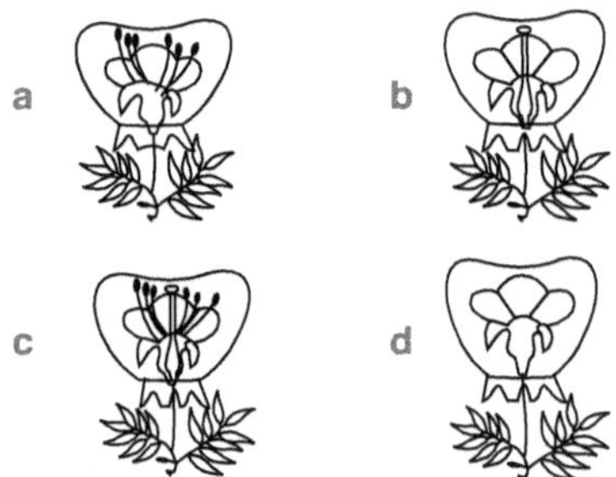

7. Which of the following shows the correct order of the processes in the life cycle of a flowering plant?

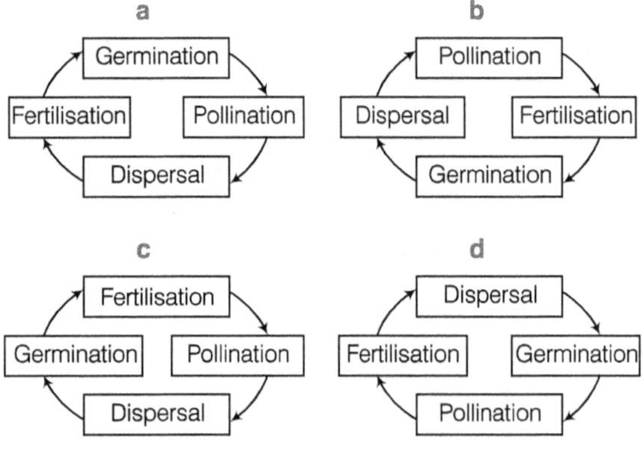

8. Observe the diagram given below. Identify '*X*'. [Hint : Reproduction]

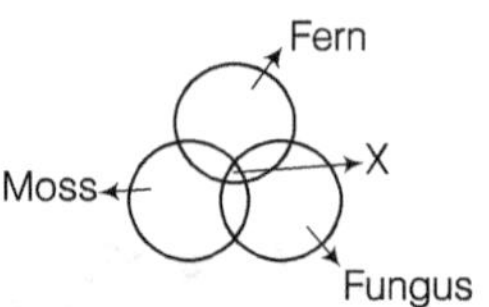

a A mode of sexual reproduction
b A mode of asexual reproduction
c Reproduce by spore formation
d Reproduce by fragmentation

9. Riya has the following parts of a rose plant. She wants to grow new rose plants. Which of the following parts she can use? Choose the correct option.

I. A leaf	II. Stem
III. A branch	IV. A flower
V. A bud	VI. Pollen grains

Codes

a II, III and VI   b Only III
c Only II   d II, III, IV and VI

10. Observe the figure given below and identify the type of pollination it shows.

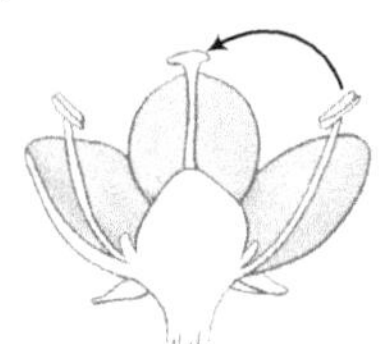

a Self-pollination   b Post-pollination
c Cross-pollination   d No-pollination

11. There are three groups given below. Each group involves an artificial method of vegetative propagation with an exception. Opt the option that correctly declares the exception

Group 1 (Cutting) : Grapes, Sugarcane, Bananas, Strawberry.

Group 2 (Layering) : Grapevine, Jasmine, Tapioca, Lime.

Group 3 (Grafting) : Guava, Mango, Sugarcane, Peach, Peas.

Codes

	Group 1	Group 2	Group 3
a	Grapes	Lime	Sugarcane
b	Grapes	Jasmine	Peach
c	Bananas	Tapioca	Guava
d	Strawberry	Tapioca	Sugarcane

12. Observe the figure given below and identify *A*, *B* and *C*.

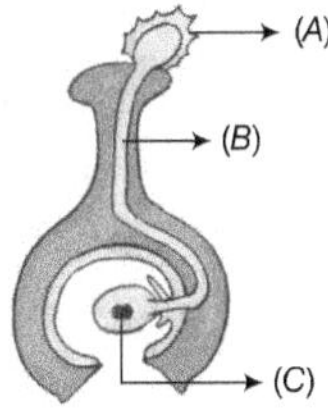

	A	B	C
a	Pollen grain	Pollen tube	Fertilised egg
b	Ovule	Pollen tube	Egg
c	Style	Pollen tube	Ovule
d	Pollen grain	Style	Ovary

13. Study the concept map shown below. Which one of these correctly shows *X*, *Y* and *Z* based on the given mapping?

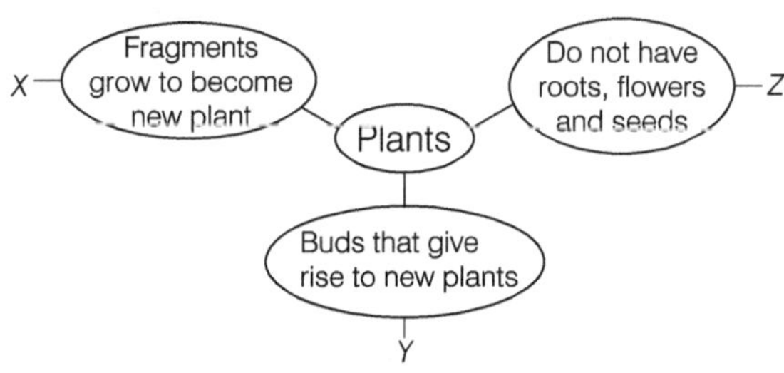

Codes

	X	Y	Z
a	Algae	Turmeric	Moss
b	Fern	Potato	Moss
c	*Oxalis*	Turmeric	Strawberry
d	*Spirogyra*	Algae	*Vallisnera*

14. Fill in the blanks below by choosing appropriate terms from the box.

1. water	2. wind
3. insect	4. jasmine
5. *Vallisneria*	6. bright
7. nectar	8. feathery
9. rice	10. scented

I. The _______ pollinated flowers have _______ to attract _______.

II. The pollination in _______ is carried by water.

III. The maize plant has _______ stigmas to catch pollen grains.

Codes

	I	II	III
a	3, 6, 2	4	7
b	1, 7, 3	9	8
c	3, 7, 3	5	8
d	3, 7, 3	5	10

15. Which of the following is/are correct match?

	Fruit	Agent of dispersal	Part which helps in dispersal
A	Drumstick	Wind	Wings of seed
B	*Madar*	Water	Hairy seeds
C	Coconut	Water	Spongy outer coat
D	*Xanthium*	Animals	Hooks in fruits

Codes
a A and B
b A, C and D
c C and D
d All are correct

16. All the flowers below have male and female parts. Seeds are likely to be formed if pollen grains are transferred from

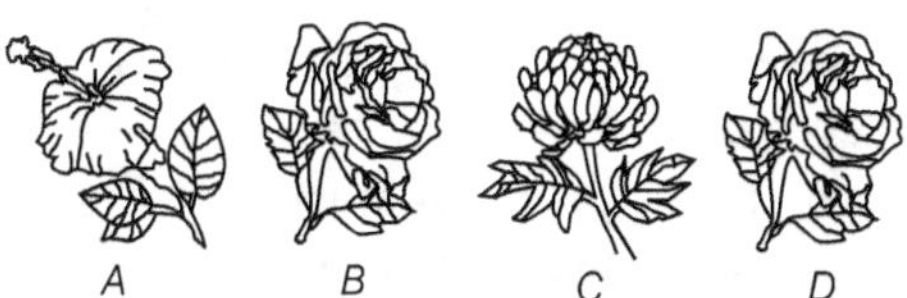

a flower B to D
b flower A to C
c flower A to any flower
d any one flower to any other flower

17. The given figure shows the parts of gynoecium of a flower. Which of the parts labelled *P*, *Q* or *R* eventually develops into a fruit?

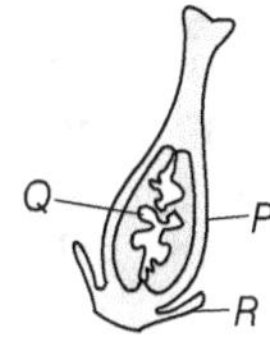

a P–ovary
b Q–ovule
c R–ovary
d None of the above

18. The diagram shows the scenario of an island where two types of plants (⬠, ▲) are growing. How fruits or seeds of the given two types of plants are most likely to be dispersed?

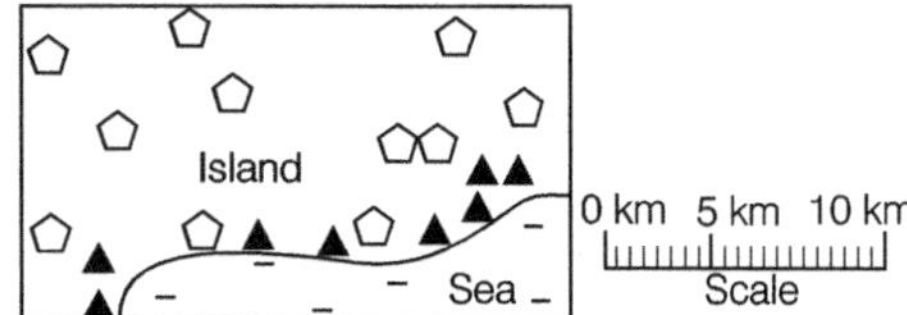

Codes

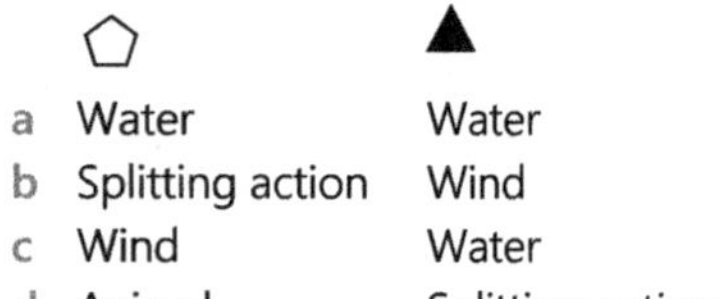

	⬠	▲
a	Water	Water
b	Splitting action	Wind
c	Wind	Water
d	Animal	Splitting action

19. Which of the following organisms reproduce by spores?

   I. *Mimosa*
  II. Bracket fungus
 III. Bird's nest fern

Codes

a I and II   b I and III
c II and III   d I, II and III

20. Arrange the following steps of germination of a pea seed.

  1. Shoot grows upwards.
  2. Seed sown in soil.
  3. Production of seedling.
  4. Tiny root grows downward.
  5. Splitting of seed coat.

Codes

a $2 \rightarrow 1 \rightarrow 4 \rightarrow 5 \rightarrow 3$
b $2 \rightarrow 5 \rightarrow 4 \rightarrow 1 \rightarrow 3$
c $3 \rightarrow 2 \rightarrow 5 \rightarrow 1 \rightarrow 4$
d $5 \rightarrow 1 \rightarrow 4 \rightarrow 2 \rightarrow 3$

21. Nividh fills an empty pot with soil. He sowed the budding points of a potato in the soil and waterered the soil regularly. What do you think Nividh will observe after some days?

a Roots can be seen emerging from bulb and shoots from tuber.
b Shoot can be seen emerging from bulb and roots from tuber.
c Roots and shoots emerge from bulb only.
d Roots and shoots emerge from tuber only.

22. The given table lists of some plants and their reproductive structures. What should be *X* and *Y*?

Plants	Reproductive structures
Gladiolus	Corns
X	Spores
Onion	Y

a X–Fern, Y–Spores
b X–Pineapple, Y–Suckers
c X–Moss, Y–Underground stems
d X–Moss, Y–Leaves

23. Study the table below. Which of the following is correct?

Plants	Reproduce by spores	Reproduce by seeds	Can make its own food	Cannot make its own food
a Dragon scales		✓	✓	
b Bracket fungus		✓		✓
c Toadstool	✓		✓	
d Moss	✓		✓	

24. Given below are the stages of budding in yeast but they are not in correct order.

   I. One of the nuclei enters the bud.
  II. An outgrowth known as bud forms on the outer surface of a parent cell.
 III. The bud cleaves to become a new daughter cell.
 IV. The nucleus then divides.
  V. A cell wall is formed between the parent cell and the bud.

Which of the following options has the correct sequence of budding in yeast?

a I, II, IV, V and III
b II, I, V, III and IV
c II, IV, I, V and III
d IV, I, II, V and III

25. Study the characteristics of a seed shown below.

> It is light and has a feathery structure attached to it which acts like a parachute.

Based on the above characteristics, how is the seed likely to be dispersed?

a By wind
b By water
c By animals
d By splitting

26. Observe the given diagrams showing the cross-section of two flowers. Which of the following statements is/are correct regarding them?

Flower X   Flower Y

  I. The flowering plants have developed from seeds.
  II. Flower *X* is a female flower and flower *Y* is a bisexual flower.
  III. Fertilisation can take place in both flowers.
  IV. Their pollen tube keeps on growing till it reaches the sepals.

Codes

a Only I

b Only II

c II and III

d II, III and IV

27. Which of thc following is/are characteristic is of insect-pollinated flowers?

  A. Nectar is present.
  B. Pollen grains are abundant and sticky.
  C. Flowers are dull coloured and scentless.
  D. Sticky stigmas.

Codes

a A and B

b B and C

c C and D

d A, B and D

28. The flow chart below shows the characteristics of some fruit.

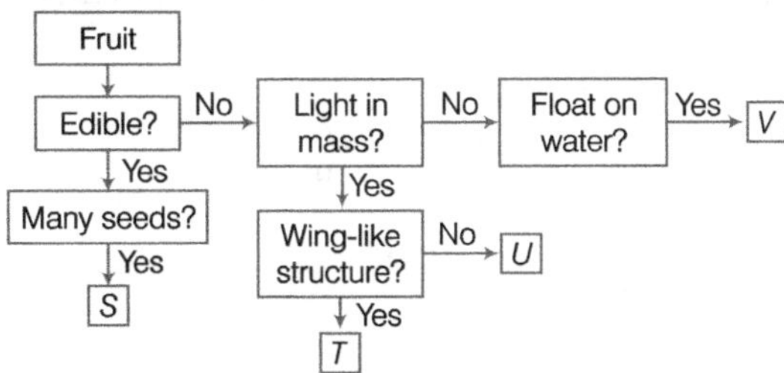

Based on the information above, which one of the following best represent fruit, *S*, *T*, *U* and *V*?

	Fruit S	Fruit T	Fruit U	Fruit V
a	Mango	*Shorea*	Rubber	Coconut
b	Tomato	Angsana	Dandelion	Pong pong
c	Watermelon	Lalang	Nipah	Lotus
d	Banana	*Urena*	Kapok	Guava

29. Study the list of plants shown below.

> Coconut, *Cassia*, Pong pong, Rubber

Which of the following characteristics can be used to group the plants into two different groups?

  I. Poisonous and non-poisonous plants.
  II. Land and water plants.
  III. Dispersal by water and dispersal by explosive action.
  IV. Flowering and non-flowering plants.

Codes

a I and II

b I and III

c I, II and III

d I, II, III and IV

30. Study the experimental set-up as shown below.

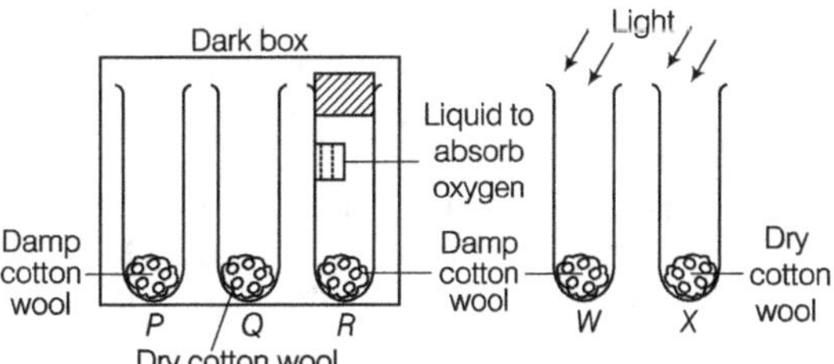

Each test tube contains bean seeds on some cotton wool. Kriti wants to study the importance of light for germination to take place. Which two test tubes from the given set-ups should she use?

a P and W

b R and W

c Q and W

d W and X

31. Study the flow chart shown below carefully.

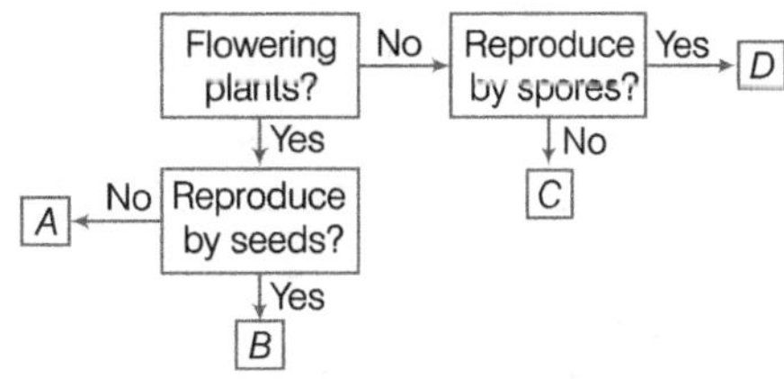

Which letters *A*, *B*, *C* or *D*, represent the flame of the forest and whisk fern, respectively?

	Flame of forest	Whisk fern
a	A	C
b	B	C
c	B	D
d	A	D

32. The development of a flowering plant given below is not listed in the correct order.

Stages of the development

A. Germination of the seeds.
B. Seeds are dispersed.
C. Fertilisation takes place.
D. Pollinated by the bees.
E. Ovary develops into a fruit while ovules become seeds.

Rearrange the stages correctly to show the development of a flowering plant.

	1st Stage	2nd Stage	3rd Stage	4th Stage	5th Stage
a	A	B	E	C	D
b	A	D	E	C	B
c	D	E	C	A	B
d	D	C	E	B	A

33. Riya likes to eat 'Langra', which is a variety of mango that looks like normal mangoes, except that it is much sweeter. What should she do if she wants to grow her own 'Langra mangoes'?

a Plant seeds from a normal mango plant and harvest the mango when they are still very small in size.
b Plant seeds from a Langra plant because the mango from the new plant would have the same size and taste as the parent plant.
c There is no way to guarantee that she can grow 'Langra' because the plant produces different types of mango at random.
d Plant seeds from a normal mango plant but use less fertiliser so that the mango will remain small in size.

34. The diagrams below show a plot of land at two different times of the year.

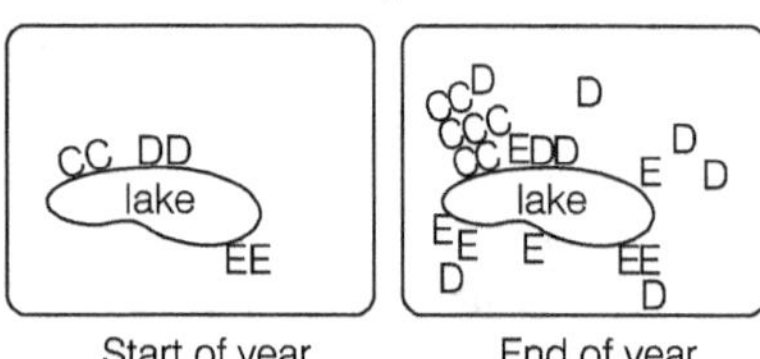

Which fruit are dispersed by wind and splitting, respectively?

	Dispersed by wind	Dispersed by splitting
a	C	D
b	D	C
c	D	E
d	E	C

35. The diagram alongside shows a cross-section of a flower.

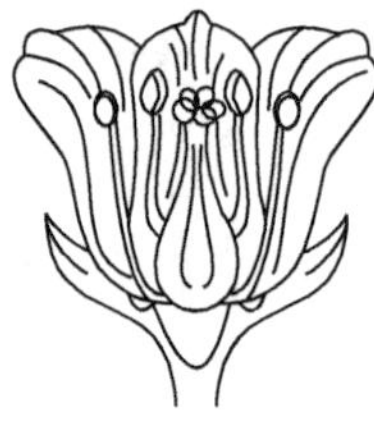

Based on what you observe in the diagram, the flower shown is likely not pollinated by wind. What is the most likely reason for this?

a The petals of the flower are huge.
b The style that joins the stigma to the ovary is short.
c All the reproductive organs are inside the flower.
d Both the male and female parts are almost of the same length.

36. Study the structure given below carefully.

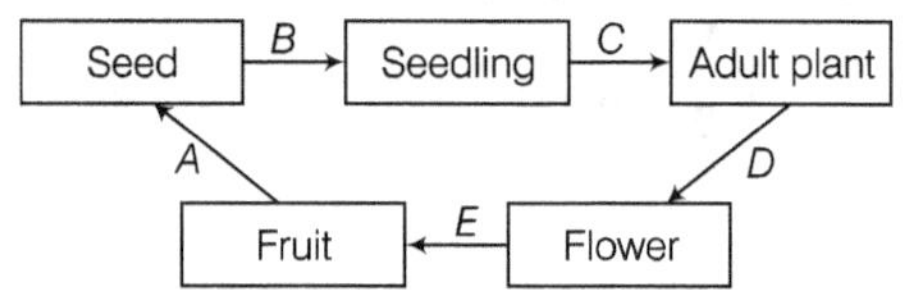

Based on the diagram above, which statement is not necessarily true ?

a At *B*, germination takes place when there is sufficient air, water and warmth
b At *C*, the seedling is able to make its own food as it develops additional leaves
c At *D*, the adult plant produces flowers to attract insects to help in pollination
d At *E*, fertilisation takes place when the male cell fuses with the female egg cell

37. I. Sepal   II. Petal   III. Stamen   IV. Anther   V. Pistil   VI. Stigma   VII. Ovary   VIII. Nectar

There are some parts of the flower mentioned above. Choose which one among them are male and female.

Codes

	Males	Females
a	III, IV	V, VI, VII
b	I, III, IV	V, VI, VII
c	IV	III, V, VI, VII
d	III, IV, V	VI, VII

38. State 'T' for true and 'F' for false statements.

I. Ovules contain the female gametes of the plant.
II. New plants produced from seeds are exactly like the female parent.
III. Potato is a root tuber.
IV. Seed dispersal prevents overcrowding of plants in an area.
V. Spores are not seeds, but asexual reproductive structures.

	I	II	III	IV	V
a	T	T	T	F	F
b	F	F	T	F	T
c	T	T	F	T	F
d	T	F	F	T	T

39. Consider the given passage and choose the option to fill it correctly.

The male and female gametes fuse to form a ____ (i)___ during the process of ____(ii)___. It grows into an ____(iii)____ which is enclosed within a seed. After fertilisation the ovule develop into ____ (iv)____ and ovary develops into fruit.

Codes

	(i)	(ii)	(iii)	(iv)
a	Egg	Fertilisation	Embryo	Seed
b	Zygote	Fertilisation	Embryo	Seed
c	Embryo	Pollination	Zygote	Seed
d	Ovule	Pollination	Zygote	Seed

40. Observe the flow chart given below and identify *X* and *Y* in it.

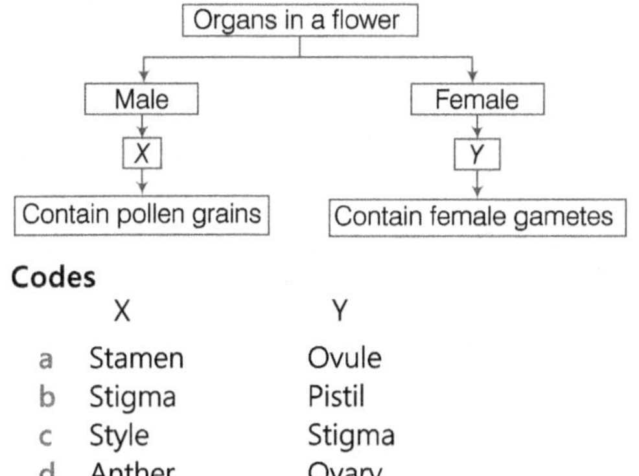

Codes

	X	Y
a	Stamen	Ovule
b	Stigma	Pistil
c	Style	Stigma
d	Anther	Ovary

41. Match the column I with column II.

	Column I		Column II
A.	Perennation	1.	Arrangement of flowers in a definite pattern
B.	Gametes	2.	Process of sending seeds away from mother plant
C.	Inflorescence	3.	Sex cells
D.	Dispersal	4.	Survival of plant from one germinating season to another

Codes

	A	B	C	D
a	2	3	1	4
b	4	3	2	1
c	1	3	2	4
d	4	3	1	2

42. The graph alongside shows the dry mass content of a seed during germination.

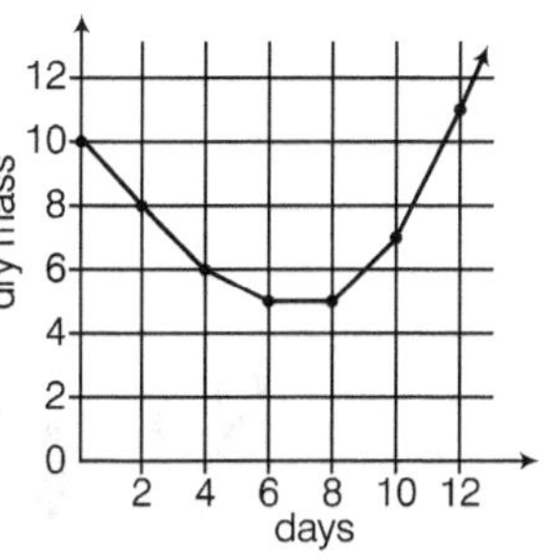

During germination, the seeds increase in size due to __A__ of water but its dry mass decreases because of __B__. After the 8th day of germination, the increase in dry mass can be related to manufacture of food in the leaves by a process called __C__. Find A, B and C in the above passage by analysing the graph.

	A	B	C
a	absorption	respiration	photosynthesis
b	respiration	absorption	photosynthesis
c	ovule formation	water retention	biomass formation
d	ovule formation	respiration	photosynthesis

43. Solve the crossword with the help of hints given below.

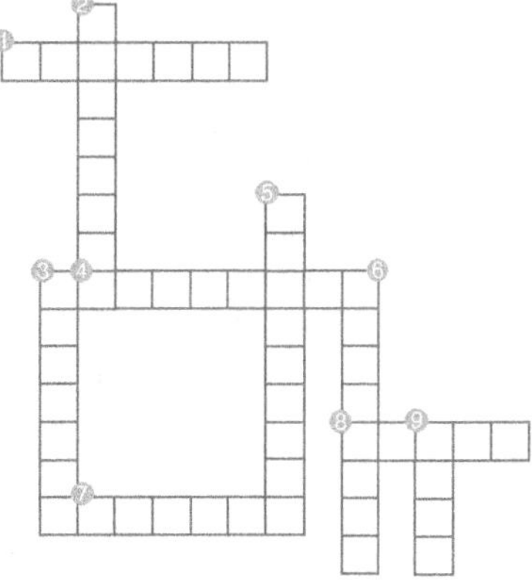

Across

1. In ginger, the stems have buds which give rise to new plants
3. Plants that can carry out sexual reproduction
7. Plant part that contain style, stigma and ovary
8. Eye on potato is located on this part

Down

2. Flowers that contain both types of sex organ
4. Process by which *Amoeba* reproduce
5. Type of flower found in corn
6. Method of artificial propagation that uses stock and scion
9. Short underground stems found in onion

Chapter 9

Motion and Time

A Motion, Its Time and Speed

1. A man walked at 2 km/h from his house to the neighbourhood park 500 m away. He then jogged around the park at 10 km/h for 30 min. To cool down, he walked back home from the park at 1.5 km/h.

If he started the journey from his home at 6:30 pm, then he would reach home at

a 7:30 pm   b 7:35 pm   c 7:40 pm   d 7:45 pm

2. Aman is standing on the platform of a station watching the trains.

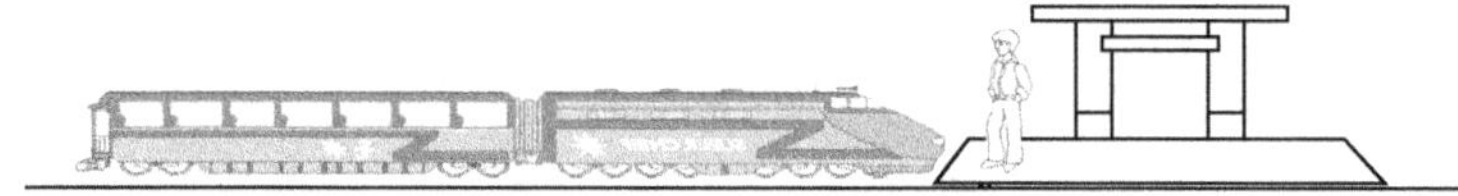

A train travelling at 30 m/s takes 3 s to pass Aman. What is the length of the train?

a 10 m   b 60 m   c 30 m   d 90 m

3. The diagrams below show some persons sitting in the moving bus and some sitting at the bus stop. With reference to the diagrams, choose the incorrect statement(s).

  I. A person sitting in the bus is at rest with respect to his/her co-passenger.

 II. A person sitting at the bus stop is in motion with respect to the person sitting in the bus.

III. A person sitting in the bus is in motion with respect to the person sitting at the bus stop.

Codes

a I and II   b II and III   c Only II   d All are correct

4. A person follows the following path as shown in the figure given below to reach to his home. What will be the average speed of the person?

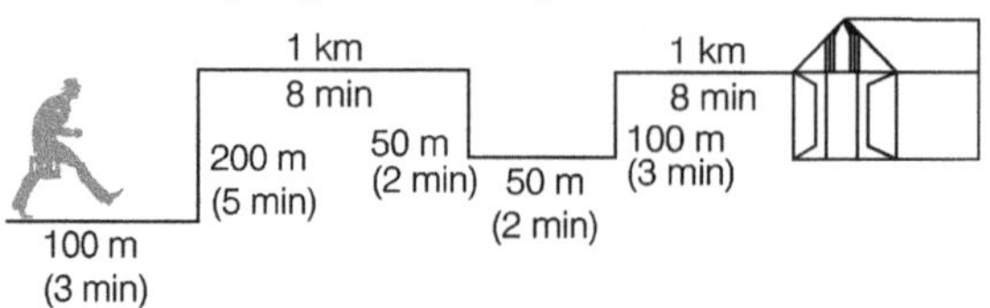

a 0.27 m/s   b 1.34 m/s   c 1.34 m/min   d 0.27 m/min

5. Allan is riding a bicycle. In the first hour, he travels at a speed of 10 km/h, in the second hour, he travels at a speed of 15 km/h, in the third hour he travels at a speed of 20 km/h. What is the total distance travelled by Allan?

  a 15 km   b 25 km
  c 45 km   d 55 km

6. Consider the following statements and choose the incorrect ones.

  I. The ratio of speed *versus* distance gives the time taken by an object to cover that distance.
  II. Odometer records the distance travelled by a vehicle in kilometers.
  III. To compare the speeds of a number of objects, units need not be same.

Codes
  a I and II   b I and III
  c II and III   d All of these

7. Consider the following statements and choose the correct ones.

  I. A speedometer measures the average speed of a vehicle.
  II. A higher speed indicates that a given distance has been covered in a shorter time.
  III. Motion of hammer in electric bell is a periodic motion.

Codes
  a I and II
  b I and III
  c II and III
  d All of the above

Direction (Q. Nos.8-10) Read the following passage and answer the questions that follow.

A school organised a picnic for the students of class VII. Some of the students enjoyed merry-go-round of radius 3.5 m for 15 min (at speed of 44 m/min) as shown in figure below.

8. How much distance they have travelled in the ride?

  a 660 m   b 30 m
  c 1320 m   d 600 m

9. Which type of motion do the children have in the figure given in above question?

  a Rectilinear motion   b Periodic motion
  c Circular motion   d Rotational motion

10. What are the number of rotations that the students took in 15 min?

  a 10   b 20
  c 30   d 40

11. The distance between starting and finishing line in a race is 800 m. In order to set the world record, an athlete needs to finish the race in 15 s. The speed of the athlete will be

  a 5.33 ms^{-1} b 53.33 ms^{-1}
  c 53.33 ms^{-2} d 53.33 kms^{-1}

12. A car having an odometer reading 234562 km as recorded at 5:20 am is moving at speed of 2 km/min. What would be the odometer reading at 6 am?

  a 234602 km   b 234682 km
  c 234642 km   d 234722 km

13. Fill in the blanks with the help of options given in the box.

(i) non-uniform	(ii) uniform
(iii) kmh^{-1}	(iv) periodic
(v) distance	(vi) odometer
(vii) ms^{-1}	(viii) position
(ix) speed	(x) rotational

  I. The distance moved by an object per unit time is termed as ....
  II. A moving body changes its .... with the passage of time.
  III. An object moving along a straight line with constant speed is in .... motion.
  IV. The SI unit of speed is ....
  V. The turning of the blades of fan is .... motion.

Codes

	I	II	III	IV	V
a	(ix)	(viii)	(ii)	(vii)	(x)
b	(iv)	(i)	(ii)	(iii)	(ix)
c	(vi)	(v)	(x)	(viii)	(ix)
d	(iii)	(vi)	(ix)	(ii)	(vii)

14. State 'T' for true or 'F' for false.

I. The motion of the earth around the sun is a uniform motion.

II. The hands of an athlete while running a race are in periodic motion.

III. The speed 36 kmh^{-1} is equivalent to 10 ms^{-1}.

IV. A slow moving object covers a particular distance in shorter time as compared to others.

V. Distance travelled by an object is the product of speed of the object to the time taken.

Codes

	I	II	III	IV	V
a	F	T	T	F	T
b	F	F	T	T	T
c	T	T	F	F	T
d	T	F	T	T	T

15. Match the given matrix.

	Column I		Column II
A.		1.	Rectilinear motion
B.		2.	Circular motion
C.		3.	Rotational motion
D.		4.	Periodic motion

Codes

	A	B	C	D
a	2	1	4	3
b	3	1	4	2
c	2	4	1	3
d	3	4	1	2

16. Assertion (A) Circular motion is a non-uniform motion.

Reason (R) The speed of a body changes at every point of the curve to be in circular motion.

a (A) and (R) are correct and (R) is the correct explanation of (A)

b (A) and (R) are correct but (R) is not the correct explanation of (A)

c (A) is correct but (R) is wrong

d (A) is wrong but (R) is correct

17. Assertion (A) If the speed of a car moving towards North is 60 ms^{-1}, its velocity is 60 ms^{-1} towards the East.

Reason (R) The velocity of a body is speed in a specified direction.

a (A) and (R) are correct and (R) is the correct explanation of (A)

b (A) and (R) are correct, but (R) is not the correct explanation of (A)

c (A) is correct but (R) is incorrect

d (A) is incorrect but (R) is correct

Direction (Q. Nos.18-20)   Read the following information and answer the questions that follow.

The earth is constantly in motion revolving around the sun and rotating on its axis. These motions account for many of the natural phenomenon, i.e. day and night changing of the seasons and climate variations in different regions. The earth spins on its axis from West to East and takes 23 h, 56 min and 4.09 s to complete one rotation. It takes the earth one full year to complete one full revolution around the sun.

18. The motion of the earth on its own axis is

a circular motion

b periodic motion

c rotational motion

d revolutionary motion

19. The radius of earth is 6371 km approximately. How much distance it travels in completing one rotation?

a 40010 km

b 400010 km

c 4000010 km

d 40000 km

20. What is the approximate speed of the earth while completing one rotation?

a 1500 km/h

b 1667 m/s

c 1667 km/h

d 1500 m/s

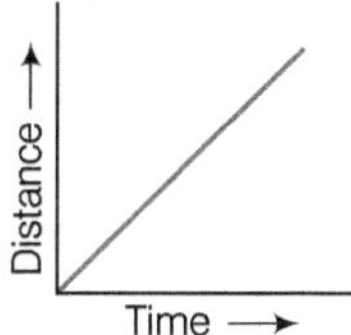

B Distance-Time Graph, Time and Simple Pendulum

1. The distance-time graph given below shows a car moving with a constant speed.

The slope of this graph indicates
   a time taken by the object
   b position of the object
   c speed of the object
   d distance moved by the object

2. The distance-time graph provides a variety of information about the motion of an object. The distance-time graph which indicates a car moving with a speed which is not constant is

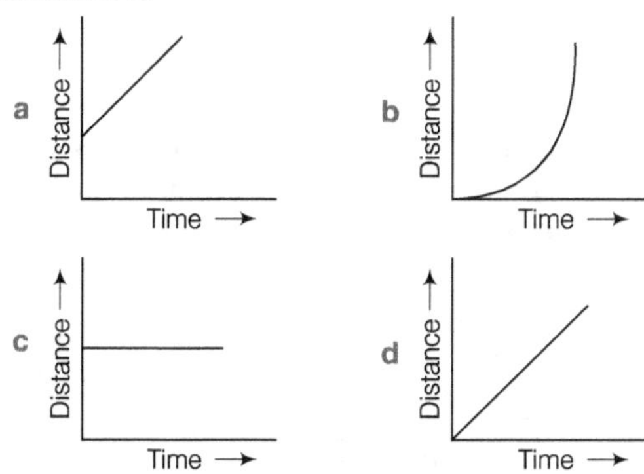

3. While drawing a distance-time graph for a moving bike, the student finds some part of the graph is parallel to the time axis. Which of the following conclusion is correct about this part of the graph?
   a This part indicates a uniform speed of the bike.
   b The bike travelled the maximum distance in this part of time.
   c The bike travelled the minimum distance in this part of time.
   d The bike was at rest in this part of time.

4. Angie was driving at a constant speed before she saw a cat on the road. She gradually increased the force on the brake pedal and managed to stop before reaching the cat.

Which of the following graphs represents the motion?

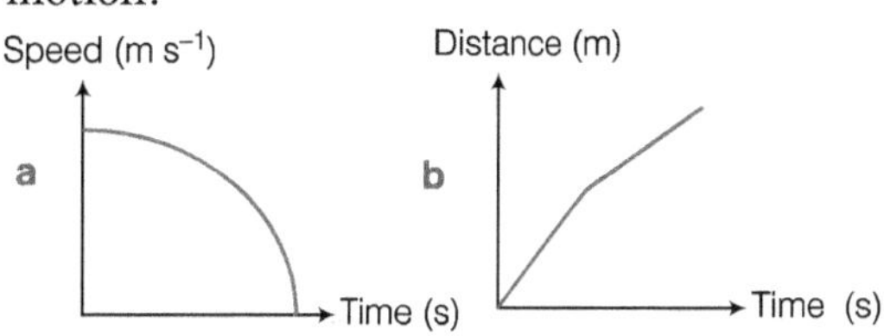

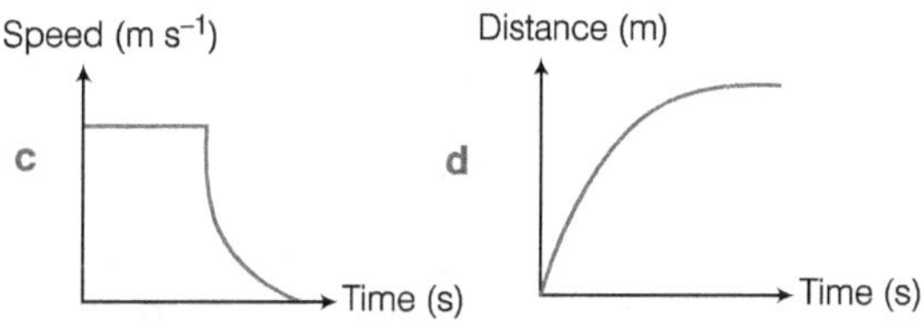

5. The distance-time graph of a moving vehicle as shown in figure indicates.

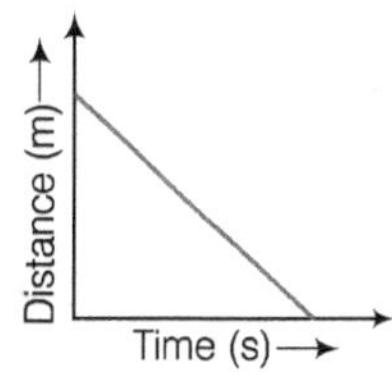

   a speed of the vehicle is increasing with time
   b speed of the vehicle is decreasing with time
   c the final speed of the vehicle is zero
   d graph is not possible

6. Which of the following distance-time graphs is not possible?

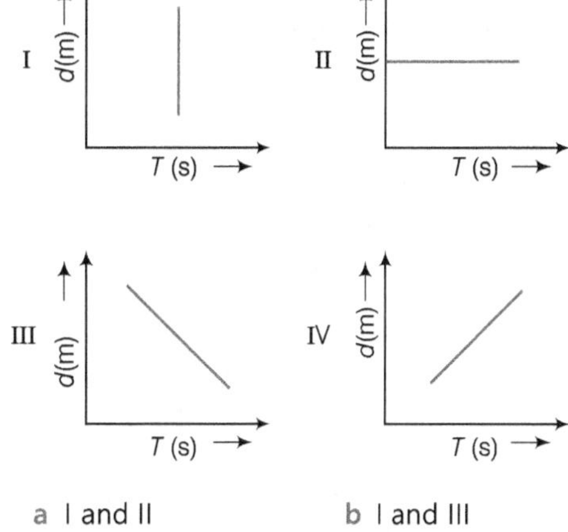

   a I and II
   b I and III
   c I and IV
   d II and III

7. The motion of a body is depicted graphically as shown in the given figure. Then,

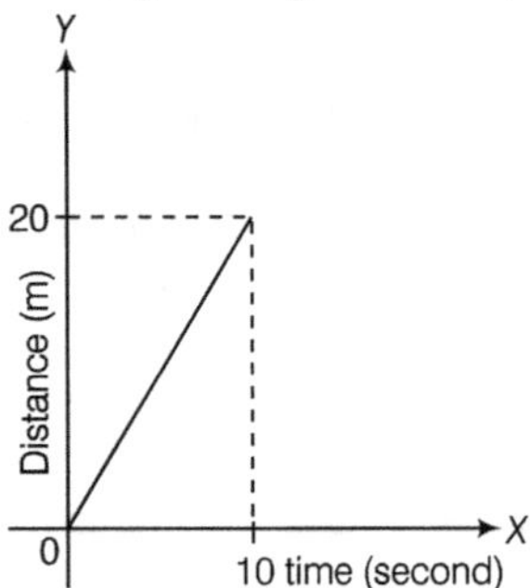

a the average speed of the body is 2 ms^{-1}
b the average speed of the body is zero
c the body changes its direction twice
d All of the above

8. Two clocks *A* and *B* are shown in figure. Clock *A* has an hour and a minute hand, whereas clock *B* has an hour hand, minute hand as well as a second hand. Which of the following statement is correct for these clocks?

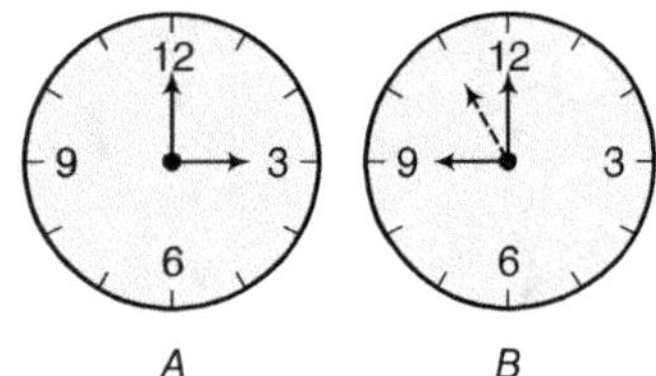

a *A* time interval of 30 s can be measured by clock *A*
b A time interval of 30 s cannot be measured by clock *B*
c Time interval of 5 min can be measured by both *A* and *B*
d Time interval of 4 min 10 s can be measured by clock *A*

9. Observe given figure as below:

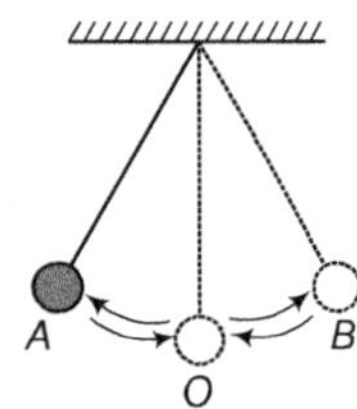

The time period of a simple pendulum is the time taken by it to travel from
a *A* to *B* and back to *A*
b *O* to *A*, *A* to *B* and *B* to *A*
c *B* to *A*, *A* to *B* and *B* to *O*
d *A* to *B*

10. The diagram below shows three pendulums of different height having different weight of bob. Which of the three will have highest time period?

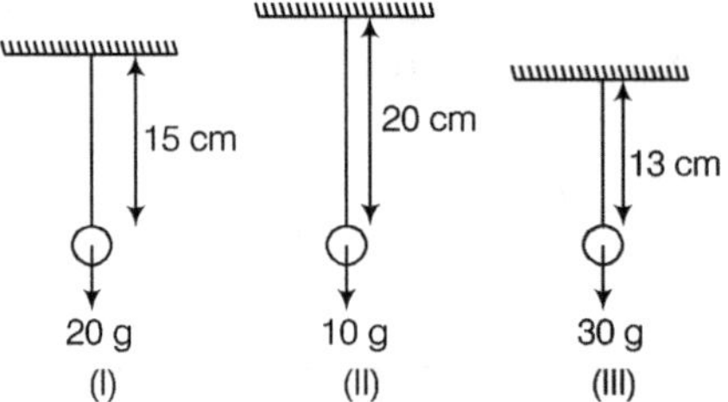

a I
b II
c III
d All have same time-period

11. A pendulum is swung periodically as shown in the figure below:

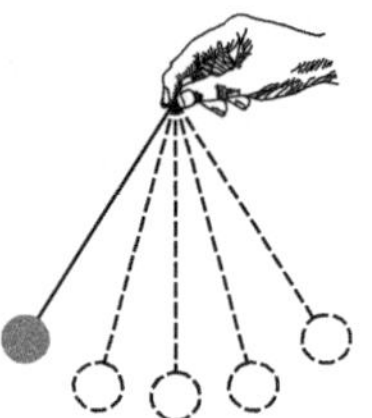

Which of the following position time graph best describes the motion of the pendulum?

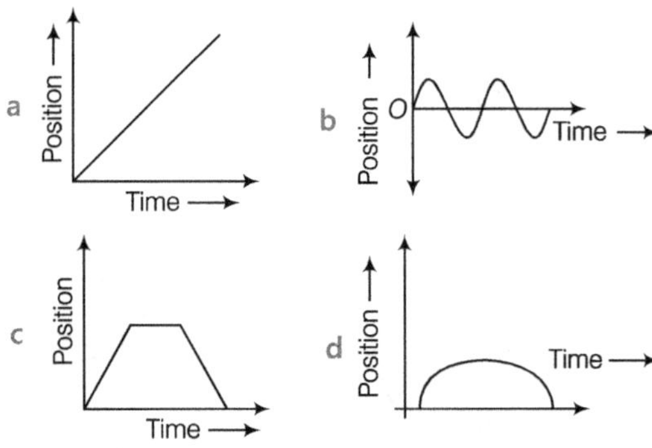

12. Time taken by a simple pendulum to travel from point *A* to *O* is 0.5 s. How much time will it take to complete 10 oscillations?

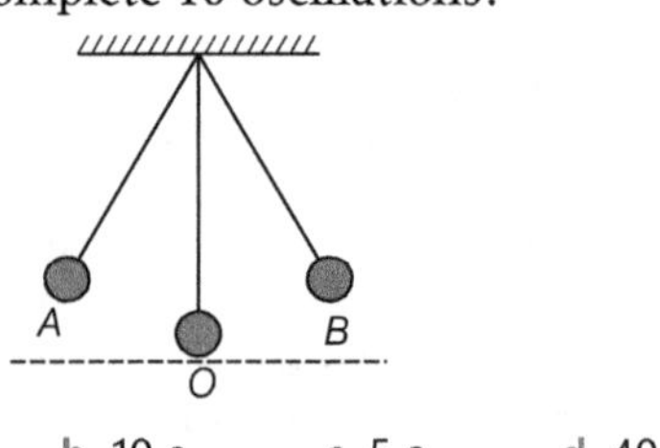

a 20 s   b 10 s   c 5 s   d 40 s

13. Fill in the blanks with the help of options given in the box.

(i) uniform	(ii) time	(iii) distance
(iv) non-uniform	(v) speed	(vi) linear
(vii) time period	(viii) periodic	(ix) parallel.

   I. The slope of distance time graph gives ....

  II. The time taken by the pendulum to complete one oscillation is called its ....

 III. The time from one sunrise to the next is a .... type of motion.

 IV. The distance-time graph of a body at rest is a straight line parallel to .... axis.

  V. If the distance-time graph of a body is a curved line, it represents body is moving with a .... speed.

Codes

	I	II	III	IV	V
a	(v)	(vII)	(viii)	(ii)	(iv)
b	(iv)	(i)	(ii)	(iii)	(ix)
c	(vi)	(v)	(ii)	(viii)	(ix)
d	(iii)	(vi)	(ix)	(ii)	(vii)

14. State 'T' for true or 'F' for false.

   I. The time-period of a given pendulum is not constant.

  II. The SI unit of time is second.

 III. The time-period of a simple pendulum depends on both length of pendulum and weight of bob.

 IV. The moment of duration in which things occur is termed as time.

  V. A sun dial measures time by the position of the shadow cast by the sun.

Codes

	I	II	III	IV	V
a	T	T	F	T	F
b	F	T	T	T	T
c	T	T	F	F	T
d	T	F	T	T	T

15. **Assertion** (A) If the length of the pendulum is increased, its time period also increases.

Reason (R) The time-period of a pendulum is always constant for a particular pendulum.

  a A and R are correct and R is the correct explanation of A

  b A and R are correct, but R is not the correct explanation of A

  c A is correct but R is wrong

  d A is wrong but R is correct

16. **Assertion** (A) Quartz clocks are more accurate than pendulum clocks.

Reason (R) The regular vibrations of a tiny quartz crystal within an electric circuit are used for measuring time.

  a A and R are correct and R is the correct explanation of A

  b A and R are correct, but R is not the correct explanation of A

  c A is correct but R is incorrect

  d A is incorrect but R is correct

17. Rahul is going from the playground back to his home. The distance-time graph of his journey is shown below. Match the statements to the marked positions of the graph correctly.

   I. He is going with high speed.

  II. He is going back.

 III. He takes rest.

 IV. He slows down.

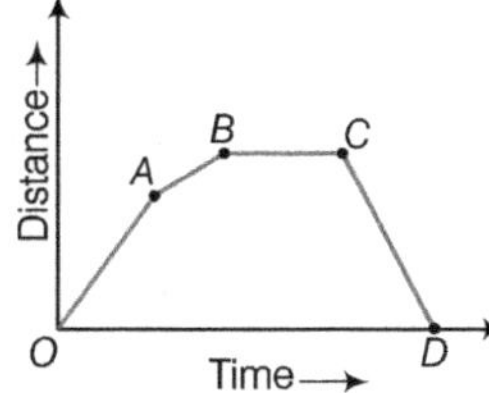

Codes

	I	II	III	IV
a	CD	OA	BC	AB
b	CD	BC	OA	AB
c	OA	CD	BC	AB
d	OA	BC	AB	CD

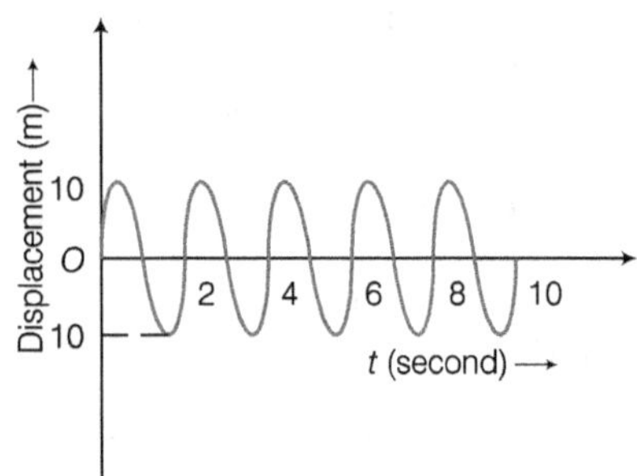

18. How many oscillations are completed by the bob at the end of 10s ?

    a 5   b 4.5

    c 6   d 2.5

19. What is the frequency of the oscillations?

    a 100 Hz   b 0.5 Hz

    c 50 Hz   d 2 Hz

20. The time-period of the oscillation is

    a 1 s   b 2 s

    c 10 s   d 0.5 s

21. The time taken to complete 20 oscillations is

    a 10 s

    b 20 s

    c 40 s

    d 50 s

22. Solve the following crossword using hints given as below:

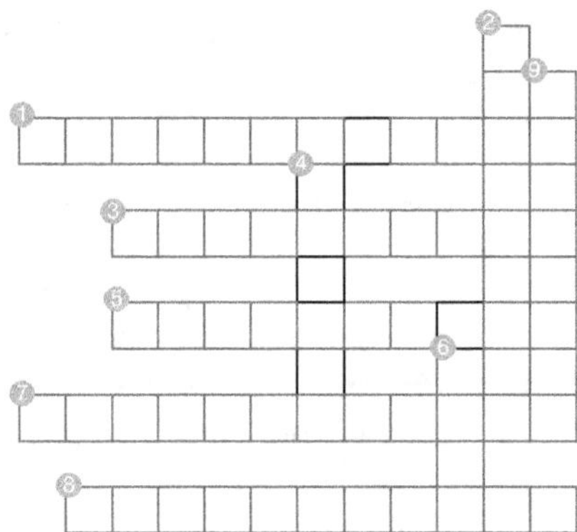

Across

1. Motion along a straight line
3. Time taken to complete one oscillation
5. Device used to measure the distance covered by a vehicle
7. Motion along a curved line
8. Device used to measure the speed of a vehicle

Down

2. Motion which repeats itself after fixed interval of time
4. Ratio of distance covered to time
6. Object covers more distance in less time is said to be
9. Device having a string suspended with a fixed point with a bob at bottom

Electric Current and Its Effects

A   Electric Current and Electric Circuit

1. A storage battery is shown in the figure below.

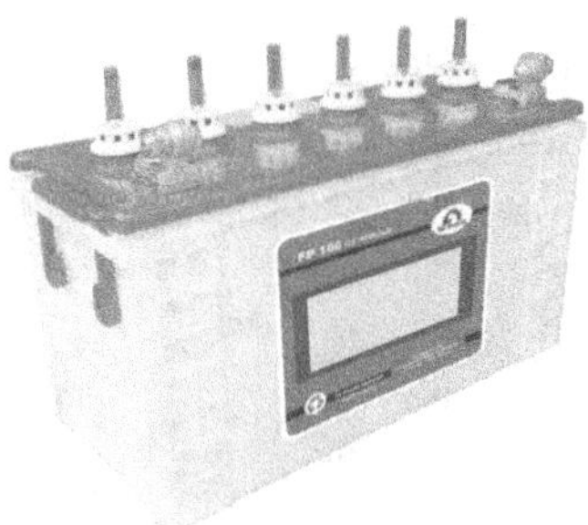

Which of the following is the symbol of battery?

 a    b   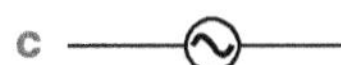 c   d

2. A conductor is a substance through which electric charge can flow easily. A current carrying conductor produces

a only heating effect   b only magnetic effect
c only chemical effect   d All of these

3. Marcus sets up an electrical circuit as shown below.

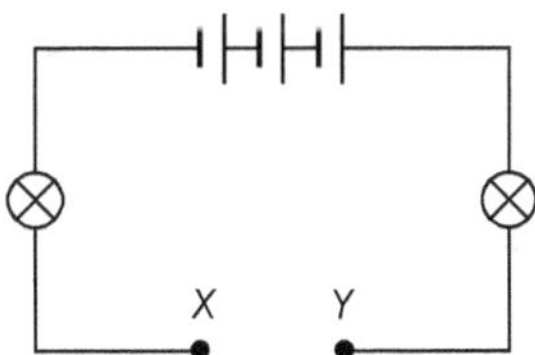

He wants to be able to control the brightness of both bulbs using a dimmer. Which of the following electrical devices should he connect between X and Y?

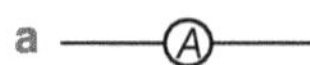 a   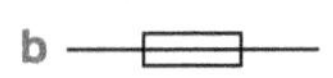 b   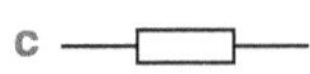 c    d

4. Which of the following statement is true in context with the circuit given below?

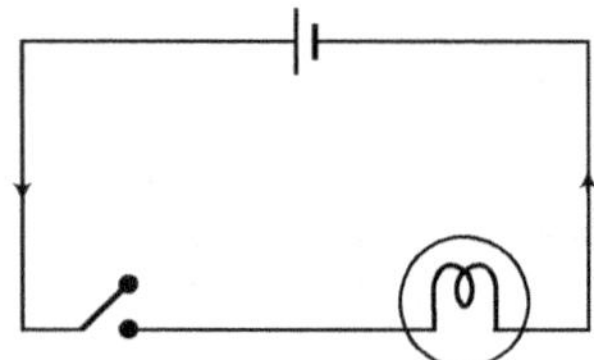

   a It is a complete circuit so current will flow through it
   b Switch is open so bulb cannot glow
   c Wire is broken
   d The direction of flow of current is not correct

5. Electric circuits consisting of a bulb (or bulbs), a key and a cell are shown below.

In which of the following circuits the bulb will glow?

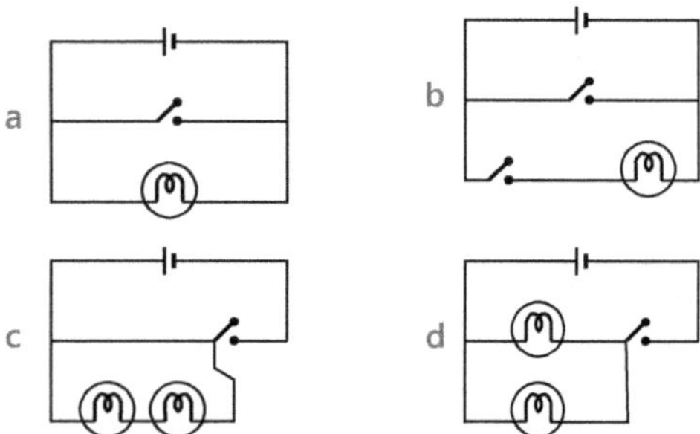

6. The bulb in the circuit below is lit at normal brightness when both switches S_1 and S_2 are closed.

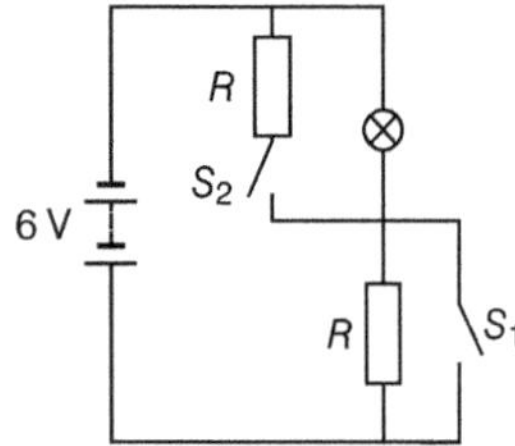

What happens to the brightness of the bulb, if only S_1 or S_2 is closed?

	Only S_1 is closed	**Only S_2 is closed**
a	Brightness increases	Brightness increases
b	Brightness increases	Brightness decreases
c	Brightness decreases	Brightness increases
d	Brightness decreases	Brightness decreases

7. Three bulbs A, B and C are connected in a circuit as shown in figure. When the switch is ON

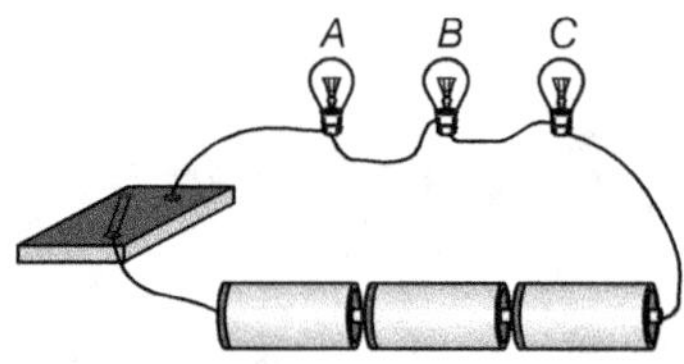

   a bulb C will glow first
   b bulb B and C will glow simultaneously and bulb A will glow after some time
   c all the bulbs, A, B and C will glow at the same time
   d the bulbs will glow in the order A, B and C

8. What is the reading shown on the ammeter as below?

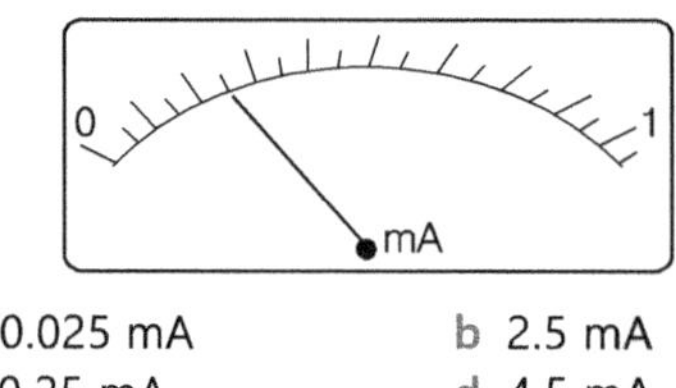

   a 0.025 mA   b 2.5 mA
   c 0.25 mA   d 4.5 mA

9. Which of the following circuit shows the correct way of connecting an ammeter and a voltmeter?

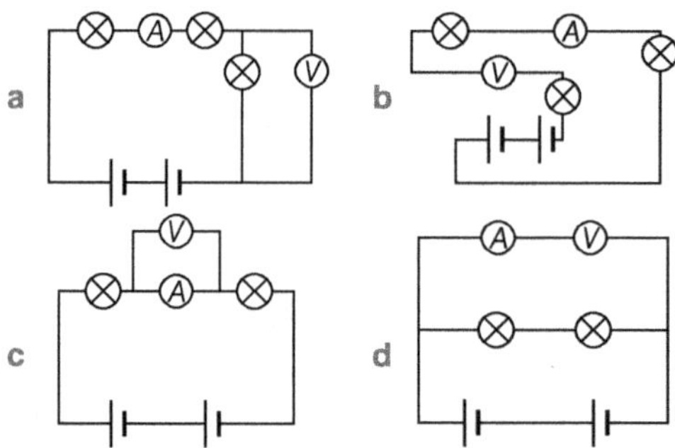

10. Below is a list of materials that can be chosen to replace material X to light up the bulb, EXCEPT ....

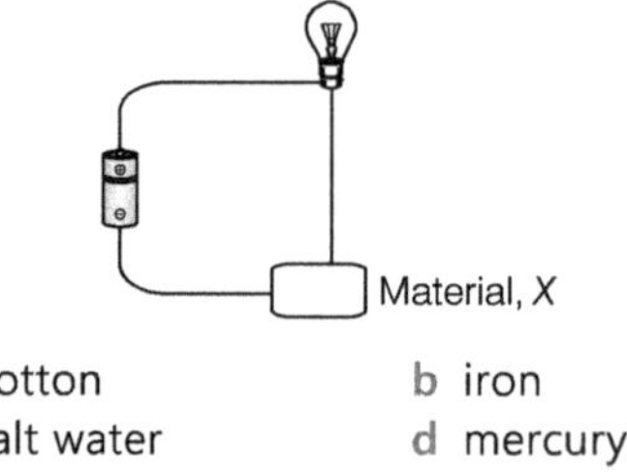

   a cotton   b iron
   c salt water   d mercury

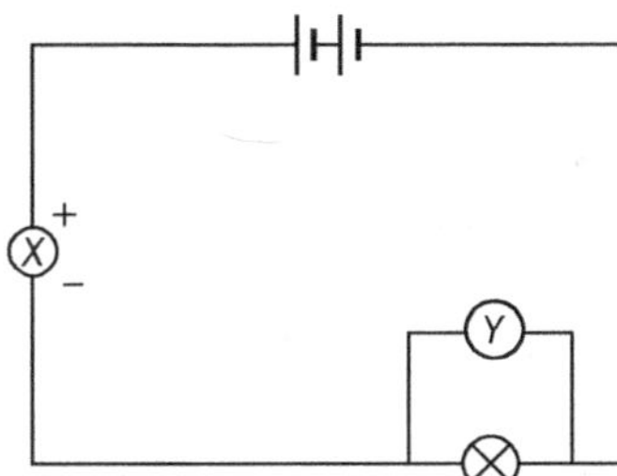

11. Which of the following statements about the circuit above is correct?

a Instrument *X* measures the voltage as the current flows through the circuit

b Instrument *X* measures the voltage of the light bulb

c Instrument *Y* measures the voltage of the light bulb

d Instrument *Y* measures the amount of current flowing through the circuit

12. Which of the following can be used to calculate the resistance of the light bulb?

a $X - Y$ b Y/X

c X/Y d $X + Y$

13. Which of the following statements are false about using household electrical appliances?

I. Metallic wires should be kept in sockets.

II. Switches may be used with wet hands.

III. Tester should be used to check the presence of current.

IV. Appliances with ISI mark is to be used.

Codes

a I and III

b I and II

c II and III

d III and IV

14. When a switch is in OFF position, then

I. current starting from the positive terminal of the cell stops at the switch.

II. circuit is open.

III. no current flows through it.

IV. current flows after some time.

Choose the combination of correct answer from the following.

a All are correct

b Both II and III are correct

c Only IV is correct

d Both I and II are correct

15. Fill in the blanks with the help of options given in the box.

(i) current	(ii) resistance	(iii) charges
(iv) potential	(v) difference	(vi) positive
(vii) resistor	(viii) circuit	(ix) fuse
(x) negative	(xi) battery	

I. Electric current is a flow of ....

II. A continuous closed path used by the current to flow through it is called ....

III. The short line in the symbol of a cell represents .... terminal.

IV. Combination of two or more cells is known as ....

V. The long thick line in the symbol of a cell represents .... terminal.

Codes

	I	II	III	IV	V
a	(iii)	(viii)	(x)	(xi)	(vi)
b	(ii)	(vii)	(ix)	(x)	(v)
c	(v)	(x)	(ii)	(viii)	(iii)
d	(viii)	(i)	(v)	(xi)	(vi)

16. State 'T' for true or 'F' for false.

I. A key or switch in circuit can be placed anywhere in the circuit.

II. To make a battery of two cells, the longer line is connected to the longer line of another cell.

III. Water is a good conductor of electricity.

IV. The bulb glows in the circuit only when key is in open position.

V. The SI unit of electric current is ampere.

Codes

	I	II	III	IV	V			I	II	III	IV	V
a	T	F	T	T	T		b	T	F	F	F	T
c	T	T	T	F	F		d	F	F	T	F	T

17. Match the given matrix.

1. Bulb	p.	(switch symbol)
2. Ammeter	q.	—(V)—
3. Key	r.	—(A)—
4. Cell	s.	—(•)—
5. Voltmeter	t.	—(m)—
	u.	—|⊢—

Codes

a 1 → t, 2 → r,t, 3 → p, 4 → u, 5 → q

b 1 → t, 2 → r, 3 → p,s, 4 → u, 5 → q

c 1 → t, 2 → q, 3 → s, 4 → u, 5 → r

d 1 → t, 2 → p, 3 → s, 4 → q, 5 → r

18. Assertion (A) All the bulbs connected in parallel glow brightly.

Reason (R) All the bulbs are connected directly to a battery and derive the required electrical energy.

   a A and R are correct and R is the correct explanation of A
   b A and R are correct but R is not the correct explanation of A
   c A is correct but R is not correct
   d R is correct but A is not correct

19. Assertion (A) The circuit is complete when key is in open position.

Reason (R) The current flows in a circuit when there is no gap in it.

   a A and R are correct and R is the correct explanation of A
   b A and R are correct but R is not the correct explanation of A
   c A is correct but R is not correct
   d R is correct but A is not correct

20. Complete the following paragraph using the words given in options below.

Electricity can be classified into two types, i.e. static electricity and ……… electricity. In case of current electricity, charges are ……… to move throughout the ……… Unlike current electricity static electricity as the name suggests is ……… in nature and charge ……… by the part of an object cannot flow through the other parts.

   a Conductor, acquired, current, free, static
   b Current, acquired, free, conductor, static
   c current, free, conductor, static, acquired
   d Static, acquired, free, current, conductor

Direction (Q. Nos. 21-23) Read the following information and answer the questions that follow.

In simple notation, batteries can be regarded as a pump that provides the energy to move charge around a circuit. In order to gain a required potential difference, a store of energy is required. One such method is a battery or a cell. A battery is a device that converts chemical energy into electrical energy. The term battery is used when several electrical cells are connected together to provide a source of potential difference in a circuit.

21. A toy car needs a 12 V battery for its operation. How many cells of 1.56 V are required to provide the needed potential difference?

   a 7   b 8   c 6   d 9

22. How many cells are connected in the battery shown as below?

   a 3   b 4   c 5   d 6

23. Four cells are fixed on a wooden board and they are connected to form a battery. Which of the following figures represent the correct connection?

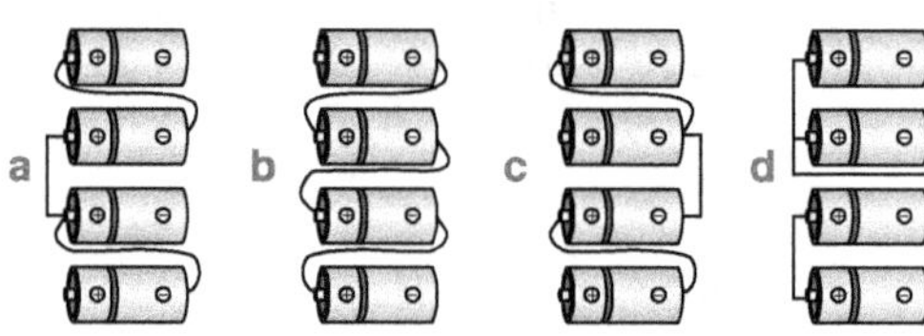

24. Consider the following circuit which shows R and S as two way switch.

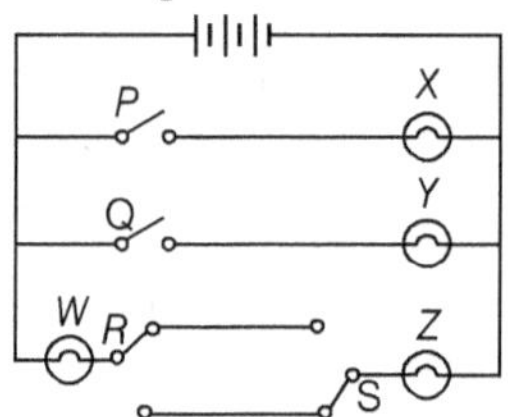

If switches P, R and S are closed simultaneously, which bulb would glow in the circuit?

   a Only X b X and Z
   c X, W and Z d W, X, Y, Z and W

25. Consider the following circuit diagram and choose the correct statement with reference to the circuit diagram.

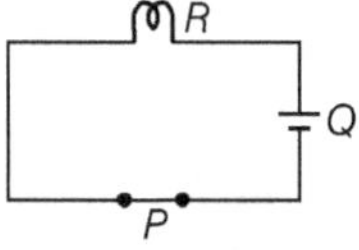

  I. Component P is in ON position so, current will flow through the circuit.
  II. An electric current transports energy from component Q to the component R.
  III. The component R uses nichrome element in order to last longer.

Codes
   a I and III   b II and III
   c I and II   d All are correct

Direction (Q. Nos. 26-27)   The circuit shown below consists of five identical bulbs P, Q, R, S and T and three switches 1, 2 and 3 all connected to a battery.

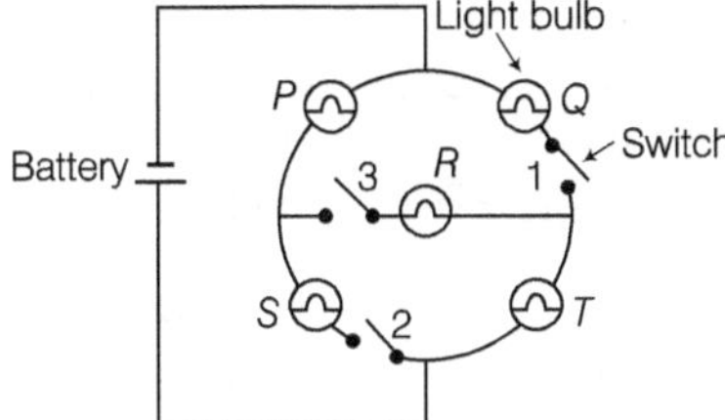

26. Which key should be closed to glow bulb T ?

   a 2
   b 1
   c 3
   d Both 1 and 2

27. Which bulb will glow when only switch 3 is closed?

   a Only R
   b P, R and S
   c P, R and T
   d P, Q, R and T

B Heating Effect of Electric Current

1. Metals are good conductors of electricity. When electric current is passed through a metallic conductor, then some amount of

   a electrical energy is converted into heat energy
   b electrical energy is converted into mechanical energy
   c mechanical energy is converted into electrical energy
   d heat energy is converted into electrical energy

2. An arrangement of cell, bulb and connecting wires to glow bulb is shown as below.

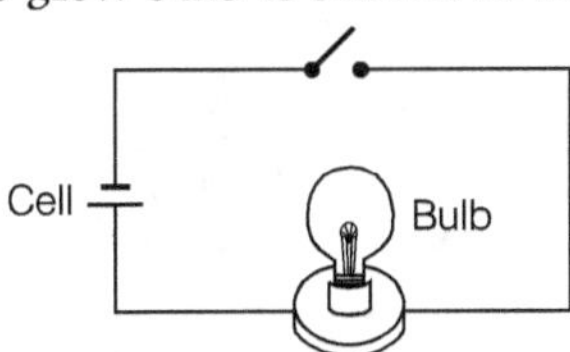

When key is closed, electric current passes through the filament of bulb and it gives off.

   a heat and sound
   b sound and magnetism
   c heat and light
   d sound and light

3. Fuse wires are made from special materials that melt quickly and break when large electric currents are passed through them. They are made up of which of the following alloy?

   a Nichrome   b Tin-lead
   c Magno-chrome   d Chrome-lead

4. An electric fuse is shown in the figure as below.

Which of the following is the symbol of fuse?

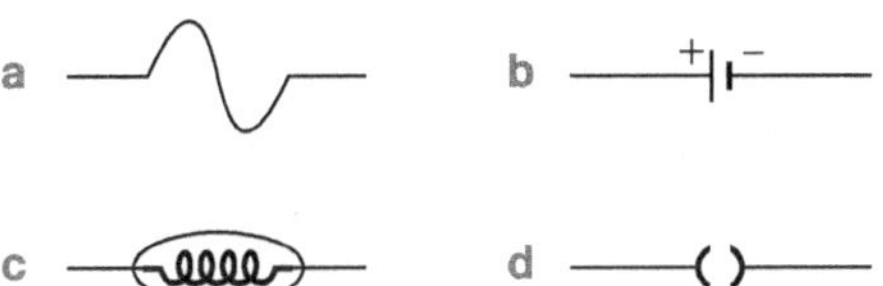

5. When an electric current is flown through a conductor, it produces heat.

The amount of heat produced in a heating element depends on

   a its length   b area of cross-section
   c nature of material   d All of these

6. Observe the circuits below carefully.

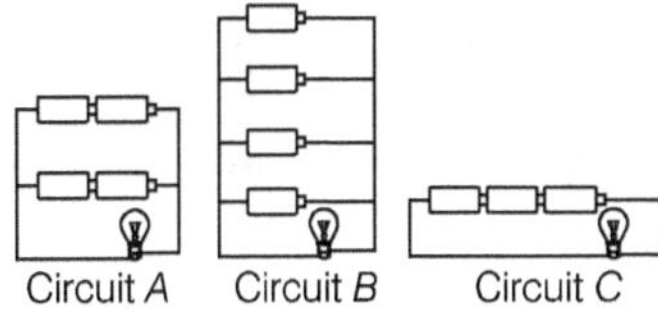

Arrange the circuits in ascending order from the least bright to the brightest.

   a A, C, B b B, A, C
   c C, A, B d B, C, A

7. Ram while studying the circuit of an electric fan observes that a plug connected to a fan contains a 3 A fuse. Why is the fuse needed ?

   a To reduce the voltage across the fan
   b To protect the fan from damage caused by a large current
   c To make it easier for the current to flow
   d To decrease the resistance of the circuit

8. A lamp is marked 24 W; 12 V. Which of the following statements given below are true?

   I. If the bulb is working for 4 h, the total energy used is 0.096 kWh.

   II. In this process, the electrical energy is converted to light energy.

   III. If electricity costs 20 paise per unit, then cost for using the lamp for 4 h will be ₹ 1.92.

   IV. The bulb is faulty.

Codes

a	Only I	b I and II
c	Only III	d II and IV

9. In the following options, at least one line in each box is correct. Identify the option in which both the lines are correct.

a	Heat produced in a conductor by electric current depends on	→ Length of conductor. → number of batteries in circuit.
b	Conductors have	→ free electrons to move. → low electrical conductivity.
c	Applications of heating effects of an electric circuit include	→ electric heater. → electric bell.
d	Fuse is a	→ device which prevents damage to electrical circuits. → wire made up of alloy of tin and lead.

10. Which of the following does not affect the brightness of a bulb in a circuit?

   I. Number of batteries in circuit

   II. Arrangement of batteries in circuit

   III. Number of bulbs in circuit

   IV. Length of wire in circuit

Codes

a	I and III	b Only II
c	II and IV	d Only IV

11. Which of the following statements about a fuse is correct?

   I. A fuse blows when the current in the circuit is larger than its current rating.

   II. A fuse blows when the current in the circuit is smaller than its current rating.

   III. A fuse can only be found in a three-pin plug

   IV. A fuse of a particular current rating can be used in a circuit.

Codes

a	I and III	b I and IV
c	II and IV	d III and IV

12. Consider the following statements and choose the incorrect one.

   I. If the current passing through the conductor is increased, heat produced will also increase.

   II. If resistance of wire is increased, heat produced in it will decrease.

   III. Heating element is made up of tungsten wire.

Codes

a	I and I	b II and III
c	I and III	d All of these

13. Choose the statements which are not correct in the case of an electric fuse.

   I. Fuses are inserted in electric circuits of all buildings.

   II. There is a maximum limit of the current which can safely flow through the electric circuits.

   III. There is a minimum limit of the current which can safely flow in the electric circuits.

   IV. If a proper fuse is inserted in a circuit, it will blow off if current exceeds the safe limit.

Codes

a	I and II	b Only II
c	Only III	d III and IV

14. Which of the conditions shown below represents short circuit or overload?

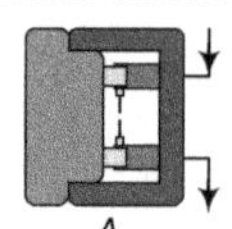 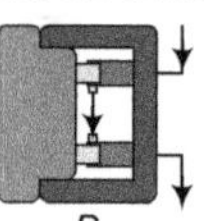

a	Only A	b Only B
c	Both A and B	d Neither A nor B

15. Fill in the blanks with the help of options given in the box.

(i) current	(ii) nichrome	(iii) element
(iv) tubelight	(v) heat	(vi) melt
(vii) tungsten	(viii) CFL	(ix) fuse
(x) overload		

   I. Higher the resistance, greater is the .... produced.

   II. The coil of wire in an electric heater is called ....

   III. When the current flowing exceeds the safety limit, the fuse wire will ....

   IV. .... is used to make the filament of a bulb.

   V. Heat energy produced by glowing bulb can be minimised by using ....

	I	II	III	IV	V
a	(v)	(iii)	(vi)	(vii)	(viii)
b	(ii)	(vii)	(ix)	(x)	(v)
c	(v)	(x)	(ii)	(viii)	(iii)
d	(viii)	(i)	(v)	(x)	(vi)

16. State 'T' for true or 'F' for false.

    I. A fuse is used to save energy in electric circuits.

    II. Fuse wire is made up of an alloy of lead and copper which are in different proportions.

    III. Electric iron works on heating effect of current.

    IV. Connecting many devices to a single socket leads to short circuit.

    V. If live wire comes in contact with neutral wire, it leads to overloading.

Codes

	I	II	III	IV	V
a	T	F	T	T	T
b	T	T	F	F	T
c	T	T	T	F	F
d	F	F	T	F	F

17. Match the given matrix.

1.	Fuse	p.	Nichrome
2.	Filament	q.	Live and neutral wire comes in direct contact
3.	Element	r.	Large current drawn from same socket
4.	Overloading	s.	High resistance and low melting point
5.	Short circuit	t.	Tungsten

  a $1 \rightarrow s, 2 \rightarrow t, 3 \rightarrow p, 4 \rightarrow r, 5 \rightarrow q$

  b $1 \rightarrow s, 2 \rightarrow p, 3 \rightarrow t, 4 \rightarrow r, 5 \rightarrow q$

  c $1 \rightarrow s, 2 \rightarrow p, 3 \rightarrow t, 4 \rightarrow q, 5 \rightarrow r$

  d $1 \rightarrow s, 2 \rightarrow t, 3 \rightarrow p, 4 \rightarrow q, 5 \rightarrow r$

18. Assertion (A) Before buying an electric appliance always look for ISI mark on them.

Reason (R) ISI mark ensures that appliance is safe and energy efficient.

  a (A) and (R) are correct and (R) is the correct explanation of (A)

  b (A) and (R) are correct and (R) is not the correct explanation of (A)

  c (A) is correct but (R) is incorrect

  d (R) is correct but (A) is incorrect

19. Assertion (A) CFL bulbs have replaced the traditional electric bulbs.

Reason (R) The filament of an electric bulb produce heat and light using electric current.

  a (A) and (R) are correct and (R) is the correct explanation of (A)

  b (A) and (R) are correct and (R) is not the correct explanation of (A)

  c (A) is correct but (R) is incorrect

  d (R) is correct but (A) is incorrect

20. Complete the following paragraph using the words given in options below.

An electric bulb works on .... effect of current. The .... of the bulb is made up of .... which heats up when .... is passed through it and hence glows. Moreover, ... which is filled inside the bulb .... the filament from catching fire.

  a Heating, filament, tungsten, current, argon gas, prevents

  b Filament, current, prevents, heating, tungsten, argon gas

  c Heating, tungsten, filament, argon gas, current, prevents

  d Tungsten, heating, filament, prevents, current, argon gas

Direction (Q. Nos. 21-23) Read the following information and answer the questions that follow.

When we apply potential difference across two ends of wire, an electric current is set up in the wire. Such a current is due to the motion of free electrons in the wire. During the motion of electrons, they collide with each other and also with ions in the wire. Due to these collisions, kinetic energy of electrons decreases. This loss in kinetic energy appears as heat and temperature of wire rises.

21. Which of the following does not work on the heating effect of current?

  a Electric bulb

  b Electric fuse

  c Miniature circuit breaker

  d Immersion rod

22. The coil of wire contained in heater is known as

  a component

  b circuit

  c filament

  d element

23. The element of a heating appliance is made of an alloy nichrome but not of tungsten. This is so because

    a tungsten catches fire in presence of air but nichrome do not

    b tungsten is not a good conductor of electricity

    c colour of nichrome makes it possible to become red hot and cause heating effect

    d All of the above

24. An electric kiln is used in pottery. A kiln has a device in it to prevent it from getting too hot. The metals in the bimetallic strip expand at different rates and the strips bend when heated. The contact points move apart and the electric current to the heating device stops.

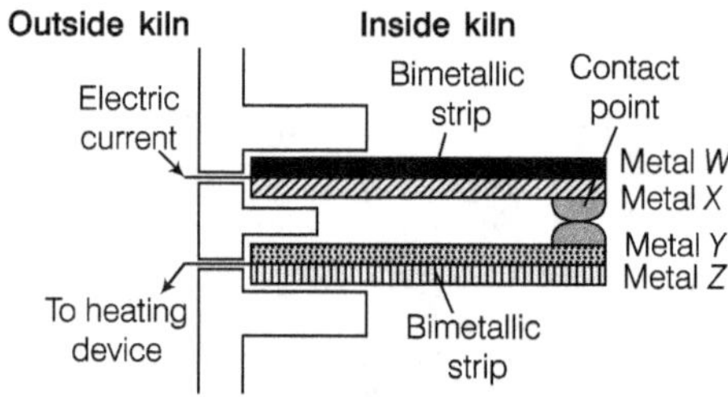

In order for this device to work,

    a X expands more than W, Y expands more than Z.

    b X expands more than W, Z expands more than Y.

    c W expands more than X, Y expands more than Z.

    d W expands more than Z, X expands more than Y.

C Magnetic Effect of Electric Current

1. The experiment below is possible to be done such that the metal nail floats in the air. Which statement is true about it?

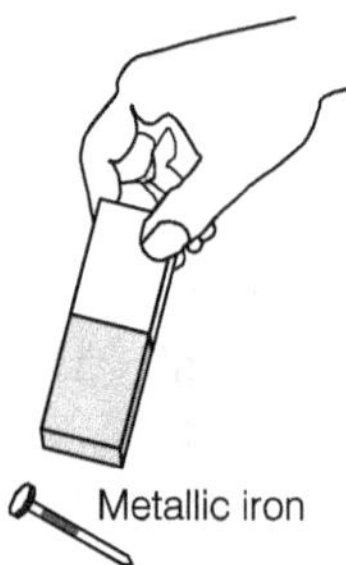

    a Magnetic force must be bigger than the weight of the nail to lift it up from the ground

    b Magnetic force must be exactly equal to the weight of the nail

    c After a few seconds, the nail will fall down to the ground as the magnetic force cannot hold the weight of the nail for long time

    d If we change the metal nail to a wooden nail, it will still be able to float in the air

2. Which of the following are not based on the magnetic effect of electric current?

    I. Fan

    II. Loudspeaker

    III. Electric bell

    IV. Electric motor

Codes

    a Only I   b I and II

    c I and III   d Only IV

3. An electromagnet is a temporary magnet, whose strength can be changed. It works only when current is

    a allowed to flow through it

    b not allowed to flow through it

    c allowed and then stopped

    d None of the above

4. Electromagnet is very strong and its power can be increased. The most suitable materials to use as its core and its application are

	Core	Application
a	Iron	Electric bell
b	Brass	Electric iron
c	Aluminium	Speaker
d	Steel	Crane

5. Which of the following does not make the electromagnet stronger?

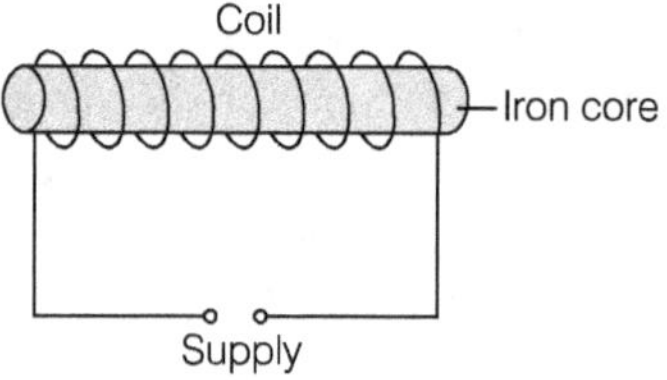

    a Increasing the number of turns of wire in the coil

    b Increasing the current in the coil

    c Using a soft iron core

    d Using a bigger resistor

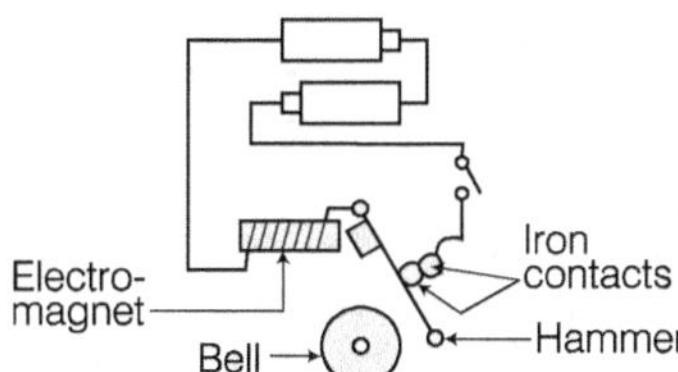

Answer the questions with reference to the circuit.

6. When the switch of an electric bell is pushed, then
   a flow of the current stops through the electromagnet in the bell
   b a current starts to flow through the electromagnet
   c voltage decreases in the current flowing through the electromagnet
   d None of the above

7. What will happen if electromagnet is replaced with a bar magnet?
   a The circuit is not correct
   b The bell will ring continuously even without circuit being complete
   c The bell will not ring when current is passed through it
   d There will be no change and bar magnet will work just like the electromagnet

8. A diagram of an electromagnet is shown below. Which of the following statements are correct regarding the circuit.

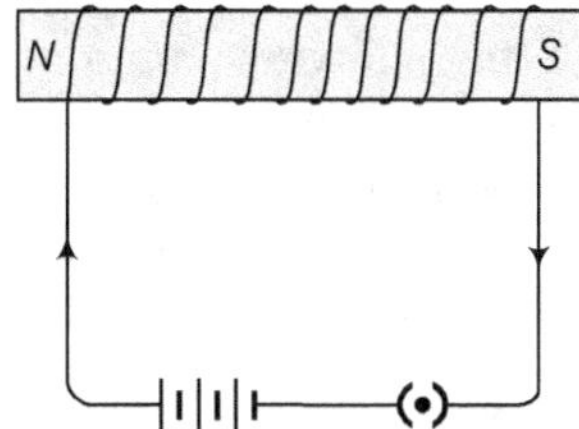

   I. Direction of current is not correct.
   II. Polarity of electromagnet is not correct.
   III. Key is open so current will not flow.

Codes
   a I and II
   b II and III
   c I and III
   d All of the above

9. There are four containers each containing different objects which are as follows.

Container I   Marble and silver coin
Container II   Copper coin and iron nail
Container III   Nickel coin and steel nail
Container IV   Steel nail and aluminium bowl

He can use an electromagnet to separate the objects in containers.
   a I and II
   b II, III and IV
   c II and III
   d II and IV

10. Which of the following statements are incorrect?
   A. Fuse is a safety device.
   B. Modern houses use Miniature Circuit Breakers.
   C. MCB needs to be replaced everytime a heavy electric current passes through it.
   D. It serves the same purpose as a CFL.
   a A and B
   b Only B
   c C and D
   d Only C

11. Which of the following statements are correct?
   I. Fuse works on heating effect of electric current.
   II. Electromagnets are used in many devices such as electric bell, cranes, etc.
   III. Fuses have replaced MCBs in modern buildings.
   IV. An electromagnet does not attract safety pins.
   a I and II
   b Only II
   c I and III
   d Only IV

12. Identify the figure given as below. On which principle does it work?

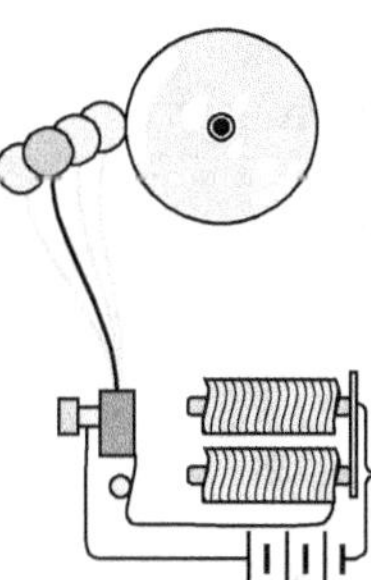

   a Electromagnet, magnetic effect of current
   b Electric bell, heating effect of current
   c Electric bell, magnetic effect of current
   d Loudspeaker, magnetic effect of current

13. Fill in the blanks with the help of options given in the box.

(i) magnet	(ii) MCB	(iii) magnetic field
(iv) current	(v) electric bell	(vi) coil
(vii) electromagnet		(viii) solenoid

   I. Current flowing in a wire gives rise to .... around it.
  II. The magnet made by using electric current is called ....
 III. A current carrying coil of an insulated wire wrapped around a piece of iron is called ....
  IV. .... works on the magnetic effect of current.
   V. The safety device based on magnetic effect of current is called ....

Codes

	I	II	III	IV	V		I	II	III	IV	V
a	iii	vii	viii	v	ii	b	ii	vii	iv	iii	v
c	v	i	ii	viii	iii	d	viii	i	v	ii	vi

14. State 'T' for true or 'F' for false.
   I. An electromagnet repels all the magnetic materials.
  II. An electric bell uses a permanent magnet.
 III. MCB stands for Miniature Circuit Breaker.
  IV. The magnetism of an electromagnet remains as long as the current is flowing in its coil.
   V. The strength of magnetic field of an electromagnet can be enhanced by increasing the number of turns of the coil.

Codes

	I	II	III	IV	V
a	T	F	T	T	T
b	T	T	F	F	T
c	T	T	T	F	F
d	F	F	T	T	T

15. Match the given matrix.

1.	Electric bell	p.	Temporary magnet
2.	ALNICO	q.	Electrical energy into sound energy
3.	Bar magnet	r.	Permanent magnet
4.	Electromagnet	s.	Electromagnet

a 1 → q, 2 → r, 3 → p, 4 → s
b 1 → q, 2 → p, 3 → r, 4 → s
c 1 → q, 2 → s, 3 → r, 4 → p
d 1 → q, 2 → p, 3 → s, 4 → r

16. Sammy designed a doorbell as shown below.

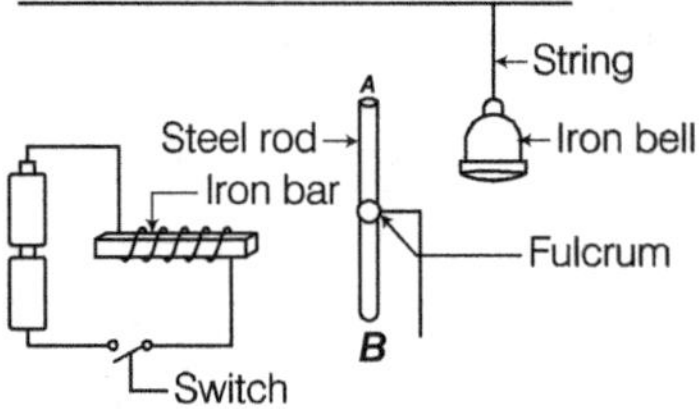

The energy changes that take place in the electric bell are

a kinetic → electrical → magnetic → sound
b electrical → kinetic → magnetic → sound
c electrical → magnetic → kinetic → sound
d electrical → chemical → magnetic → sound

17. **Assertion** (A) An electromagnet is a temporary magnet.

   Reason (R) The magnet made by using electric current is called an electromagnet.

   a A and R are correct and R is the correct explanation of A
   b A and R are correct but R is not the correct explanation of A
   c A is correct but R is incorrect
   d R is correct but A is incorrect

18. **Assertion** (A) Current flowing through a conductor produces a magnetic field.

   Reason (R) A current carrying conductor is able to deflect a compass needle.

   a A and R are correct and R is the correct explanation of A
   b A and R are correct but R is not the correct explanation of A
   c A is correct but R is incorrect
   d R is correct but A is incorrect

19. Complete the following paragraph using the words given in options below:

It was observed by Oersted that when a .... compass is brought near a current carrying .... the needle of the compass gets deflected in the .... of flow of electricity. This shows that electric current produces a magnetic effect. The .... which are formed using a coiled current carrying conductor and soft iron .... are being used in many instruments like big cranes and electric door bells.

   a electromagnets, direction, core, conductor, magnetic
   b magnetic, conductor, direction, electromagnets, core
   c magnetic, direction, core, conductor, electromagnets
   d electromagnets, core, direction, magnetic, conductor

 (Q. Nos.20-22)   Read the following information and answer the questions that follow.

An electromagnet is simply a coil of wire. It is usually wound around an iron core. (However, it could be wound around an air core, in which case it is called a solenoid). When connected to a DC voltage or current source, the electromagnet becomes energised, creating a magnetic field just like a permanent magnet. The strength of an electromagnet can be controlled.

20. What is the name given to the coil of an electromagnet?

    a Magnetic coil   b Toroid   c Solenoid   d Element

21. The strength of an electromagnet does not depend upon

    a number of turns in the coil   b current passing through the coil
    c nature of core material   d None of the above

22. An electromagnet is operated on which type of power supply?

    a Alternating Current (AC) power supply   b Direct Current (DC) power supply
    c Either AC or DC   d Neither AC nor DC is needed

23. Solve the following crossword using hints given as below.

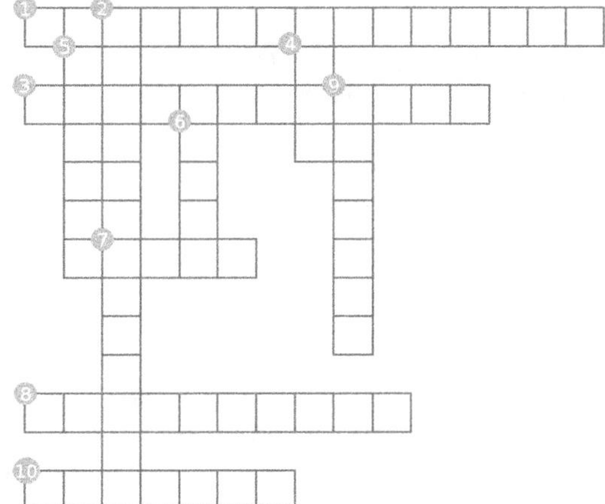

Across

1. The flow of electric charge is also known as
3. A device which is used to produce electric current from chemicals
7. When current does not flow into the circuit, it is said to be
8. Metal used for making elements of heating appliances
10. A group of cells is known as

Down

2. Magnetic device used in electric bells
4. The problem of replacement of fuse can be overcome using these safety devices
5. When current flows into the circuit it is said to be
6. It is a safety device which works on heating effect of current
9. It is a path through which electric charge moves

Light

(A) Light, Reflection and Mirror

1. Geeta stood 4 m away from a plane mirror, then she moved again 1 m away. Now, the distance between her and image is

   a 5 m   b 6 m   c 8 m   d 10 m

2. Reflection of light is the change in direction of light by a mirror or any shiny surface that acts as a mirror. Reena held a stainless steel spoon to see her reflection. She saw that her reflection was

   a inverted on the outer side of the spoon   b erect on the inner side of the spoon
   c erect on the outer side of the spoon   d inverted on the inner side of the spoon

3. I am a spherical mirror. My bulging out face performs the reflection. I am used as a rear view mirror in vehicles. I give a wide field of view. Who am I?

   a Spherical mirror   b Convex mirror   c Plane mirror   d Concave mirror

4. I am a spherical mirror. Unlike my other companion I can form real and inverted as well virtual and erect images. Dentists rely on me to cure their patients. Who am I?

   a Convex mirror   b Plane mirror
   c Concave mirror   d Either convex or concave mirror

5. If an object is placed at a distance of 0.5 m in front of a plane mirror, then distance between the object and the image formed by the mirror will be

   a 2 m   b 1 m   c 0.5 m   d 0.25 m

6. The final image seen after two reflections at mirror 1 and mirror 2, respectively is

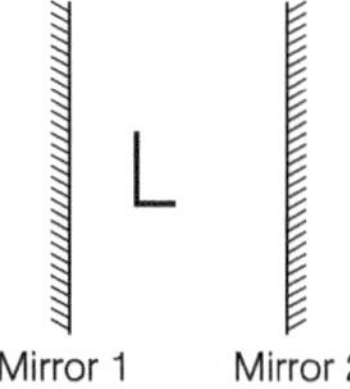

   a real, erect and laterally inverted   b virtual, erect and laterally inverted
   c virtual, erect and not laterally inverted   d virtual, inverted and laterally inverted

7. Boojho and Paheli were given one mirror each by their teacher. Boojho found his image to be erect and of the same size whereas Paheli found her image erect and smaller in size. This means that the mirrors of Boojho and Paheli are respectively

   a plane mirror and concave mirror   b concave mirror and convex mirror
   c plane mirror and convex mirror   d convex mirror and plane mirror

8. An object *O* is placed between two plane mirrors as shown below. At which position will an image not be seen?

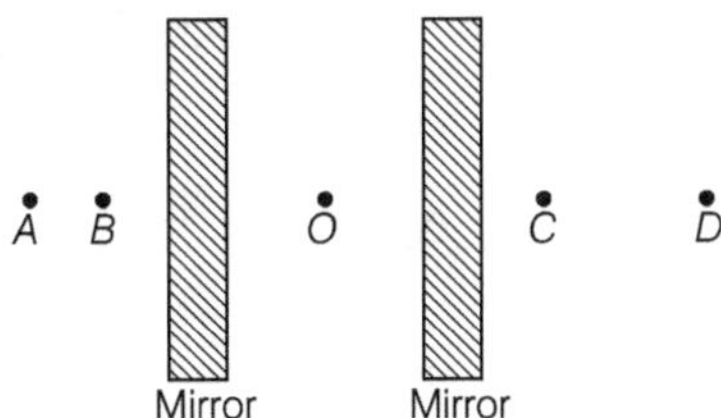

a Only *A*
b Both *B* and *C*
c Only *C*
d Only *D*

✎ **Direction** (Q. Nos. 9-10) Consider the following statements and choose the incorrect ones.

9. I. The incident ray, reflected ray and normal ray never lies on the same plane.
II. The angle made by the incident ray with the plane of mirror is equal to the angle made by reflected ray with the plane of mirror.
III. The angle made by incident ray with the normal is equal to the angle made by reflected ray with the normal.

Codes
a I and II
b II and III
c I and III
d All are incorrect

10. I. When an object is placed close to a concave mirror, the image will be virtual, erect and magnified.
II. Convex mirrors always form virtual, erect and diminished images.
III. Lateral inversion is possible only with plane mirrors.

Codes
a I and II
b II and III
c I and III
d All are correct

11. What is the angle of reflection in the figure given as below?

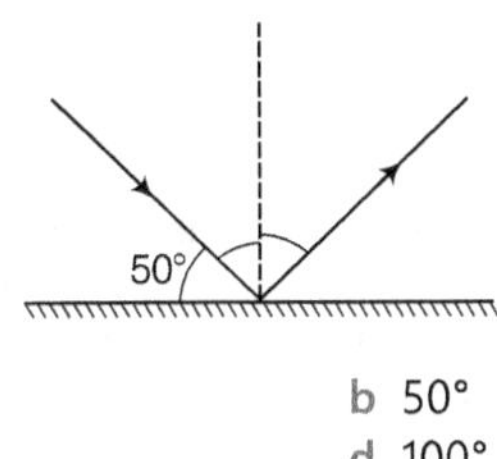

a 40°
b 50°
c 90°
d 100°

12. A wall separates a person from a ball but he is still able to see it.

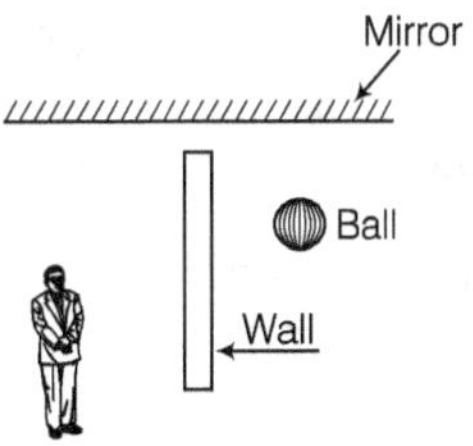

Which one of the following shows how this was possible?

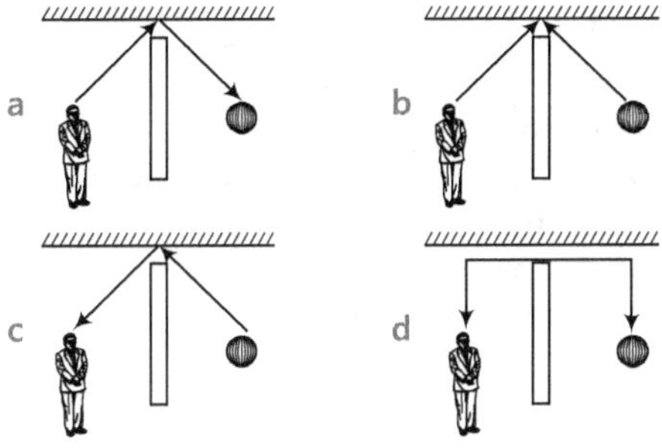

13. The letter G is placed in front of a plane mirror. How would its image look like when seen in the mirror?

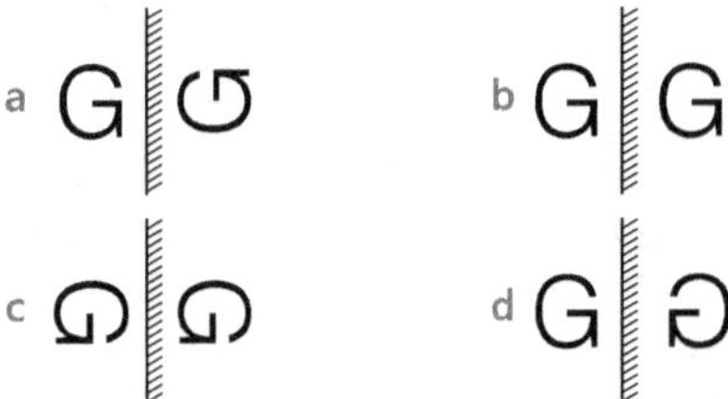

14. Fill in the blanks with the help of options given in the box.

(i) Non-luminous	(ii) virtual	(iii) plane
(iv) convex	(v) real	(vi) concave
(vii) luminous	(viii) reflection	
(ix) diffraction	(x) dispersion.	

I. .... images are the one which can be taken on screen.
II. The image formed in a plane mirror is ....
III. Dentists use .... mirrors to see the infected tooth.
IV. A periscope works on the principle of .... of light.
V. .... bodies emit their own light.

Codes

	I	II	III	IV	V
a	(v)	(ii)	(vi)	(viii)	(vii)
b	(vii)	(viii)	(ix)	(ii)	(v)
c	(v)	(x)	(iii)	(vii)	(ix)
d	(i)	(iv)	(iii)	(ix)	(vii)

15. State 'T' for true and 'F' for false.

I. The distance of the object from the mirror is equal to the distance of the image from the mirror in case of a plane mirror.

II. Like plane mirror, spherical mirrors also produce laterally inverted images.

III. The angle between the incident ray and reflected ray is the angle of reflection.

IV. Reflection is the bouncing back of light from a surface.

V. The nature of images formed by a concave mirror varies with the position of the object.

Codes

	I	II	III	IV	V
a	T	F	F	T	T
b	T	T	F	F	T
c	T	T	T	F	F
d	F	F	T	F	T

16. Assertion (A) A convex mirror always form a diminished and virtual image.

Reason (R) The laws of reflection are not applicable in the case of spherical mirrors.

a A and R are correct and R is the correct explanation of A

b A and R are correct but R is not the correct explanation of A

c A is correct but R is incorrect

d Both A and R are incorrect

17. Assertion (A) Concave mirrors are used as rear view mirrors in vehicles.

Reason (R) Concave mirrors form diminished images with a wide field of view.

a A and R are correct and R is the correct explanation of A

b A and R are correct, but R is not the correct explanation of A

c A is correct, but R is incorrect

d Both A and R are incorrect

18. Match the given matrix.

p. Angle of incidence   q. Normal
r. Reflected ray   s. Angle of reflection
t. Incident ray   u. Spherical mirror
v. Plane mirror

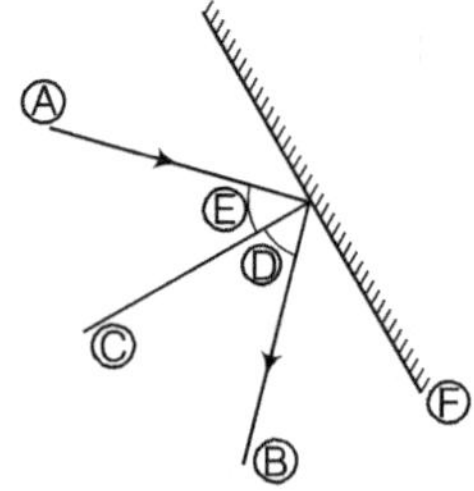

Codes

	A	B	C	D	E	F
a	t	q	r	p	s	v
b	t	r	q	s	p	v
c	t	r	q	p	s	u
d	t	r	q	p	s	v

Direction (Q. Nos.19-21) Read the following information and answer the questions that follow:

Eyes are wonderful gift given by God to all the living beings. The ability of our eyes to visualize the world is because of light. When a person looks into the mirror, he is able to see himself due to reflection of light from the mirror. The mirror image will be laterally inverted. Multiple images can be obtained by introducing two mirrors and altering their alignment.

19. The term lateral inversion refers to

a appearance of inverted images

b appearance of erect images

c appearance of left side of object on right side of image and *vice-versa*

d appearance of left side of object on left side of image and *vice-versa*

20. How many images will form if two mirrors are placed perpendicular to each other and an object is kept between them?

a 2   b 3
c 4   d infinite

21. A ray of light is incident on a plane mirror placed in a horizontal plane making an angle of 30° with the vertical, then the angle between the reflected ray and normal will be

a 35°   b 30°
c 90°   d 60°

B) Lens, Types of Lens and Dispersion

1. The distance between an object and a convex lens is changing. The size of the image formed has been observed to be decreasing. In which direction does the object moving with respect to lens?

a Towards the lens
b Away from the lens
c Initially towards and then away from the lens
d Initially away from the lens and then towards the lens

2. I always form virtual, erect and diminished image. If you want to know who I am just observe an air bubble in water, Then

a spherical lens
b concave lens
c convex lens
d cylindrical lens

3. Sir Newton discovered me using a simple experiment of glass prism. The secret of rainbow formation was revealed when I came into existence. Who am I?

a Reflection
b Refraction
c Dispersion
d Polarization

4. A lens is a piece of refracting medium bounded by two surfaces at least one of which is a curved surface. An image formed by a lens is erect. Such an image could be formed by a

a convex lens provided the image is smaller than object
b concave lens provided the image is smaller than object
c concave lens provided the image is larger than object
d concave lens provided the image is of the same size

5. Rama takes a prism to see the dispersion of white light through it. She observes when a ray of light passes through prism,

a the deviation of red light is maximum
b the deviation of violet light is maximum
c the deviation of blue light is maximum
d All rays deviate equally

6. The human eye has a converging lens system that produces an image at the back of the eye. If the eye views a distant object, then which type of image is produced?

a Real, erect, same size
b Real, inverted, diminished
c Virtual, erect, diminished
d Virtual, inverted, magnified

7. The diagrams below show the passage of light through glass blocks. Which diagram is not correct?

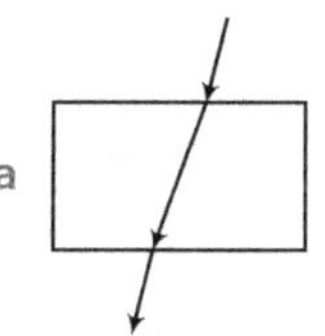

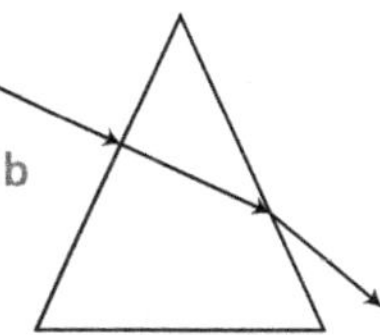

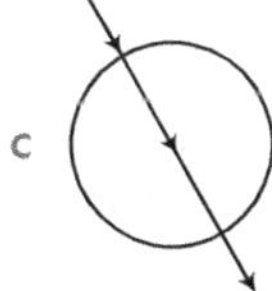

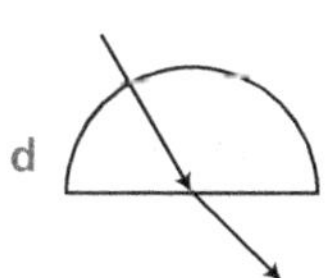

8. During an experiment, a lens X was kept on a table and a lighted candle was placed at a distance from the focus. The image was found to be real, inverted and diminished. When the candle was moved closer to the lens, the size of the image was found to be increasing. The lens X is

a concave lens
b convex lens
c prism
d Both (a) and (b)

9. Light travels at different speeds in different mediums. Which is the correct order of increasing speed of light in the following materials?

a Air, water, glass
b Water, glass, air
c Glass, air, water
d Glass, water, air

10. A ray of light XY travels from medium P into medium Q as shown below

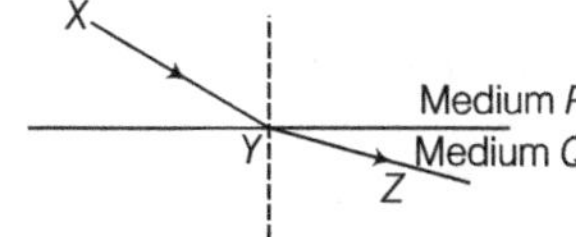

Which of the following statements is correct?

a Medium P is less dense than medium Q and the ray YZ travels faster than XY

b Medium P is denser than medium Q and the ray YZ travels faster than XY

c Medium P is less dense than medium Q and the ray YZ travels slower than XY

d Medium P is denser than medium Q and the ray YZ travels slower than XY

11. In the following options, at least one line forming in each box is correct. Identify the option in which both the lines are correct.

a	Spherical lens is	→	a piece of refracting medium bounded by two curved surfaces.
		→	Widely used in spectacles.
b	A prism	→	is transparent object rectangular in shape.
		→	disperses white light into a band of seven colours.
c	Convex lens is	→	thicker in middle than at the edges.
		→	also known as converging lens.
d	Concave lens is	→	thicker in middle than at edges.
		→	also known as diverging lens.

12. Stained glass can be seen in windows of many medieval buildings throughout Europe. It is a colourful art form and is best viewed when light is passing through it. How are we able to see the different colours of the glass?

a There must be reflection and refraction of the sun's rays inside the raindrops

b Light is refracted into our eyes

c Light is reflected into our eyes

d When light passes through the coloured glass, only light rays of that colour enter our eyes

13. The given figures show the path of light through two lenses A and B represented by rectangular boxes. The nature of lenses A and B are

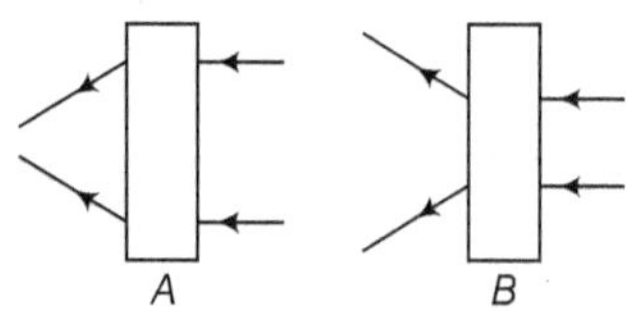

a A convex, B concave

b A concave, B convex

c A concave, B concave

d A convex, B convex

14. A light passes through a prism as shown in the figure below:

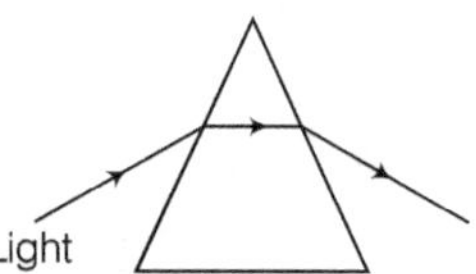

The light that comes out from the prism goes to the different direction with the initial direction. What causes this deviation of light?

a Reflection

b Refraction

c Interference

d Diffraction

15. A convex lens has a focal length of 15 cm. At which of the following distance should an object be placed in front of this convex lens so that it may act as a magnifying glass?

a 15 cm   b 10 cm

c 25 cm   d 30 cm

Direction (Q. Nos.16-17) Consider the following statements and choose the incorrect one.

16.
I. Convex lens is thicker at the edges and thinner in the middle.

II. Concave lens is thinner in the middle and thicker at the edges.

III. Convex lens is also known as converging lens.

IV. Concave lens is also known as converging lens.

Codes

a I and III

b II and III

c I and IV

d II and IV

17.
I. The role of glass prism is only to separate the seven colours of white light.

II. Focus is a point where parallel rays of light converge or appear to converge on principle axis.

III. Real image of the sun can be formed using a convex lens.

Codes

a Only I

b Only II

c Only III

d All are correct

18. The image formed by certain lens is always virtual, erect and smaller in size for an object kept at different positions in front of it. The lens must be

   a Convex lens

   b Concave lens

   c Plano-convex lens

   d Either convex or concave lens

19. The distance between an object and a convex lens is changing such that image formed on the screen is decreasing. The object will be

   a moving in a direction towards the lens

   b moving away from the lens

   c initially moving towards then moving away from the lens

   d initially moving away then moving towards the lens

20. Fill in the blanks with the help of options given in the box.

(i) Concave	(ii) diverging
(iii) spectrum	(iv) convex
(v) reflection	(vi) converging
(vii) seven	(viii) refraction
(ix) dispersion	(x) real

   I. A magnifying glass is a .... lens used to magnify small objects.

   II. Convex lens is also known as .... lens.

   III. Splitting of light into constituent colours is called ....

   IV. A prism splits sunlight into .... colours.

   V. The band of seven colours of white light is called ....

Codes

	I	II	III	IV	V
a	(iv)	(vi)	(ix)	(vii)	(iii)
b	(vii)	(viii)	(ix)	(ii)	(v)
c	(v)	(x)	(iii)	(vii)	(ix)
d	(i)	(iv)	(iii)	(ix)	(vii)

21. State 'T' for true or 'F' for false.

   I. The image in a concave lens is always smaller than the object.

   II. Convex lens gives a wide field of view.

   III. It is possible to recombine the lights of seven colours to obtain white light.

   IV. Infrared rays are responsible to give the heating effect in light.

   V. Lenses work on the reflection of light bouncing from them.

Codes

	I	II	III	IV	V
a	T	F	T	T	F
b	T	T	F	F	T
c	T	T	T	F	F
d	F	F	T	F	T

22. Match the given matrix.

A.	Lens	1.	Dispersion
B.	Convex lens	2.	Divergent
C.	Concave lens	3.	Seven colours
D.	Prism	4.	Refraction
E.	White light	5.	Convergent

Codes

	A	B	C	D	E			A	B	C	D	E
a	4	2	5	3	1		b	4	2	5	1	3
c	4	5	2	1	3		d	4	5	2	3	1

23. Assertion (A) A rainbow is formed when white light is incident on raindrops.

Reason (R) White light contains seven colours which undergoes dispersion inside a raindrop.

   a A and R are correct and R is the correct explanation of A

   b A and R are correct but R is not the correct explanation of A

   c A is correct but R is incorrect

   d Both A and R are incorrect

24. Assertion (A) Lenses work on the refraction of light.

Reason (R) Lenses are transparent, so light can pass through them.

   a A and R are correct and R is the correct explanation of A

   b A and R are correct but R is not the correct explanation of A

   c A is correct but R is incorrect

   d Both A and R are incorrect

25. Complete the following passage using hints given as below:

A .... causes the .... light to get dispersed into its constituent components. When a ray .... into the prism, it undergoes .... twice. It is because of its non-parallel refracting sides that cause ....

   a Prism, refraction, dispersion, white, passes

   b White, prism, passes, dispersion, refraction

   c Refraction, dispersion, prism, white, dispersion

   d Prism, white, passes, refraction, dispersion

A spectacular application of the phenomenon of refraction is the lens. Just as a focusing mirror is used to obtain an image of a distant object, a lens is used to focus light by refraction. The only difference between the two is that when a ray of light is incident on a lens, it gets refracted twice, i.e. once entering the lens and again while passing out of the lens from the other side.

26. Which phenomenon of light describes the propagation of light through a transparent object?
   a Reflection of light   b Refraction of light   c Dispersion of light   d Diffraction of light

27. In which type of lens, images formed are always diminished?
   a Concave lens   b Convex lens   c Spherical lens   d Plane lens

28. Which of the following is not an application of concave lens?
   a Flashlights   b Correction of myopia or short-sightedness
   c Peepholes in doors   d Correction of hypermetropia or far- sightedness

29. Solve the following crossword using hints given as below.

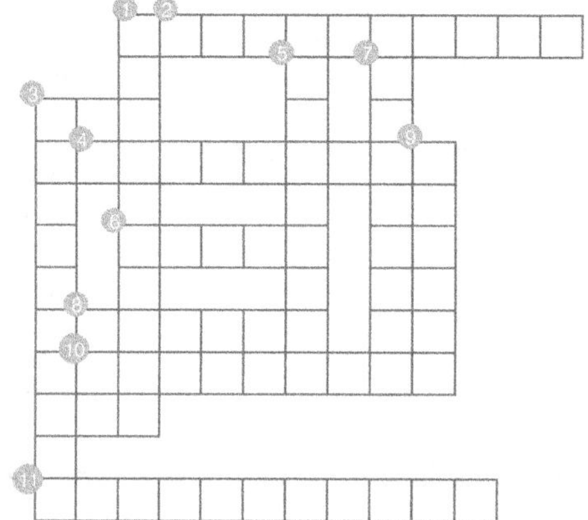

Across
   2. The phenomenon of bending of light while changing its medium
   4. Band of constituent colours of white light.
   6. Images formed on cinema screen
   8. A form of energy which enables us to see
   10. This mirror is converging in nature
   11. Objects which reflect back light incident on them to make themselves visible

Down
   1. Splitting of white light into seven constituent colours
   3. The phenomenon of bouncing back of light
   5. Images which are just illusion
   7. Objects having their own light
   9. Shop security mirrors

Practice Sets

Practice Set 1

A Whole Content Based Test for Class 7th Science Olympiad

1. There is a flow chart given below, it shows the components involved in the replenishment of nutrients in soil. Identify P, Q, R and S.

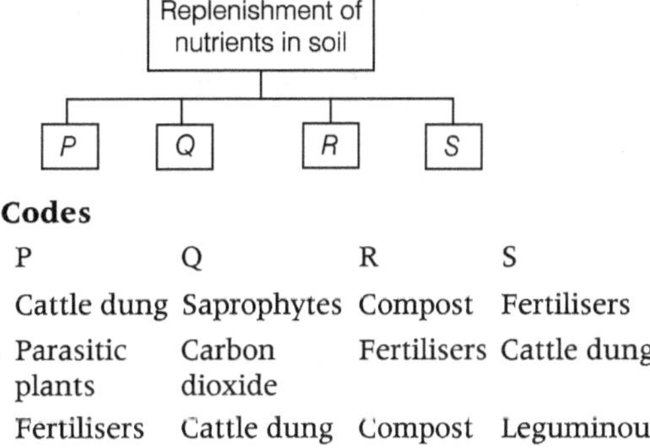

Codes

	P	Q	R	S
a	Cattle dung	Saprophytes	Compost	Fertilisers
b	Parasitic plants	Carbon dioxide	Fertilisers	Cattle dung
c	Fertilisers	Cattle dung	Compost	Leguminous crops
d	Chlorophyll	Carbon dioxide	Compost	Fertilisers

2. Two bicycles are approaching each other with speed 15 km/h. Initially, the distance between them is 60 km. How long will they hit each other?

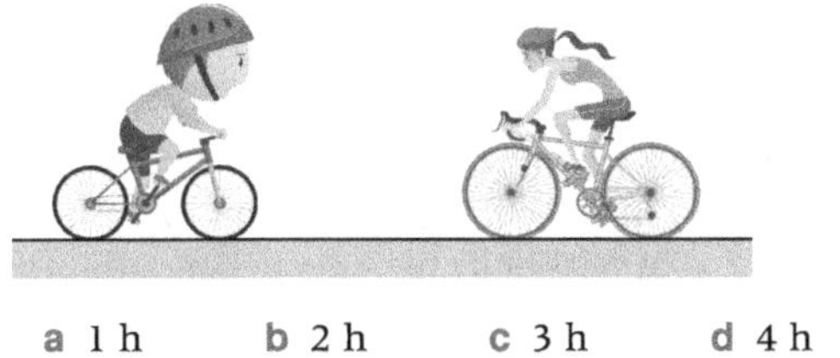

  a 1 h   b 2 h   c 3 h   d 4 h

3. Seema took some turmeric powder in a cup and made a paste by adding some water to it. Then, she take some paper strips and apply the paste over them. She dried the strips and use them to test the nature of following solution by keeping a few drops of the solution on the strips as shown below.

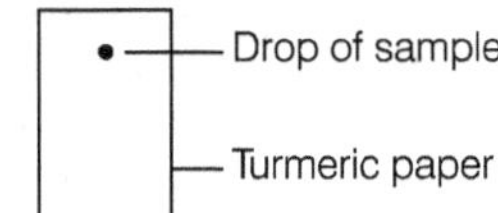

If the solutions used by her are (i) solution of common salt (ii) solution of baking soda (iii)lemon juice (diluted) and (iv) lime water, then the change in colour observed by her is

	(i)	(ii)	(iii)	(iv)
a	Yellow	Red	Yellow	Red
b	Yellow	Red	Red	Yellow
c	Yellow	Yellow	Red	Red
d	Red	Red	Yellow	Yellow

4. Observe the figure given below of excretory system and identify the part through which the waste carrying blood reach kidney and clean blood flows out of it.

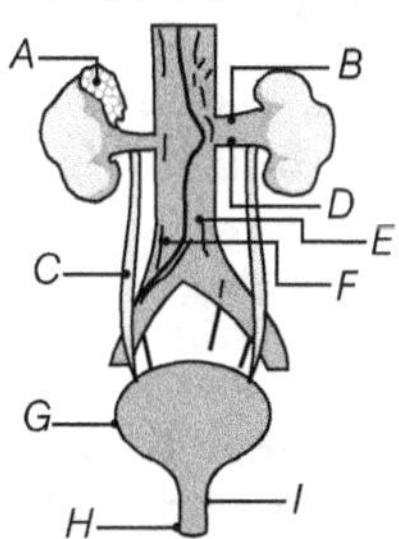

Choose the correct option

	Waste blood carrier	Clean blood carrier
a	A	B
b	B	C
c	B	D
d	B	F

5. A mirror is tilted at an angle of 30° to the bench. A ray of light is directed so that it hits the mirror at an angle of 20° to the surface of the mirror.

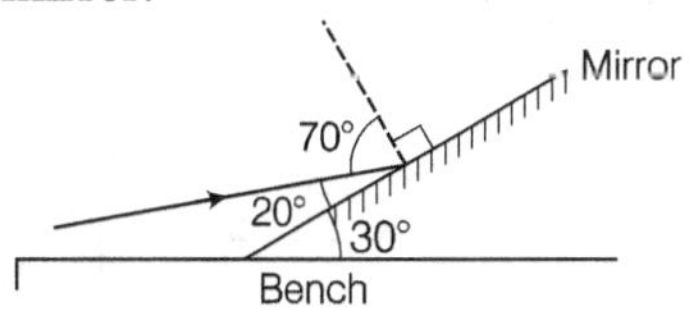

What is the angle of reflection?

  a 20°   b 50°   c 30°   d 70°

6. Classify the following processes into physical P or chemical changes C.
(i) Beating of aluminium metal to make aluminium foil.
(ii) Digestion of food.
(iii) Cutting of a log of wood into pieces.
(iv) Burning of crackers.

Codes

	(i)	(ii)	(iii)	(iv)		(i)	(ii)	(iii)	(iv)
a	P	C	P	C	b	P	P	C	C
c	P	C	C	P	d	C	P	P	C

7. Consider the following statements.

I. Wasp sting venom can be neutralised by an acid.

II. Indicators become green in neutral solution.

III. Salts obtained from nitric acid are called nitrates.

The correct statements are

a I and II
b II and III
c I and III
d I, II and III

Direction (Q. Nos. 8-10) Ah May leaves home at 8:15 am. She drives at 70 km/h to work. She reaches her office at 8:30 am.

8. How far is Ah May's office from her home?

a 4.7 km
b 17.5 km
c 280 km
d 1050 km

9. How fast must Ah May drive if she wants to reach her office at 8:25 am?

a 47 km/h
b 105 km/h
c 170.5 km/h
d 176.7 km/h

10. Ah May wants to reach her office by 8:15 am. but, because of the heavy traffic she can only travel at 50 km/h. What time would you advise Ah May to leave her home?

a 7:30 am
b 7:40 am
c 7:54 am
d 7:56 am

11. In which of the following circuits would the bulb light up?

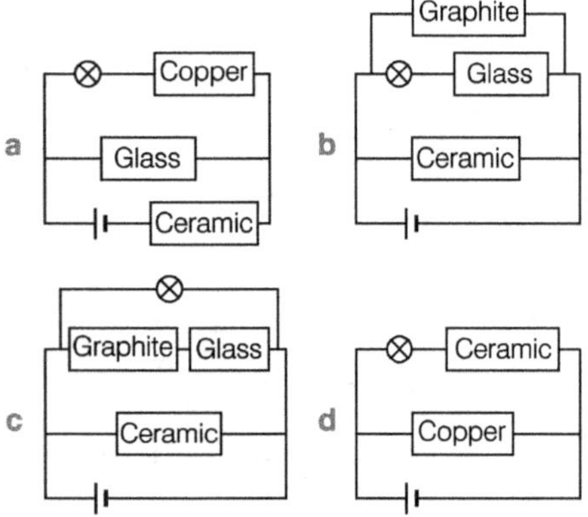

12. A convex lens is also called converging lens. Which statement about the image formed by a converging lens is correct?

a It is always real and erect
b It is always real and inverted
c It is always virtual and erect
d It may be either real or erect

13. 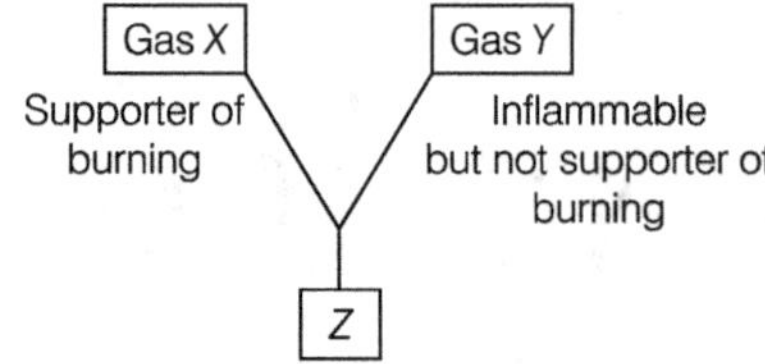

The above process is an example of

a reversible change
b temporary change
c physical change
d chemical change

14. The diagram below shows three connecting wires from part of a circuit. The current in wire RS is 5 A and the current in wire QR is 2 A.

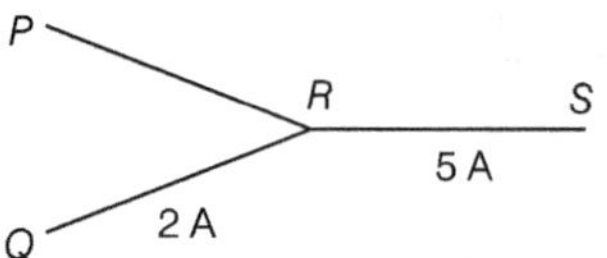

What will the current in wire PR be?

a 3 A
b 5 A
c 7 A
d 9 A

15. **Assertion** (A) Blood is red in colour.

Reason (R) Blood contains RBCs with haemoglobin.

a Both A and R are true and R is the correct explanation of A
b Both A and R are true, but R is not the correct explanation of A
c A is true, but R is false
d Both A and R are false

16. The diagrams below show two beakers X, and Y, filled with different amounts of water. The water in both beakers is heated upto 80°C.

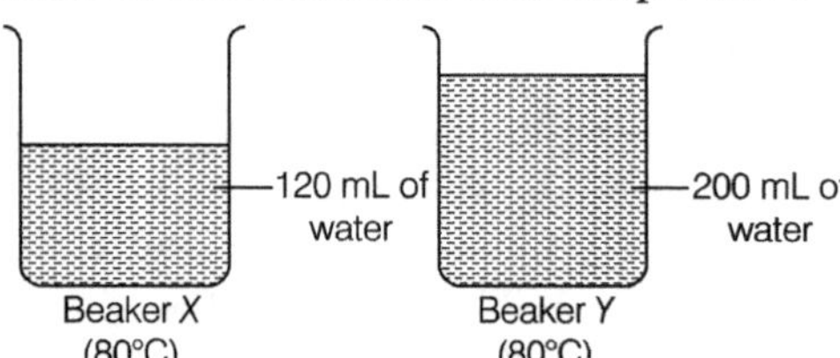

Which of the following statements is true about the two beakers of water?

a The water in both beakers has the same amount of heat energy and temperature
b The water in both beakers has different amount of heat energy
c The water in both beakers has the same amount of heat but different amount of energy
d The water in beaker Y will evaporate faster than the water in beaker X

17. Solve the given crossword.

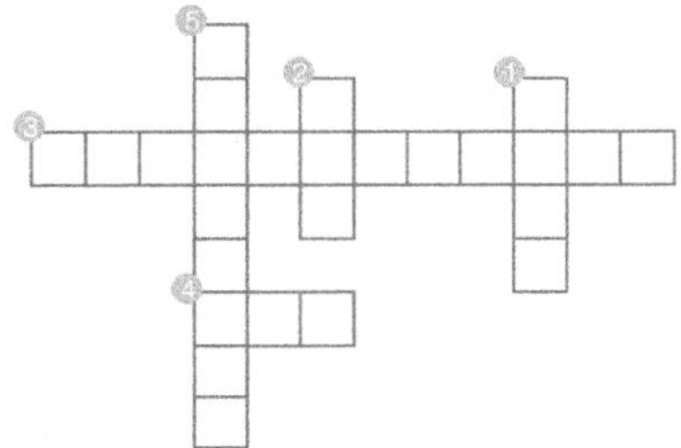

Across

3. Wear and tear of insulated wires cause
4. The safety mark necessary on all the electrical appliances

Down

1. Safety device used in circuits
2. Safety switches which work on the principle of magnetic effect of current
5. Connecting an electric circuit with ground to avoid an electric shock

18. Some process alongwith their reversibility and chemical composition are tabulated below.

	Process	Reversible	Chemical composition
I.	Combustion	✗	Different
II.	Crystallisation	✓	Different
III.	Curd formation	✗	Same
IV.	Digestion	✗	Same

Key	✓ Yes
	✗ No

The correct matching(s) is/are

  a I and II   b Only I
  c I, III and IV   d All of these

19. Which of the following correctly shows the direction of the convection currents when water is heated?

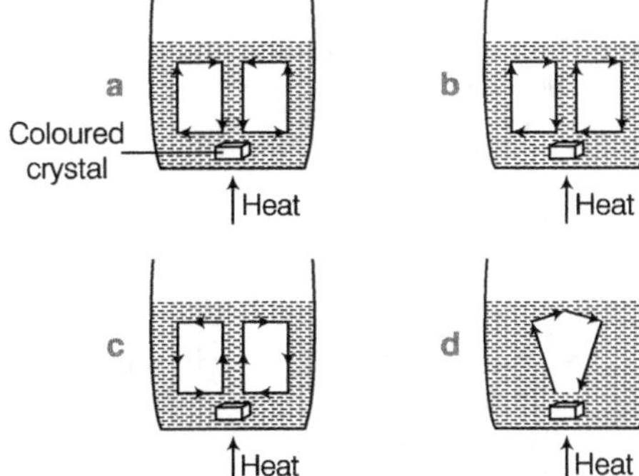

20. Consider the given below statements.

  I. In plants, the extra food is stored as starch.
  II. Minerals from soil travel throughout the plants through vascular tissues.
  III. Cortex lies in between the epidermis and vascular cylinder.
  IV. Sunlight and carbon dioxide enters into the leaves through stomata.
  V. *Cuscuta* is an example of a saprophytic plant

Which of the above statement(s) is/are true?

  a I, II and III   b I and III
  c Only III   d I and IV

21. Bernard did a simple experiment as shown below:

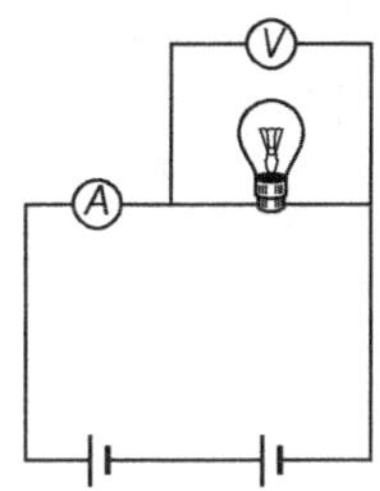

Here, he plots the readings of the voltmeter (V) and the ammeter (A).

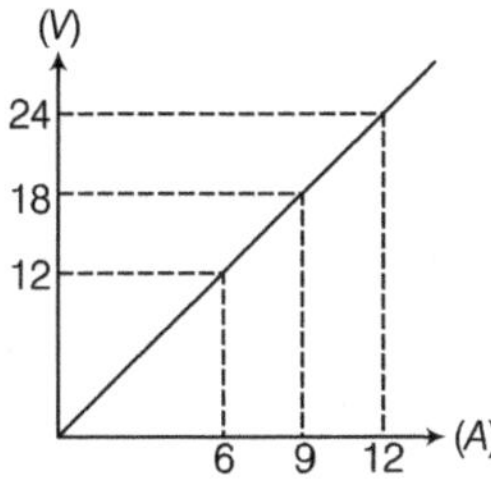

Which of the following statement is true?

  a Bernard used a fixed number of batteries throughout the experiment
  b Bernard used a $2\,\Omega$ resistor
  c Bernard used 12 V batteries only
  d Bernard used several numbers of bulbs in his experiment

22. Observe the given below table and identify A, B, C, D and E.

Description of parts of plants
A. Stacks of thylakoids.
B. Fluid matrix in a chloroplast
C. Tiny vessels that transport water from roots of a plants to its leaves.
D. Vessels that transport food from leaves to the other parts of the plant.
E. Leaves of a plant.

	A	B	C	D	E
a	Grana	Stroma	Xylem	Phloem	Foliage
b	Stroma	Grana	Phloem	Xylem	Foliage
c	Grana	Foliage	Stroma	Xylem	Phloem
d	Foliage	Grana	Xylem	Phloem	Stroma

Direction (Q. Nos. 23-25) The graph below shows the change in pH value of liquid X as liquid Y is mixed with it. One of the liquids is an acid and the other an alkali.

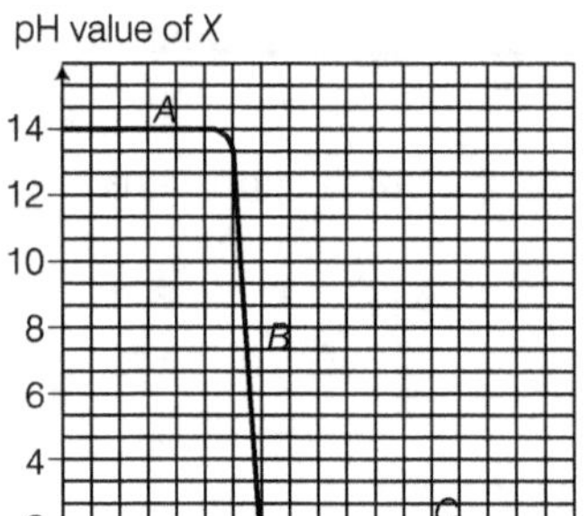

23. At which part of the curve will the red litmus paper turn blue?

   a A b B
   c C d A, B and C

24. What is the minimum volume of Y required to neutralise the solution?

   a 10 mL   b 20 mL   c 30 mL   d 40 mL

25. What does part C of the graph indicate?

   a X is in excess
   b Y is in excess
   c Y neutralises X completely
   d Y neutralises X partially

26. **Statement I** For respiration, plants take in oxygen and release carbon dioxide.

Statement II Respiration is a chemical process which takes place with the release of heat energy.

Which of the above statement(s) is/are true?

   a Only I   b Only II
   c Both a and b   d Neither a nor b

27. Observe the table given below and identify P and Q.

Types of teeth	Permanent teeth	Milk teeth
M	4	4
N	8	8
Q	8	0
P	12	8
Total	**32**	**20**

	P	Q
a	Molars	Premolars
b	Canines	Incisors
c	Molars	Canines
d	Incisors	Premolars

28. Denise has a faulty digital thermometer. When she placed the thermometer in a bucket of ice, the reading obtained was 2°C. When she placed it in a pot of boiling water, the new reading was 102°C. If the temperature reading of a glass of water at room temperature is 30°C, what is the actual temperature of the water?

   a 34°C   b 32°C   c 28°C   d 26°C

29. The table provides information about four different indicators.

Indicator	Colour at pH 4	pH at which colour changes	Colour at pH 12
P	Colourless	10	Red
Q	Red	3	Yellow
R	Blue	4	Red
S	Blue	6	Colourless

What colours will be obtained if each of the indicators are added separately to distilled water?

	P	Q	R	S
a	Colourless	Red	Red	Blue
b	Colourless	Yellow	Blue	Blue
c	Red	Yellow	Blue	Colourless
d	Colourless	Yellow	Red	Colourless

30. The diagram shows a root hair, surrounded by a dilute solution of mineral ions.

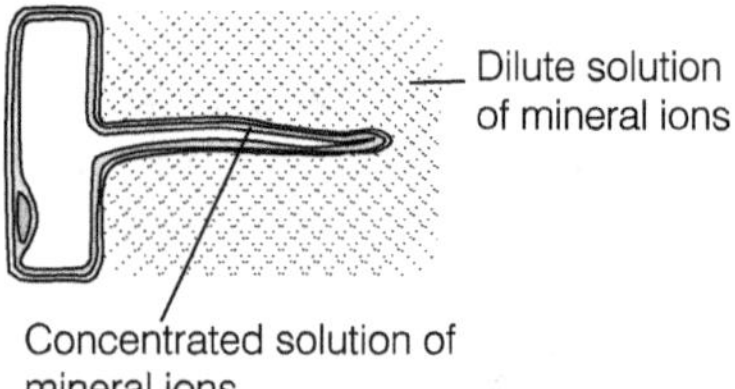

Which statement is correct?

   a Water molecules move into the root hair by osmosis.
   b Water molecules move out of the root hair by osmosis.
   c Water molecules move into the root hair by diffusion.
   d Water molecules move out of the root hair by diffusion.

Answers

1. (c) Fertilisers, cattle dung and compost add nutrients to soil and improve its quality.
   Nitrogen fixing leguminous crops also help in soil improvement.

2. (b) Since, both the bicycles are approaching with same speed. So, they both will cover same distance before hitting each other.
   $$\Rightarrow \text{Distance covered} = \frac{60}{2} = 30 \text{ km}$$
   $$\text{Speed} = 15 \text{ km/h}$$
   $$\text{Time taken} = \frac{\text{Distance}}{\text{Speed}}$$
   $$= \frac{30}{15} = 2 \text{ h}$$

3. (a) Colour of turmeric is yellow in acidic medium and red in basic medium.

4. (c) The blood brings wastes to the kidney through the renal artery. Nephrons purify the blood and clean blood flows out of the kidneys through the renal vein.

5. (d) According to second law of reflection, angle of incidence is always equal to the angle of reflection.
   Here, $\qquad \angle i = 70°$
   So, $\qquad \angle r = 70°$

6. (a) Chemical change involves change in chemical composition which remain unaffected in case of physical change. Thus, beating of aluminium foil and cutting of wood log are the examples of physical changes while remaining two are the chemical changes.

7. (d) Wasp sting inject some base, which can be neutralised by some acid.
   Appearance of green colour shows the neutral nature of a solution.
   Salts of nitric acid are called nitrates, e.g. $NaNO_3$ (sodium nitrate).

8. (b) Time taken = 15 min = 15×60 s
   Speed $\quad = 70$ km/h
   $$= 70 \times \frac{5}{18} \text{ ms}^{-1}$$
   Distance $=$ Speed $\times$ time
   $$= 70 \times \frac{5}{18} \times 15 \times 60 = 17500 \text{ m}$$
   $$= 17.5 \text{ km}$$

9. (b) Time taken = 10 min
   $$= 10 \times 60 \text{ s} = 600 \text{ s}$$
   Distance = 17500 m
   $$\text{Speed} = \frac{\text{Distance}}{\text{Time}}$$
   $$= \frac{17500}{600} \times \frac{18}{5} \text{ km/h} = 105 \text{ km/h}$$

10. (c) Distance = 17500 m = 17.5 km
    Speed $\quad = 50$ km/h
    $$\text{Time} = \frac{\text{Distance}}{\text{Speed}} = \frac{17.5}{50} = 0.35 \text{ h}$$
    $$= 0.35 \times 60 \text{ min} = 21 \text{ min}$$
    $$8:15 \text{ am} - 21 \text{ min}$$
    $$= 7:54 \text{ am}$$

11. (c) Ceramic and glass are insulators whereas copper and graphite are conductors. In case of option (c), circuit is complete with the bulb even if insulators are connected.

12. (d) The image formed by a converging lens can be real and inverted for, e.g. in camera or virtual and erect e.g. in magnifying lens depending upon the distance between the object and surface of lens.

13. (d) During a chemical change, a new substance is formed. Since, Z is quite different from X and Y, so it is a chemical change.

14. (a) Current in PR will be $RS - QR$
    $$= 5 \text{A} - 2 \text{A} = 3 \text{A}$$

15. (a) Blood contains RBCs, which has haemoglobin protein that gives blood its red colour.

16. (b) In case of beaker Y, heat energy will be more.

17.

18. (b) Combustion, curd formation and digestion all involve change in chemical composition, so these are the examples of chemical changes. All these are irreversible processes.
    Crystallisation is a reversible process but no new substance is formed during this process.

19. (c)   20. (a)

21. (b) Resistance, $R = \dfrac{V}{I} = \dfrac{12}{6}$
    $$R = 2 \, \Omega$$

22. (a)

23. (a) Litmus paper is blue when pH is more than 7. Thus, at point A.

24. (b) 20 mL of Y neutralises the liquid X.

25. (b) It shows excess of Y after neutralisation of X completely.

26. (c)

27. (a) $M \rightarrow$ Canines
    $N \rightarrow$ Insisors
    $Q \rightarrow$ Premolars
    $P \rightarrow$ Molars

28. (c) The temperature of ice = 0°C
    Obtained reading = 2°C
    So, error in thermometer = 2°C
    Hence, actual temperature of glass of water at room temperature = Obtained reading – error
    $$= 30 °C - 2°C = 28°C$$

29. (b) pH of distilled water is 7. So, P remains colourless, Q becomes yellow, R remains blue and S also remains blue.

30. (a)

Practice Set ②

A Whole Content Based Test for Class 7th Science Olympiad

1.

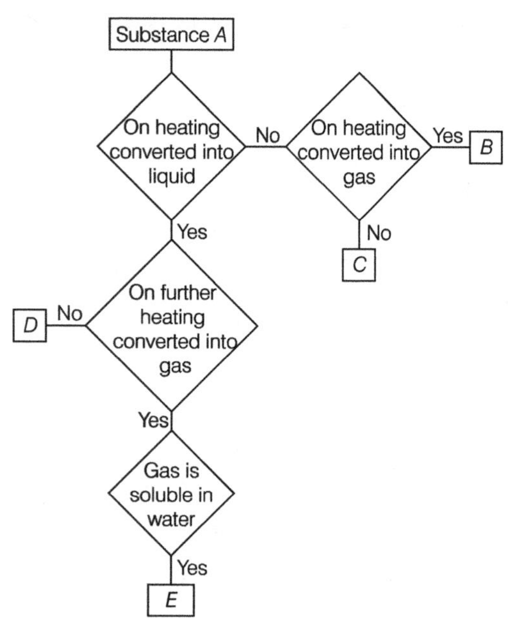

The correct term/substance A, B, C and D are

	A	B	C	D
a	ICl	NH_3	HCl	Chlorine
b	Solid	NH_3	HCl	Bromine
c	Solid	Na_2CO_3	NH_4Cl	Mercury
d	Solid	NH_4Cl	Na_2CO_3	Mercury

2. A helicopter takes 5 min to travel from terminal X to terminal Y. If the distance between terminals X and Y is 2000 m, then which of the following is the average speed of the helicopter?

a 24 km/h
b 40 km/h
c 400 km/h
d 1440 km/h

3. The diagram shows a section of a stem. Which tissue transports sugars and amino acids from the leaves to other parts of the plant?

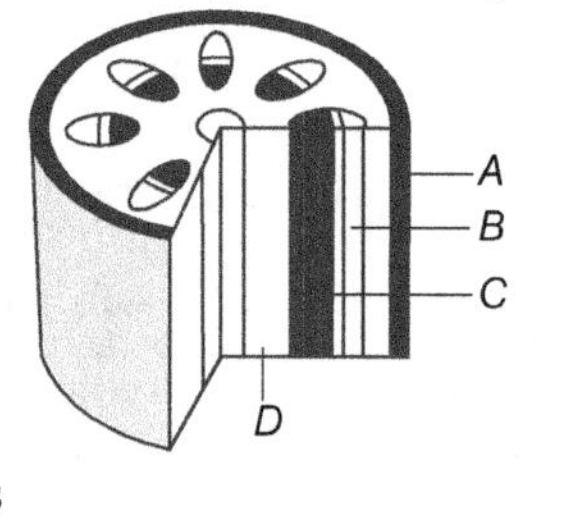

Codes

a B   b A   c D   d C

4. The distance-time graph of an object in motion is shown as below:

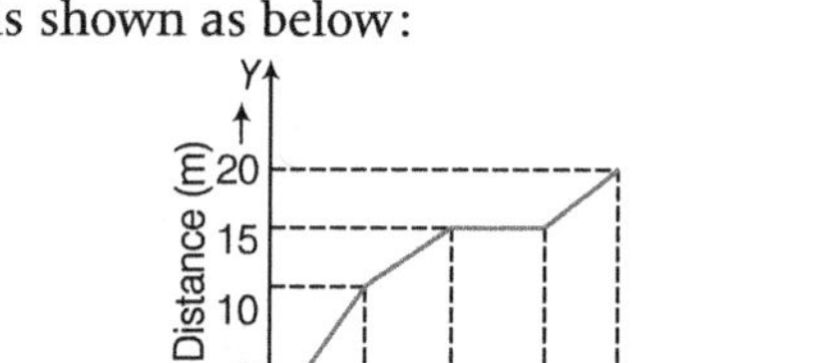

What will be the average speed of the object?

a 1 ms^{-1} b 2 ms^{-1} c 0.5 ms^{-1} d 0.08 ms^{-1}

5. Match the items of Column I with the items of Column II.

	Column I		Column II
p.	Large crystals	i.	Turns lime water milky
q.	Depositing a layer of zinc on iron	ii.	Physical change
r.	Souring of milk	iii.	Rust
s.	Carbon dioxide	iv.	Sugar candy (Mishri)
t.	Iron oxide	v.	Chemical change
u.	Dissolving common salt in water	vi.	Galvanisation

Codes

	p	q	r	s	t	u
a	(iv)	(vi)	(i)	(v)	(iii)	(i)
b	(iv)	(vi)	(i)	(iii)	(v)	(ii)
c	(iv)	(vi)	(v)	(i)	(iii)	(ii)
d	(iv)	(v)	(vi)	(i)	(ii)	(iii)

6. Eric conducted an experiment to find out which material was a better conductor of heat. He placed four identical spoons made of silver, copper, aluminium and iron into a beaker of very hot water.

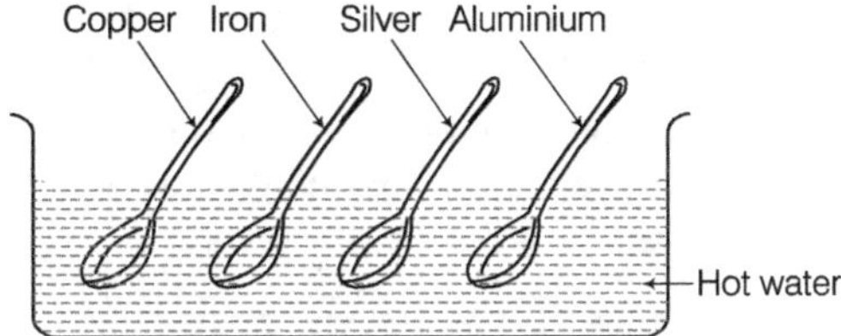

Rank the spoons from the best to the worst conductor of heat.

   a copper, silver, iron, aluminium
   b copper, iron, aluminium, silver
   c silver, iron, copper, aluminium
   d silver, copper, aluminium, iron

7. An object is placed in front of a spherical mirror. The image formed by the spherical mirror is virtual. The mirror will be

   a concave
   b convex
   c Either concave or convex
   d metallic

8. If one litre of water at 20°C is mixed with one litre of water at 60°C. The temperature of mixture will be

   a 30°C
   b 40°C
   c between 20°C and 60°C
   d 60°C

Direction (Q. Nos. 9-11) Read the following information and answer the questions that follow:

The founding concept of the Jantar Mantar is rooted in the conquest of science and the betterment of knowledge. The Jantar Mantar observatory is also known as time machine. It contains 14 numerical devices which are used in time measurement.

9. Which device is used in Jantar Mantar to measure time?

   a Sand dial   b Sun dial
   c Sand clock   d Quartz dial

10. The main principle used in time machine to measure time is

   a position of moon in the sky
   b position of sun in the sky
   c Both (a) and (b)
   d Neither (a) nor (b)

11. Modern clocks are based on

   a number of heart beats
   b number of vibrations of quartz crystal
   c number of ticks of second hand in a clock
   d None of the above

12. **Assertion** (A) Baking soda does not have sour taste.

   Reason (R) The taste of acids is sour while that of bases is bitter.

   a Both (A) and (R) are true and (R) is the correct explanation of (A)
   b Both (A) and (R) are true but (R) is not the correct explanation of (A)
   c (A) is true but (R) is false
   d (R) is true but (A) is false

13. Which of the following is the correct diagram when light passes through a piece of glass?

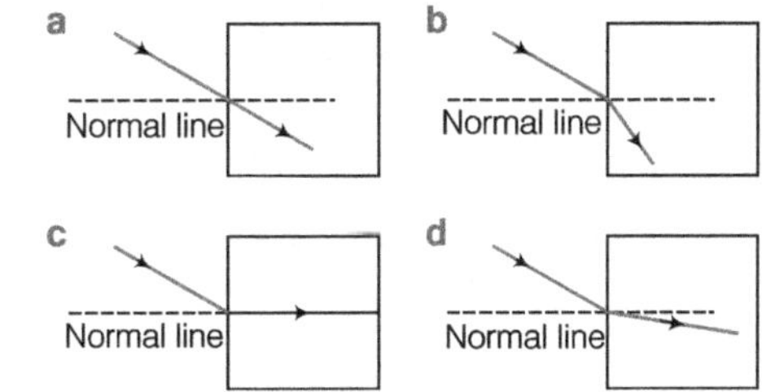

14.

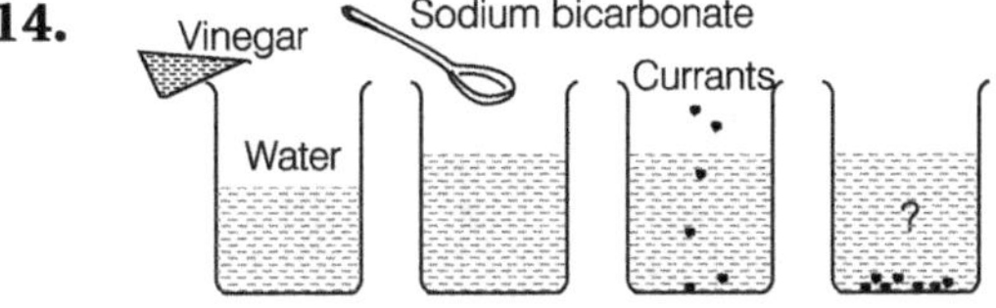

What happens to the currants? Why?

   a They will grow bigger, as they absorb water
   b They will float as sodium bicarbonate produces bubbles when it releases CO_2
   c They will disintegrate as the vinegar and sodium bicarbonate break it down
   d There is no change in the currants

15. Solve the given puzzle.

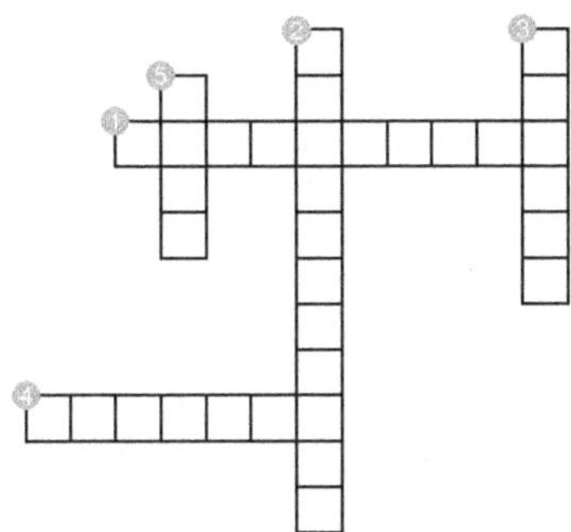

Across

1. Bending of light when it changes its medium.
4. Sequence of colours of spectrum

Down

2. This mirror always form virtual image and of the same size as that of object.
3. This mirror gives wide field of view
5. A piece of refracting medium bounded by two surfaces

16.

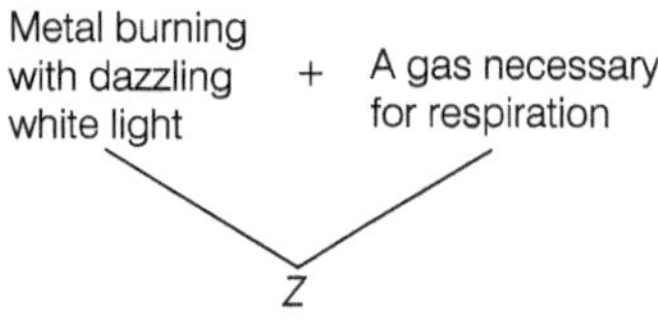

Z is

a magnesium oxide
b manganese dioxide
c magnesium carbonate
d magnesium sulphate

For questions 17 and 18, refer to the diagrams below which show the transverse sections of a young root and three types of cells found in it.

Transverse section of root — Cell type 1 — Cell type 2 — Cell type 2

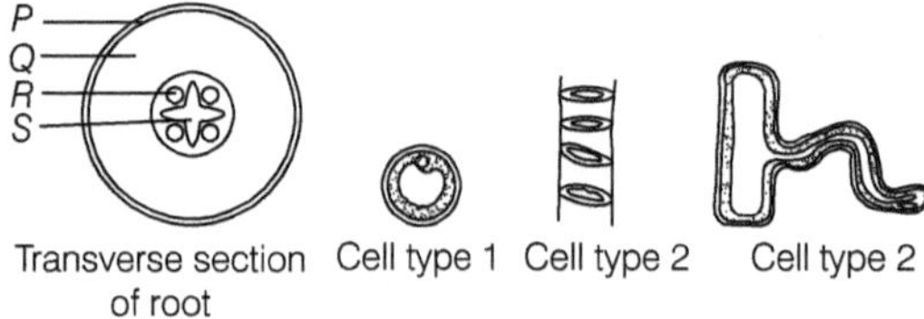

17. Which of the following correctly lists the locations of the three types of cells?

	Cell type 1	Cell type 2	Cell type 3
a	Q	P	S
b	Q	S	P
c	R	S	Q
d	R	Q	P

18. Which of the following correctly states the functions of *P*, *Q* and *R*?

	P	Q	R
a	Absorption	Transport	Support
b	Support	Protection	Food storage
c	Protection	Food storage	Transport
d	Transport	Support	Protection

19. Which of the following statements about alkalis is not true?

a Alkalis taste bitter and feel slippery
b Alkalis can be corrosive and hence need to be handled carefully
c Alkalis turn phenolphthalein colourless
d Alkalis turn red litmus paper blue

20. The figure below shows a mercury thermometer. The distance between −10°C and 110°C is 30 cm.

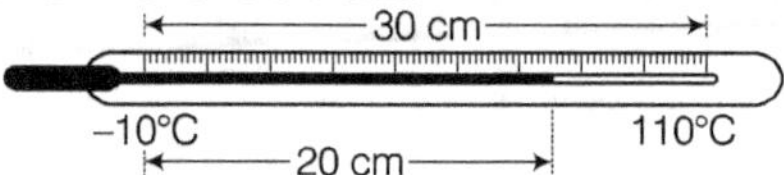

At what temperature will the mercury thread be 20 cm long?

a 67°C　　b 70°C
c 73°C　　d 80°C

21. Which of the following circuits produce the brightest bulbs?

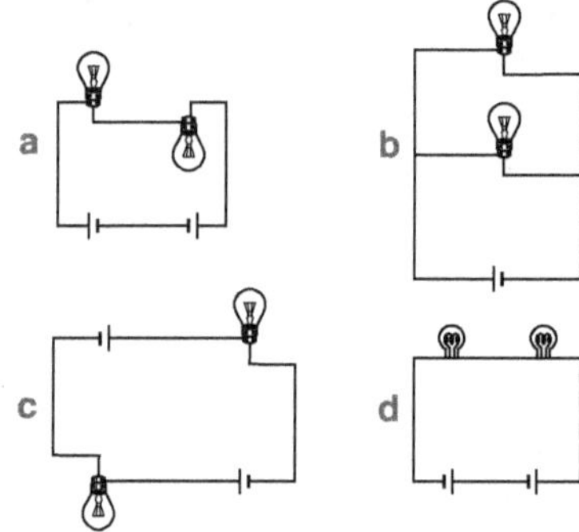

22. Factories are allowed to flow their wastes into river water only after its proper treatment. Which of the following shows the correct treatment and reason for applying this?

a Sorting, as bigger wastes pollutes the river most
b Detoxification, as the wastes may contain poisonous substances
c Neutralisation, as the waste is acidic and will kill the aquatic life
d Decomposition as the waste may contain several chemicals

23. The diagram shows a section through the heart.

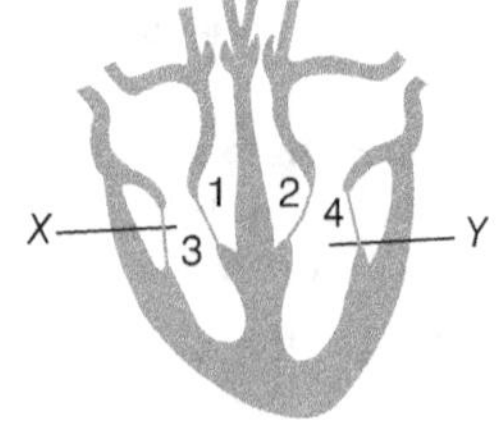

While chambers *X* and *Y* are emptying blood, which valves are open and which are closed?

	Valves 1 and 2	Valves 3 and 4
a	closed	closed
b	open	closed
c	closed	open
d	open	open

24. Which of the angles shown below is the anlge of reflection?

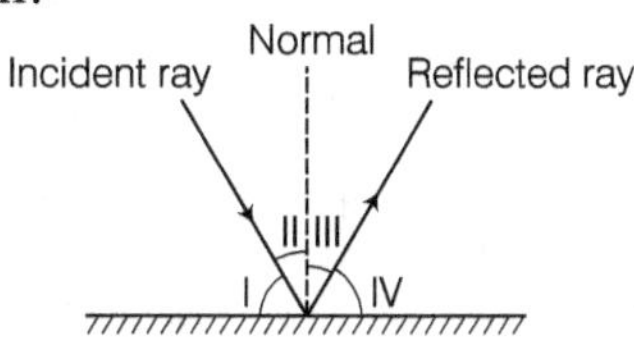

    a I   **b** II   **c** III   **d** IV

25. Due to overloading and short-circuiting, electrical circuits suffer a huge damage. Which of the following devices is used to prevent the flow of excess current in a circuit?

    a switch   **b** bulb   **c** fuse   **d** wire

26. The chain of boxes given below show a type of process occurring in plants.

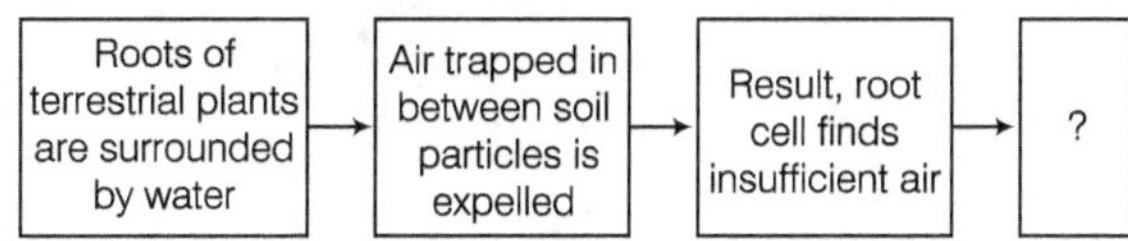

Identify the option from the following that correctly fills the last box.

Codes

    a The plant will die.

    b The plant will start aerobic respiration.

    c The plant will start photosynthesis.

    d The plant will start anaerobic respiration.

27. During rainy season, you can see a number of earthworms around you. They look little moist. This is because __*A*__. The Respiration is caused __*B*__.

	A	*B*
a	Water transport in their body	Pulmonary respiration
b	Rainy season	Branchial respiration
c	Their living habitat is under the soil	Tracheal respiration
d	They exchange respiratory gases through skin	Cutaneous respiration

28. The heating of seawater is called ______ and the product(s) is/are ________ .

    a boiling, hydrogen and oxygen

    b evaporation, salt and steam

    c electrolysis, salt and water

    d crystallisation, salt and water

29.

Mushroom

Above plant mushroom gets its food from ___________. The type of nutrition is ___________.

    A. From dead and decaying plants

    B. From photosynthesis

    C. By eating small insects which come near it

    D. From the water we pour near it

    1. Parasitic

    2. Autotrophic

    3. Saprophytic

    4. Symbiotic

Codes

    a A–3   **b** B–2

    c C–1   **d** D–4

30. Which of the following would happen when an acid is slowly added to an alkaline solution?

    I. The acid would lose its properties.

    II. The alkali would lose its properties.

    III. The pH value of the acid will increase.

    IV. The pH value of the alkaline solution will decrease.

        a I and III

        b II and IV

        c I, II and IV

        d All of the above

Answers

1. (d) Na_2CO_3 remains unaffected by heat, whereas NH_4Cl on heating sublimes (i.e. directly converted into gas) and decomposed to give ammonia (NH_3) and CO_2.

   Solid on heating converts into liquid which on further heating generally converts into gas with the exception of mercury.

2. (a) Average speed $= \dfrac{2000}{5 \times 60}$ ms^{-1}

   $= \dfrac{2000}{5 \times 60} \times \dfrac{18}{5}$ km/h

   $= 24$ km/h

3. (a) Phloem is the vascular tissue responsible for transporting organic nutrients around the plant body. It carries dissolved sugars from the leaves to other parts of the plants.

4. (d) Average speed $= \dfrac{\text{Total distance}}{\text{Total time}}$

   $= \dfrac{20}{4 \times 60}$

   $= 0.08$ ms^{-1}

5. (c) Mishri is in the form of large crystals. Galvanisation is the process of deposition of a layer of zinc over iron to protect it from rusting. Souring of milk is a chemical change whereas dissolution is a physical change. Iron oxide (hydrated) is called rust. CO_2 turns lime water milky.

6. (d) Silver and copper are very good conductors of heat. Iron is worst among the given for the conduction of heat.

7. (c)   8. (c)

9. (b)

10. (b) As, the position of sun changes in the sky, the position of shadow of blade on the dial also changes. This position of shadow of vertical blade on the dial gives the time of the day.

11. (b) The regular vibrations of quartz crystal when connected to an electric circuit is used to measure time very accurately.

12. (a) Baking soda is a base and have somewhat bitter taste.

13. (d) Since, glass is optically denser medium. So, ray will bend towards the normal.

14. (b)

15. 1. Refraction   2. Plane mirror

    3. Convex   4. VIBGYOR

    5. Lens

16. (a) Magnesium burns with dazzling white light and oxygen is necessary for combustion. Magnesium oxide (MgO) is formed when oxygen reacts with magnesium.

17. (a) P $\rightarrow$ Epidermis

    Q $\rightarrow$ Cortex

    R $\rightarrow$ Primary phloem

    S $\rightarrow$ Primary xylem.

18. (c) Epidermis (P) protects the underlying cells.

    Cortex (Q) contains stored carbohydrates or other substances such as resins, latex, essential oils and tannins.

    Primary phloem (R) transport organic nutrient, (Sucrose) to all parts of the plant.

19. (c) In alkalis, colour of phenolphthalein is pink, whereas it is colourless in acidic medium.

20. (b) 30 cm corresponds to $- 10°$-$110°$C

    $\Rightarrow$ 30 cm is equivalent to 120 readings.

    So, 1 cm $\Rightarrow \dfrac{120}{30}$ readings

    $= 4$ readings

    and 20 cm $\Rightarrow 4 \times 20$

    $= 80$ readings

    $\Rightarrow$ $80 - 10 = 70$°C

21. (b) When the bulbs are connected in parallel circuit, then overall resistance decreases because of which brightness of the bulb increases.

22. (c) Most of the times the waste coming from the factories is acidic and may kill aquatic life, so its neutralisation is necessary.

23. (b) The figure shows systolic condition. Both atrioventricular values, i.e. tricuspid (3) and mitral (4) are closed and the aortic (2) and pulmonary (1) valves are open.

24. (c) The angle between reflected ray and normal at the point of incidence is known as angle of reflection.

25. (c)

26. (d) Anaerobic respiration takes place in plants in the presence of little or no O_2 e.g. Roots of plants in waterlogged condition.

27. (d)

28. (b) When sea water is heated below its boiling point water evaporates leaving the salt as residue. This process is called evaporation.

29. (a) Mushroom is a fungi that saprophytic in nature. It gets its food from dead and decaying plants.

30. (d) During neutralisation process, acid as well as alkali loses its properties. The pH of acid increases while that of alkali decreases.

Practice Set ③

A Whole Content Based Test for Class 7th Science Olympiad

1. The regular vibrations of which electrically driven crystal is used to measure the time very accurately?
   a Calcite crystal
   b Quadric crystal
   c Chrome crystal
   d Quartz crystal

2. Iron pillar near the Qutub Minar in Delhi is famous of the following facts. Which of these facts is responsible for its long stability?
   a It is more than 7 metres high
   b It weighs about 6000 kg
   c It was built more than 1600 years ago
   d It has not rusted after such a long period

3. The diagram represents blood flow through the human body.

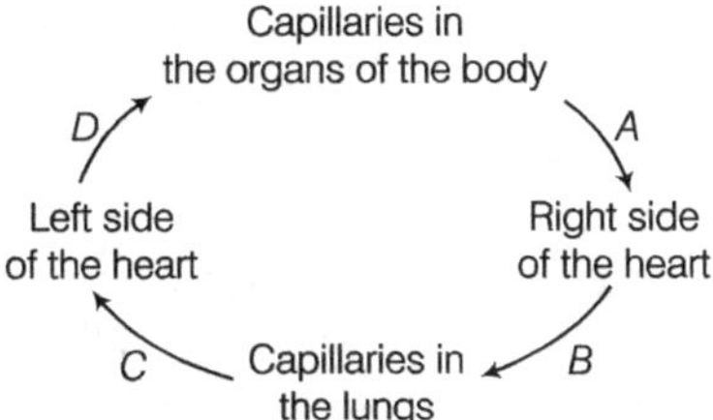

   At which stages does the blood contain maximum oxygen?
   a A and B   b B and C
   c C and D   d D and A

4.
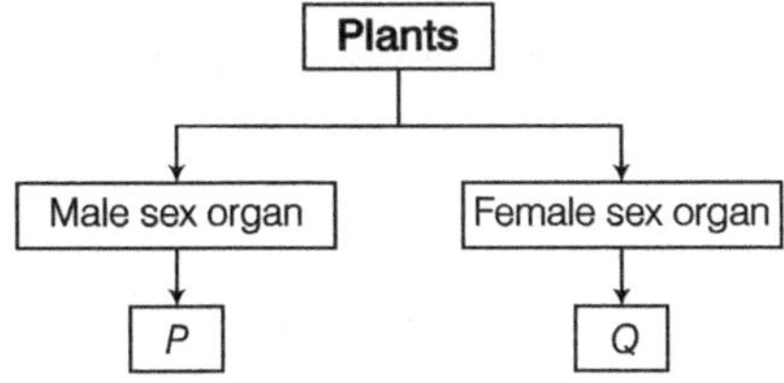

   Observe the above flow chart carefully. Identify P and Q with their respective description.
   a P–stamen, it contains pollen grains
   Q–carpel, its lower part is ovary that contains ovule.
   b P–carpel, it contains pollen grains.
   Q–stamen, it contains ovule which is the lower part of ovary.
   c P–pistil, it contains ovule.
   Q–style, it contains pollen grains.
   d P–style, it contains pollen grains.
   Q–pistil, it is the lower part of the ovary that contains ovule.

5. The ammeter reading in the following circuit diagrams consisting of a cell, a resistor, a key and an ammeter will be

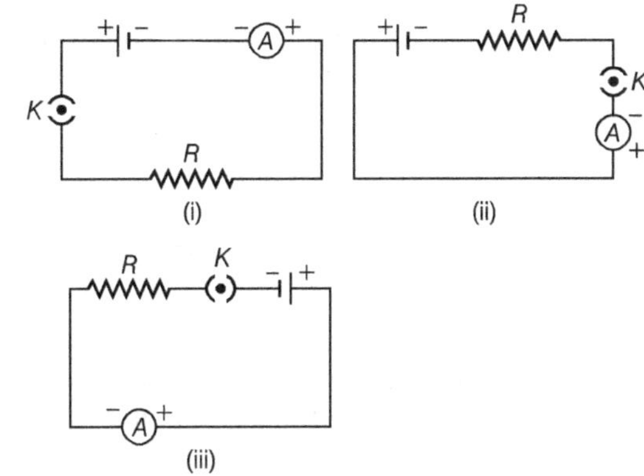

   a Maximum in (i)
   b Maximum in (ii)
   c Maximum in (iii)
   d The same in all the cases

6. A car takes 10 h to travel from town A to town B and 7 h to travel from town B to town C.

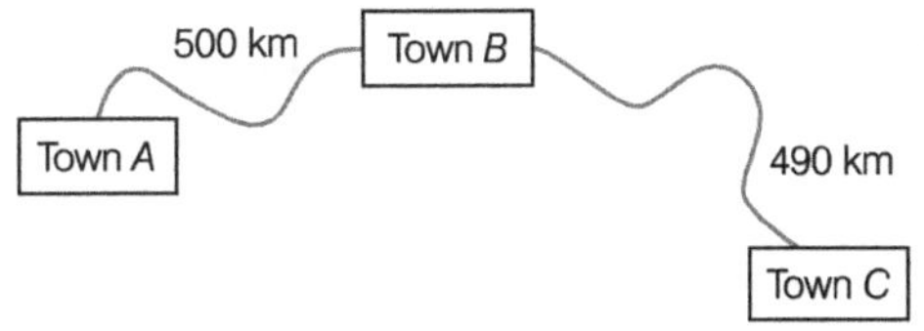

   What is the average speed of the car in the whole journey?
   a 116.47 km/h
   b 29.12 km/h
   c 58.24 km/h
   d 60 km/h

7. Reema needs to examine the type of lens. She is provided during her science practical. The image she obtained is erect. Which type of lens would it be?

   a Convex lens provided image is smaller than object

   b Concave lens provided image is smaller than object

   c Concave lens provided image is larger than object

   d Concave lens provided image is of the same size

8. Mr. Sharma started a shipping corporation but he was facing huge loss because of the rusting of ironships.

What was the cause and solution to this problem?

   a The bodies of the ships are in contact of salty water, so he can paint the ships

   b The bodies of the ships are in contact of salty seawater, so galvanisation is a solution to it

   c The bodies of the ships are not made up of good quality metal, so he must improve the quality of metal

   d The bodies of the ships are in contact of non-salty water, so he can paint them

9. After studying photosynthesis, Neelima drew the illustration of a plant shown below.

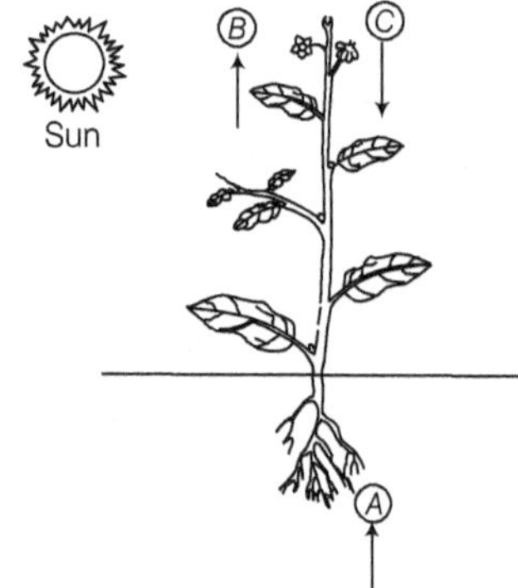

Arrow A represents

   a release of water and minerals by the plant into soil

   b release of carbon dioxide into the soil

   c absorption of water and minerals by the roots from the soil

   d release of oxygen into the atmosphere

10.

Indicator	Colour	
	Acidic medium	Basic medium
Litmus	Red	...A...
...B...	Colourless	Red
...C... juice	Yellow	Red-brown
Red-cabbage juice	...D...	Green
China-rose juice	Red	...E...

The correct option for *A*, *B*, *C*, *D*, *E* are

   a Red, Methyl orange, Lemon, Pink, Green

   b Blue, Methyl orange, Lemon, Yellow, Green

   c Red, Phenolphthalein, Lemon, Yellow, Pink

   d Blue, Phenolphthalein, Turmeric, Red, Green

11. Study the diagrams below, carefully. In which circuit will at least one bulb remain lit if the bulb marked *X* blows?

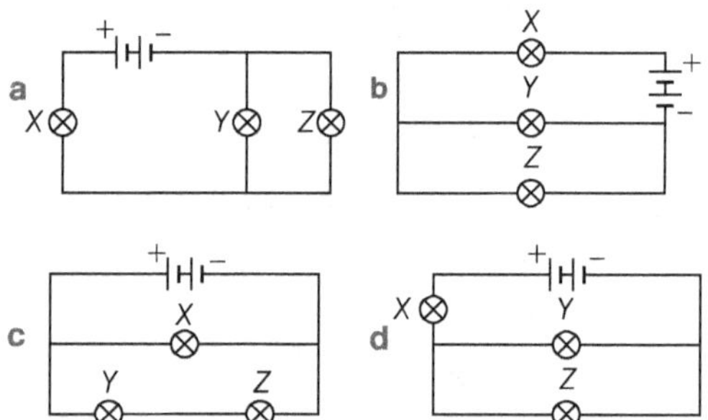

12. The speed of light increases when it passes from medium *X* to medium *Y*. Which of the following statements is correct about this observation?

   a Medium *Y* is denser than medium *X*

   b The light bends towards the normal

   c The light bends away from the normal

   d The light does not bend or change its direction

13. Consider the following statements.

   I. The common name of hydrochloric acid is aqua fortis.

   II. Acids taste sour.

   III. Term alkali is used for water soluble bases.

The incorrect statement(s) is/are

   a I and II

   b II and III

   c Only I

   d Only III

14. Consider the following figure shown below. Which of the following processes are involved in the figure?

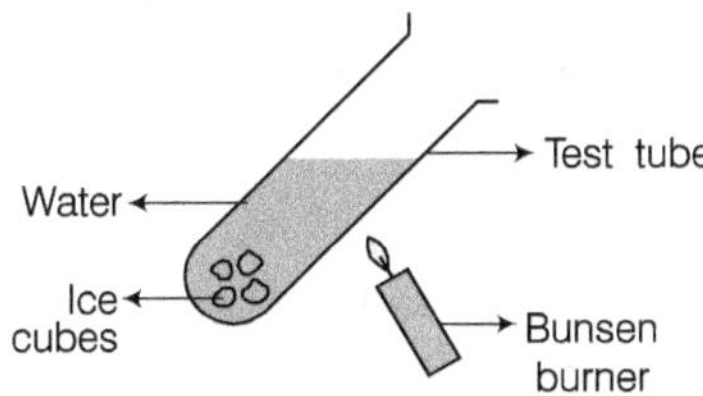

   a Conduction and melting
   b Insulation and heating
   c Conduction and contraction
   d Expansion and contraction

15. **Assertion** (A) Asexual reproduction does not require two opposite sexes.

Reason (R) New organism is formed by the fusion of sperm and ova.
   a Both A and R are true and R is the correct explanation of A
   b Both A and R are true, but R is not the correct explanation of A
   c A is true, but R is false
   d A and R are false

16.

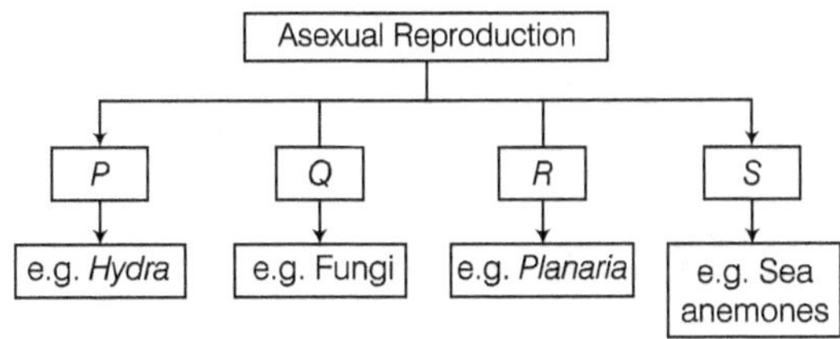

Use your analytical skills and observe the above flow chart. Identify *P*, *Q*, *R* and *S* correctly.

Codes

	P	Q	R	S
a	Binary fission	Budding	Regeneration	Fragmentation
b	Budding	Spore formation	Regeneration	Fragmentation
c	Spore formation	Budding	Fragmentation	Regeneration
d	Budding	Binary fission	Fragmentation	Regeneration

17. When you stand on bare feet with one foot on a stone floor and the other on a carpet, the stone floor feels colder than the carpet. What is the most likely explanation?
   a Air is unable to circulate through the carpet fibres
   b The stone is at a lower temperature than the carpet
   c More heat energy flows from the carpet to your foot than from the stone floor to your foot
   d More heat energy flows from your foot to the stone floor than from your foot to the carpet

18. This is a bimetallic trip. It is made up of 2 different strips of metals, *X* and *Y* joined together. Before heating, the strips are of the same length.

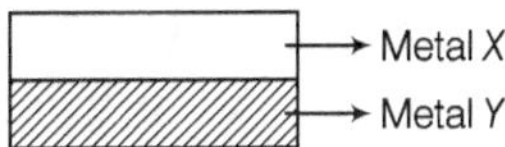

After heating, the following is observed.

The following inference can be deduced from the above observation.
   a Metal *X* is better conductor of heat
   b Metal *Y* is better conductor of heat
   c Metal *X* is poor insulator
   d Metal *Y* is poor insulator

19. In which of the following parts of the digestive system is hydrochloric acid produced?

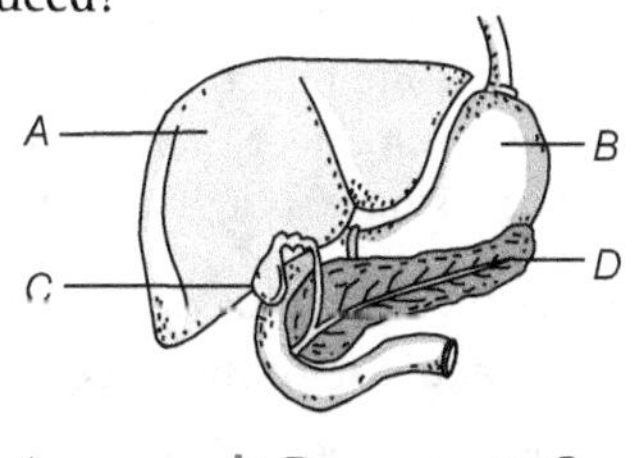

   a A   **b** B   **c** C   **d** D

20. Study the three glasses of tea that are placed on the table.

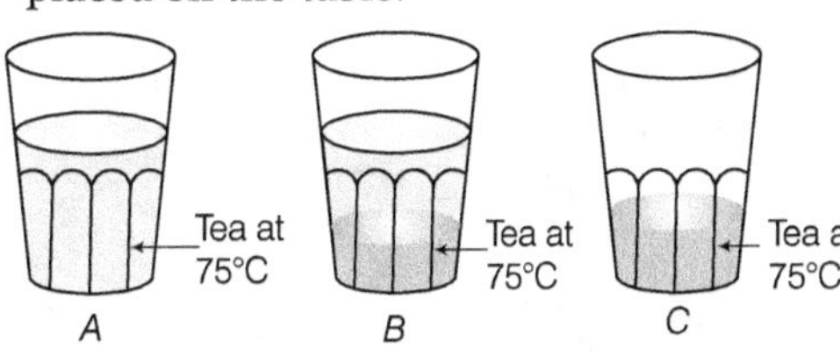

Which of the following statements are true about the glasses of tea?

   I. The tea in the three glasses have the same amount of heat.

  II. The tea in the three glasses are at the same temperature.

 III. There is more heat in glass A than in glass B.

 IV. There is less heat in glass C than in glass B.

  V. More heat is needed to warm up glass B than glass C.

Codes

a I and II   b II and III
c III and IV   d II, III and V

21. Which of the following are similarities between acids and alkalis?

   I. Both are colourless liquids.

  II. Both are hazardous when concentrated.

 III. Their pH value decreases to 7 when they are neutralized.

 IV. Both contain water.

Codes

a I and II

b III and IV

c I, II and IV

d All of the above

22. Rama went to a shop to buy some cooking utensils. She asked the shopkeeper, why the cooking utensils are always fitted with plastic handles?

a Plastics are good thermal conductor

b Plastics are not strong

c Plastics are poor thermal conductor

d Plastics have a high density

23. Consider the following statements.

   I. It is made up of living cells.

  II. It helps in the transport of food and hormones in the plants.

 III. Structurally, its cells join end to end.

 IV. Its cells form sieve plates.

Which of the following structural component is this?

a Cambium

b Tracheids

c Xylem

d Phloem

24. One of the ways to prevent us from getting electric shock is by wearing rubber shoes. What is the reason?

a Rubber is a very good insulator

b Shoes are placed at the lowest part of our body

c All metals conduct electricity except shoes

d Copper conducts electricity better than rubber

25. Root hairs absorb water

Take it to xylem tube

Xylem tubes reach to leaves of plant

Observe the above flow of steps that shows the job of root hairs. Which of the following statement is correct regarding this?

A. Water enters into xylem vessels through root hairs, where vessels are formed by dead cells.

B. Root hairs lie in between soil particles

C. The cells of xylem vessels have tapering ends.

D. Cells of xylem vessels are joined with open ends.

Codes

a A and B   b B and C
c A, B and D   d None of these

26. Assertion (A) A laboratory thermometer cannot be used to measure the human body temperature.

Reason (R) The kink is a narrow and sharp curve in the bore of a clinical thermometer tube.

a Both A and R are true and R is the correct explanation of A

b Both A and R are true, but R is not the correct explanation of A

c A is true, but R is false

d A is false, but R is true

27. The diagram below shows some of the food molecules which are digested to become small molecules by the action of enzymes.

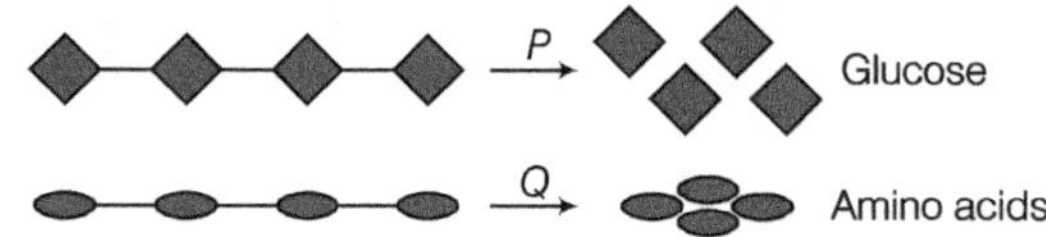

What are the enzymes *P* and *Q*?

	P	*Q*
a	Carbohydrase	Protease
b	Lipase	Carbohydrase
c	Protease	Lipase
d	Amylase	Carbohydrase

28. When electric current is passed through an electromagnet, it behaves like a temporary magnet. Which of the following figures correctly depicts the direction of magnetic field lines?

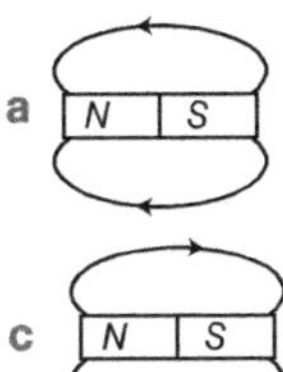

29. Mannu was investigating how a certain factor affected the growth of plants. The table shows how the experiment was set up.

Location of pot	Soil	Water	Number of seeds in each pot	Number of earthworms in the soil
Pot *A* Window ledge	Garden Soil	500 mL	2	8
Pot *B* Window ledge	Garden Soil	500 mL	10	8

Which of the following characteristics of the seedlings should Mannu observe to tell which pot of plant was growing better.

   a Colour of the leaves
   b Height of the seedlings
   c Thickness of the seedling
   d a and b

30. Consider the following circuits and choose the one in which all the components are connected properly.

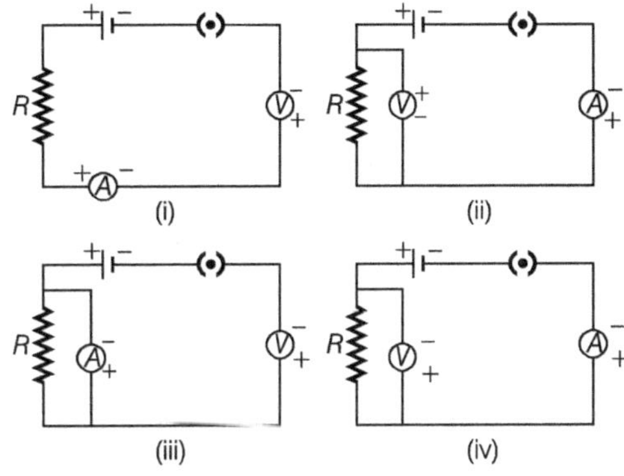

   a (i)
   b (ii)
   c (iii)
   d (iv)

Answers

1. *d*	2. *d*	3. *c*	4. *a*	5. *d*	6. *c*	7. *b*	8. *b*	9. *c*	10. *d*
11. *c*	12. *c*	13. *c*	14. *b*	15. *c*	16. *b*	17. *d*	18. *b*	19. *b*	20. *b*
21. *c*	22. *c*	23. *d*	24. *a*	25. *c*	26. *a*	27. *a*	28. *b*	29. *d*	30. *b*

Practice Set 3

Answer & Explanations

7

① Nutrition in Plants

1. *b*	2. *b*	3. *c*	4. *c*	5. *a*	6. *d*	7. *a*	8. *c*	9. *c*	10. *b*
11. *b*	12. *a*	13. *b*	14. *c*	15. *d*	16. *b*	17. *b*	18. *b*	19. *a*	20. *c*
21. *b*	22. *c*	23. *b*	24. *b*	25. *a*	26. *b*	27. *b*	28. *c*	29. *c*	30. *c*
31. *c*	32. *c*	33. *b*	34. *c*	35. *a*	36. *b*	37. *b*	38. *a*	39. *a*	

② Nutrition in Animals

1. *c*	2. *c*	3. *b*	4. *d*	5. *d*	6. *a*	7. *d*	8. *b*	9. *b*	10. *a*
11. *b*	12. *b*	13. *c*	14. *c*	15. *b*	16. *c*	17. *b*	18. *c*	19. *d*	20. *d*
21. *c*	22. *d*	23. *b*	24. *d*	25. *c*	26. *a*	27. *b*	28. *a*	29. *d*	30. *a*
31. *c*	32. *c*	33. *c*	34. *b*	35. *d*	36. *a*	37. *c*	38. *b*	39. *b*	40. *c*
41. *a*	42. *c*	43. *d*	44. *d*	45. *a*	46. *a*				

③ Heat

A. Heat, Temperature and Types of Thermometers

1. *a*	2. *d*	3. *a*	4. *a*	5. *c*	6. *d*	7. *a*	8. *b*	9. *a*	10. *a*
11. *b*	12. *b*	13. *c*	14. *c*	15. *d*	16. *b*	17. *b*	18. *c*	19. *b*	20. *c*
21. *b*	22. *b*	23. *d*							

B. Transfer of Heat, Conduction, Convection and Radiation

1. *b*	2. *d*	3. *d*	4. *d*	5. *d*	6. *b*	7. *b*	8. *b*	9. *a*	10. *d*
11. *d*	12. *a*	13. *c*	14. *a*	15. *b*	16. *a*	17. *b*	18. *c*	19. *b*	20. *d*
21. *c*	22. *d*	23. *b*	24. *c*	25. *a*	26. *b*	27. *a*	28. *a*	29. *a*	30. *c*
31. *c*									

④ Acids, Bases and Salts

A. Acids and Bases

1. *b*	2. *c*	3. *b*	4. *c*	5. *c*	6. *c*	7. *d*	8. *c*	9. *c*	10. *a*
11. *a*	12. *c*	13. *a*	14. *a*	15. *c*	16. *a*	17. *d*	18. *d*	19. *c*	20. *c*
21. *c*	22. *b*	23. *b*	24. *d*						

B. Indicators (Strength of Acids and Bases)

1. *c*	2. *b*	3. *d*	4. *a*	5. *b*	6. *d*	7. *a*	8. *c*	9. *b*	10. *d*
11. *d*	12. *b*	13. *a*	14. *c*	15. *c*	16. *c*	17. *d*	18. *a*	19. *b*	20. *d*
21. *d*	22. *c*	23. *c*							

C. Salts

1. *c*	2. *d*	3. *a*	4. *a*	5. *a*	6. *b*	7. *b*	8. *d*	9. *a*	10. *b*
11. *c*	12. *c*	13. *b*	14. *a*	15. *b*					

5 Physical and Chemical Changes

A. Physical Changes

| 1. *d* | 2. *c* | 3. *a* | 4. *c* | 5. *c* | 6. *a* | 7. *c* | 8. *d* | 9. *d* | 10. *c* |
| 11. *d* | 12. *a* | 13. *c* | | | | | | | |

B. Chemical Changes and Rusting

1. *d*	2. *a*	3. *b*	4. *c*	5. *a*	6. *a*	7. *c*	8. *c*	9. *b*	10. *d*
11. *b*	12. *d*	13. *d*	14. *b*	15. *a*	16. *b*	17. *c*	18. *c*	19. *b*	20. *a*
21. *a*	22. *d*								

C. Physical as well as Chemical Changes

| 1. *c* | 2. *b* | 3. *c* | 4. *c* | 5. *c* | 6. *b* | 7. *c* | 8. *c* | 9. *c* | 10. *b* |

6 Respiration in Organisms

1. *d*	2. *b*	3. *b*	4. *b*	5. *a*	6. *d*	7. *b*	8. *b*	9. *d*	10. *d*
11. *c*	12. *a*	13. *d*	14. *c*	15. *b*	16. *c*	17. *b*	18. *b*	19. *b*	20. *b*
21. *d*	22. *a*	23. *b*	24. *a*	25. *d*	26. *b*	27. *b*	28. *c*	29. *c*	30. *d*
31. *c*	32. *a*	33. *c*	34. *b*	35. *b*	36. *b*	37. *c*	38. *b*	39. *a*	40. *d*
41. *a*	42. *b*	43. *b*	44. *b*	45. *a*	46. *d*				

7 Transportation in Plants and Animals

1. *b*	2. *b*	3. *a*	4. *a*	5. *a*	6. *b*	7. *c*	8. *d*	9. *c*	10. *b*
11. *d*	12. *a*	13. *a*	14. *d*	15. *b*	16. *d*	17. *a*	18. *c*	19. *d*	20. *c*
21. *a*	22. *b*	23. *b*	24. *c*	25. *a*	26. *b*	27. *c*	28. *b*	29. *b*	30. *c*
31. *a*									

8 Reproduction in Plants

1. *b*	2. *c*	3. *c*	4. *c*	5. *a*	6. *c*	7. *d*	8. *c*	9. *c*	10. *a*
11. *d*	12. *a*	13. *a*	14. *c*	15. *b*	16. *c*	17. *a*	18. *c*	19. *c*	20. *b*
21. *a*	22. *c*	23. *d*	24. *c*	25. *a*	26. *c*	27. *d*	28. *c*	29. *b*	30. *a*
31. *c*	32. *d*	33. *b*	34. *b*	35. *c*	36. *c*	37. *a*	38. *d*	39. *b*	40. *d*
41. *d*	42. *a*								

9 Motion and Time

A. Motion, Its Time and Speed

| 1. *b* | 2. *d* | 3. *d* | 4. *b* | 5. *c* | 6. *b* | 7. *c* | 8. *a* | 9. *c* | 10. *c* |
| 11. *b* | 12. *c* | 13. *a* | 14. *a* | 15. *d* | 16. *c* | 17. *d* | 18. *c* | 19. *a* | 20. *c* |

B. Distance-Time Graph, Time and Simple Pendulum

1. *c*	2. *b*	3. *d*	4. *d*	5. *d*	6. *b*	7. *a*	8. *c*	9. *a*	10. *b*
11. *b*	12. *a*	13. *a*	14. *b*	15. *b*	16. *a*	17. *c*	18. *a*	19. *b*	20. *b*
21. *c*									

10 Electric Current and Its Effect

A. Electric Current and Electric Circuit

1. *d*	2. *d*	3. *d*	4. *b*	5. *a*	6. *a*	7. *c*	8. *c*	9. *c*	10. *a*
11. *c*	12. *b*	13. *b*	14. *b*	15. *a*	16. *b*	17. *b*	18. *a*	19. *d*	20. *c*
21. *b*	22. *b*	23. *b*	24. *c*	25. *c*	26. *b*	27. *c*			

B. Heating Effect of Electric Current

1. *a*	2. *c*	3. *b*	4. *a*	5. *d*	6. *b*	7. *b*	8. *a*	9. *d*	10. *d*
11. *b*	12. *b*	13. *c*	14. *a*	15. *a*	16. *d*	17. *a*	18. *a*	19. *a*	20. *a*
21. *c*	22. *d*	23. *a*	24. *a*						

C. Magnetic Effect of Electric Current

1. *a*	2. *a*	3. *a*	4. *a*	5. *c*	6. *b*	7. *b*	8. *b*	9. *d*	10. *c*
11. *a*	12. *c*	13. *a*	14. *d*	15. *c*	16. *c*	17. *b*	18. *a*	19. *b*	20. *c*
21. *c*	22. *b*								

11 Light

A. Light, Reflection and Mirror

1. *d*	2. *c*	3. *b*	4. *c*	5. *b*	6. *b*	7. *c*	8. *d*	9. *a*	10. *d*
11. *a*	12. *c*	13. *d*	14. *a*	15. *a*	16. *c*	17. *d*	18. *b*	19. *c*	20. *b*
21. *b*									

B. Lens, Types of Lens and Dispersion

1. *b*	2. *b*	3. *c*	4. *b*	5. *b*	6. *b*	7. *c*	8. *b*	9. *d*	10. *b*
11. *c*	12. *d*	13. *a*	14. *b*	15. *b*	16. *c*	17. *d*	18. *d*	19. *b*	20. *a*
21. *a*	22. *c*	23. *a*	24. *a*	25. *d*	26. *b*	27. *a*	28. *d*		

1. In animals, the glucose is stored as glycogen. Digestion is the hydrolysis process by which starch in them is broken into glucose and then glycogen. In green plants, glycogen is not formed and glucose made in photosynthesis is stored as starch. These are converted into substances such as cellulose for cell walls, proteins for growth, repair, etc.

3. The part of leaf shown in the figure is stomata. These are small pores on the epidermis of a leaf. Surrounded by guard cells which fill with water in order to open and allow exchange or drain themselves to stop the gaseous exchange and water loss.

4. The part labelled as 'A' is chloroplast (palisade mesophyll). It is part of leaf that is filled with pigment chlorophyll. This pigment which traps energy from sunlight for plants to conduct photosynthesis.

5. Photosynthesis can be represented by using a chemical equation.

The overall balanced equation is

$$\underset{\substack{\text{Carbon}\\\text{dioxide}}}{6CO_2} + \underset{\text{Water}}{6H_2O} \xrightarrow[\text{Chlorophyll}]{\text{Sunlight}} \underset{\text{Glucose}}{C_6H_{12}O_6} + 6O_2$$

7. During photosynthesis, light energy splits water into oxygen and hydrogen ions. Carbon dioxide gas combines with the hydrogen to make glucose.

So, if oxygen (^{18}O) is incorporated into water, then radioactive ^{18}O will be found only in oxygen.

8. The two mineral ions needed by plants are
(i) **Nitrate** which is used for making proteins.
(ii) **Magnesium** which is used for making chlorophyll and thus for making starch.

12.

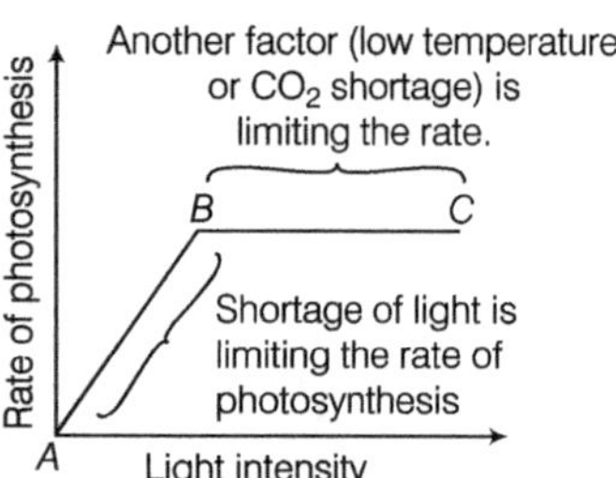

Photosynthesis needs light, so in the graph region A-B of low light becomes the limiting factor. On increasing light upto a certain level, photosynthesis increases. Further increasing light cannot increase the ratio. Some other factor limits the rate now.

14. The gas is nitrogen. Plants use nitrogen by absorbing N compounds as nitrate through the roots. N is converted into these compounds by nitrogen fixing organisms such as *Rhizobium* bacteria (lives in the roots of leguminous plants.

15. *Rhizobium* is a nitrogen-fixing bacteria. It forms an endosymbiotic nitrogen-fixing association with roots of legumes and thus, shows symbiosis.

17. Lichen is a composite organism that emerges from algae or cyanobacteria living among filaments of a fungus in a mutually beneficial manner.

18. The incorrect statements can be written in correct form as:
(i) Energy is utilised during photosynthesis. It is an anabolic process that uses energy to build up complex molecules.
(ii) A plant kept in dark fails to photosynthesise. (Sunlight supplies energy for the process and is necessary for photosynthesis to take place).

20. Temperature affect the rate of photosynthesis, upto a certain range. Increase in temperature beyond that range stops photosynthesis as enzymes are destroyed by heat.

21. *R* will photosynthesise at slowest rate. The pigment responsible for light harvesting by plants is chlorophyll that is a green pigment.

The green colour indicates that it is absorbing non-green light. On other hand temperature is also a factor shown in the figure. The chemical reactions of photosynthesis can takes place slowly at low temperature.

Thus, photosynthesis will occur in *P*, but it will be at a slow rate.

In *Q*, the photosynthesis will be the fastest as it has the optimum condition of temperature as well as red light in which the rate of photosynthesis is maximum.

25. *P* is water and *Q* is sugar. Leaves take water and other components, i.e. light and carbon dioxide, to make sugar (glucose) by the process of photosynthesis and distribute it to other parts of the plant.

33. Plant cuticle is a protective film covering the epidermis of leaves, young shoots and other aerial plant organs without periderm.

40.

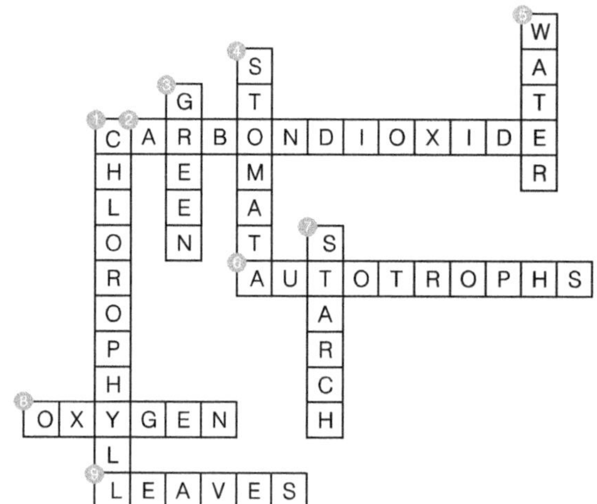

1. Bile is a yellowish brown fluid produced by the liver for the digestion of fats in the small intestine.

2. Protein digestion is mediated in the stomach chamber by an enzyme called pepsin, which is secreted by chief cells present in the stomach in an inactive form called pepsinogen.

   Along with it, mucus that protects the inner lining of stomach and HCl which kills bacteria and provides an acidic medium for digestion are also secreted.

3. Small intestine is the principal organ of the digestive tract. The primary function of small intestine is absorption of nutrients. It involves processes that solubilise carbohydrates, proteins and fats and reduce them to relatively simple inorganic compounds.

   The large intestine absorbs most of the water from the undigested food material.

4. Insulin is a peptide hormone produced by beta cells of the pancreas. It regulates the metabolism of carbohydrates and fats by promoting the absorption of glucose from the blood to skeletal muscles and fat tissues.

5. pH of stomach is 2-4. It is acidic due to the presence HCl
   pH of enzyme (amylase) in mouth ranges from 6.2-7.4
   pH of enzyme in small intestine is usually 6-7.4.

6. X is blood capillary shown in the figure.

7. Stomach has specialised cells that secrete hydrochloric acid (HCl) helps to convert pepsinogen to pepsin and also kills many microorganisms present in the food.

   After leaving the stomach, the food enters the small intestine. Most part of digestion takes place in the small intestine.

   The undigested food leaves the small intestine and reaches large intestine as liquid paste, where absorption of water occurs and liquid paste turns into solid waste.

   The solid waste collects in the rectum at the end of the large intestine and finally leaves the body through an opening called the anus.

8. The teeth in mouth increase the surface area of the food. There are different types of teeth with different shapes which are adapted for distinct actions, e.g. incisors cut food, molars grind the food and canines tear the food, etc.

9. Peps is secreted by chief cells of the stomach. It breaks down proteins. Trypsin is an enzyme secreted by pancreatic acinar cells. It digests proteins.

   Peptidases are secreted in small intestine. These digest smaller pieces of proteins (peptides) into their individual amino acids.

11. Saliva contains enzyme called amylase, that breaks down starch present in food into maltose.

12. B has the highest concentration of dissolved amino acids. It is coming from the small intestine where most of the amino acid are absorbed and are carried to the liver.

14. R and S shows premolar and molar, respectively. These are specialised for chewing and grinding the food.

15. Y is large intestine, which absorbs most of the water from the undigested food.

16. Z shows small intestine which has very large surface area due to the presence of numerous villi.

17. Cellulose is the main constituent of plant cell walls. It is resistant to enzymes, i.e. cannot be broken down by digestive enzymes present in the animal body.

18. Rumen is the first chamber of alimentary canal in ruminant animals. It is present between oesophagus and small intestine.

19. Rennin is a protein digesting enzyme that curdles milk.

24. Peristalsis is a series of wave-like muscle contractions that moves food to different parts of the digestive tract.

26. X shows finger-like projections called villi. It has thin walls to facilitate efficient absorption.

28. Protein digestion begins in the stomach with the action of an enzyme called pepsin.

34. The stomach produces pepsinogen enzyme for protein digestion. The small intestine also contains enzymes like trypsin and chymotrypsin that convert proteins into amino acids.

40. Y contains maximum amount of fat as well as a high amount of proteins. It therefore has the highest energy value.

43. The labelled part N shows the gall bladder from which bile enters into the small intestine.

47.

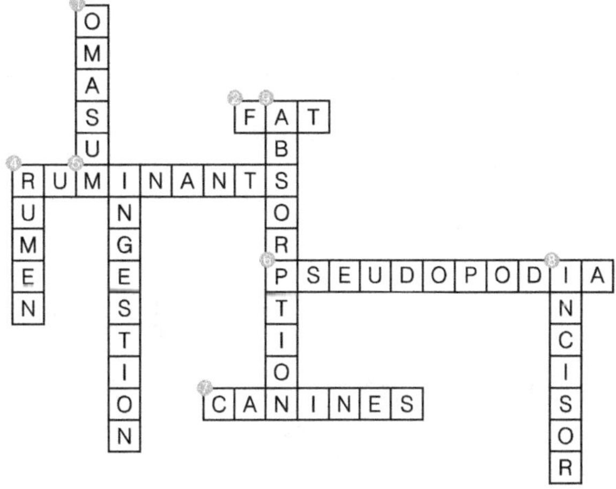

A) Heat, Temperature and Types of Thermometers

2. Since, heat flows from high temperature to low temperature. So, hot milk will loose heat to the cold water and the temperature of cold water rises.

4. Both (i) and (iii) are clinical thermometers and (ii) is laboratory thermometer.

5. The bulb should have a thin glass wall so that heat can rapidly reach the mercury in order for the mercury to expand. This makes the thermometer to give a faster reading. The bore needs to be narrow in order to increase the sensitivity of the temperature scale.

7. The thermometer bulb should be surrounded from all sides by the substance whose temperature is to be measured. Also, the thermometer bulb should not touch the sides or bottom of the container and it should be upright while measuring temperature.

8. For her left hand, the temperature of tub *C* will be lower and for her right hand the temperature of tub *C* will be higher.

10. Since, black is a better absorber of heat, so thermometer *A* will show higher temperature.

13. The more the bunsen burners are used, more will be the amount of heat given and hence less time will be taken by ice to melt.

14. The normal body temperature of a human body is 37°C or 98.6°F.

16. The kink is present in clinical thermometer. Kink is a narrow and sharp bent in the tube of clinical thermometer.

23. Heat always flows from hot region to cold region.

B) Transfer of Heat, Conduction, Convection and Radiation

1. Air is a bad conductor of heat. Hence, it does not allow the heat from the body of beggar to transfer to the cold surroundings.

3. The vapours of tea are at higher temperature than the surrounding air which is comparatively at lower temperature can cause the formation of convection currents above the tea.

4. In convection process, the heated particles move as a whole to circulate heat.

8. White or shiny surfaces reflect back the heat from the sun and prevent the fuel to get ignited.

11. This is a popular experiment used to demonstrate the poor conductivity of water. Since, the water is heated at the top, the heat is forced to travel downwards *via* conduction. Although, convection occurs in water, it does not occur in the water below the heat source. The metal gauze is to prevent the ice from floating.

14. Pouring hot water inside the bottle will expand the bottle neck from inside.

15. This is because the two thin blankets joined together will have a layer of air trapped in between them which prevents the body heat to transfer to the surroundings more efficiently and hence will help to keep the body more warm.

18. When a fluid is heated, it expands. Its density decreases and the fluid rises producing convection currents.

21. During summers, iron tracks get heat up by the process of conduction and hence expand. This expansion compensates the gap between the tracks.

22. Radiation process do not require any medium for transmission of heat.

23. Wool is a bad conductor of heat due to which it does not allow heat to transmit to the surroundings.

Water transfers heat by the process of convection.

32.

								H	K	I	N	K
		K	E	L	V	I	N	E			T	
		M			C			A			E	
T	H	E	R	M	O	M	E	T	E	R	M	
		R			N					I	P	
		C			D					N	E	
		U			U					S	R	
		R			C					U	A	
		Y			T					L	T	
					O					A	U	
				B	R	E	E	Z	E	T	R	
C	O	N	V	E	C	T	I	O	N	O	E	
										R		

A) Acids and Bases

1. Oxalic acid is present in spinach (palak). Ascorbic acid is present in amla and citrus fruits.
Tartaric acid is present in unripe grapes and unripe mangoes.

2. Magnesium hydroxide is a mild base which is used as an antacid. Another antacid is baking soda, i.e. sodium hydrogen carbonate. Both are used to cure indigestion. Potassium hydroxide is a strong base and sodium carbonate is washing soda.

3. Soapy touch and bitter taste are the characteristics of bases.

5. Ant or bee sting contains formic (or methanoic acid). Oxalic acid is present in spinach. Amla is a source of ascorbic acid and grapes contain tartaric acid.

6. Antacids are used to neutralise excess acid secreted in the stomach. So, they must be basic. Curd contains lactic acid, so its nature is acidic.

7. Bases are known to turn red litmus paper blue, taste bitter and feel soapy. A common example of a base is washing soda used for washing purposes.

8. (i) acid   (ii) base   (iii) organic   (iv) base

9. Lactic acid is present in milk. So, its source is natural. Carbonic acid (H_2CO_3) is a mineral acid. Other two matches are correct.

10. Only I is correct as all alkalis are bases but only water soluble bases are alkalis. Further, acids may be strong or weak.

Strong and weak both types of acids may be in dilute or concentrated form.

11. Ravi's answer is correct. Lime water, soap solution, slaked lime and ammonia solution all are basic.

13. Fizzing occurs in both the test tubes due to the evolution of H_2 gas, but it is faster in test tube A because HCl is a strong acid and CH_3COOH is a weak acid.

14.
$$2CH_3COOH + MO \longrightarrow (CH_3COO)_2M + H_2O$$
$$M = \text{Metal}$$
$$CH_3COOH + \underset{\text{Baking soda}}{NaHCO_3} \longrightarrow CH_3COONa + CO_2 + H_2O$$
$$CH_3COOH + \underset{\text{(Alkali)}}{NaOH} \longrightarrow CH_3COONa + H_2O$$

17. Inert metals like gold and platinum are soluble in aqua-regia (a mixture of conc. HCl and HNO_3).

18. Acids react with metals to form poisonous salts. That's why, sour substances like lemon are generally not prescribed to store in metallic containers.

19. Dilute acid contains acid in very less amount and water in large quantity.

20. Sulphuric acid may be present in bathroom acid.

21. Sodium hydroxide is soft and slippery to touch, so, X may be sodium hydroxide.

22. This experiment suggests the presence of acidic substances in the juice.

23. Acids as well as bases both are corrosive and their strength is measured in terms of hydrogen ion concentration.

24. All mineral acids except the carbonic acid (H_2CO_3) are strong and all organic acids are weak.

25. 1. Malic acid   2. Lactic acid
    3. Alkali   4. Amino acid
    5. Ammonia   6. Tartaric acid
    7. Citric acid   8. Acetic acid

(B) Indicators (Strength of Acids and Bases)

1. (i) Litmus solution turns blue in alkali.
   (ii) Methyl orange turns red/pink in acidic solution and yellow in basic solution.
   (iii) Phenolphthalein is colourless in acidic solution and pink in basic solution.

2. Sour taste means the solution is acidic and acidic solutions turn blue litmus red but have no effect on red litmus.

3. All the given substances/techniques can be used to test acids/bases.

4. The indicators among the given substances are red cabbage, turmeric, litmus paper and phenolphthalein.

5. Lime water is most basic, so possesses highest pH while soft drink being least basic or most acidic, has the lowest pH.

6. Sugar solution is neutral, so, have no effect on the indicator, juice being acidic turns it in magenta and lime water being basic turns it in green.

7. Sugar solution being neutral has no effect over acidic or basic solutions.
   Washing soda turns red litmus blue but has no effect on blue litmus.
   Rest two matches are correct.

9. The colour of methyl orange indicator is pink in acidic medium and yellow in basic/alkaline medium. So, X is methyl orange.

10. If X is an acid,
    (i) it will turn blue litmus red.
    (ii) shows a pH below 7.
    (iii) release CO_2 with carbonate which turns lime water milky.
    (iv) release hydrogen with metal which burns with 'pop' sound.

11. Turmeric is a natural indicator, colour of which is red in alkaline/basic medium. The nature of soap solution is basic. So, stain turns red.

12. A turns blue litmus red, so it is an acid. B turns red litmus blue, so it is a base.
    Common salt (NaCl) is produced when NaOH (base) reacts with hydrochloric acid (HCl).
    Thus, A = HCl, B = NaOH

13. Window cleaner being basic has no effect on blue litmus paper. Sugar is neutral, so also does not affect the litmus.
    Vinegar turns blue litmus red and baking soda has no effect on blue litmus paper.

14. X is litmus, which is obtained from a plant, called lichen.

15. Because of sulphatic fertilisers, the nature of soil gets acidic, so lime water (basic) is a solution to neutralise it.

16. The colour of methyl orange is yellow in basic medium while of turmeric is red.

17. Solution of common salt is neutral as it is a salt of strong acid and strong base.
    Thus, it has no effect on blue litmus paper, i.e. blue litmus remains blue.

18. Z produces no colour with phenolphthalein, so, it must be an acidic salt like $CuSO_4$. Which is prepared from CuO (basic, i.e. X) and H_2SO_4 (acidic, i.e. Y).

19. Wash the hand with plenty of water which washes away most of the acid and whatever little acid is left is neutralised with the weak base, sodium hydrogen carbonate.

20. The colour of phenol red remains yellow upto pH 7 and afterwards turns to red.

21. Methyl orange shows a colour change at pH 4, so, at pH, its colour is yellow.

22. Phenol red shows colour change at pH 7, so its colour is yellow at pH 6 and red at pH 9.

23. 100 g lime is required to raise the pH of $1\ m^2$ by 1.
    Change in pH = $7.5 - 5.5 = 2$
    $\therefore$ 200 g lime is required to raise the pH of $1\ m^2$ by 2.
    Area of land = $25\ m \times 15\ m = 375\ m^2$
    For raising pH of $1 m^2$ soil, lime required = 200 g
    $\therefore$ For $375\ m^2$ soil, lime required
    $$= 200 \times 375\ g = 375 \times 0.2\ kg = 75\ kg$$

(C) Salts

1. Sodium chloride (common salt) is formed by the reaction between hydrochloric acid (an acid) and sodium hydroxide (a base).
   $$\underset{\substack{\text{Hydrochloric} \\ \text{acid}}}{HCl} + \underset{\substack{\text{Sodium hydroxide} \\ \text{(Base)}}}{NaOH} \longrightarrow \underset{\substack{\text{Sodium chloride} \\ \text{(Salt)}}}{NaCl} + \underset{\text{Water}}{H_2O}$$

2. Mixing of solution of an acid with the solution of base (neutralisation) is exothermic, i.e. temperature increases and salt formation takes place.

3. The reaction between an acid and a base is called neutralisation reaction.

CuO is a base and HNO_3 is an acid.

$PbCO_3$ is a salt and Mg, K, etc., are metals.

4. P = Salt Q = water R = exothermic S = neutral

5. Because $CaCO_3$ and Na_2CO_3 are salts and water is neutral (not an acid).

6. Because base (like baking soda or lime water) neutralises the acidic impurities.

7. A should add quicklime to neutralise excessive fertilisers (mainly sulphatic).

Run off of clothes makes the soil basic, so organic matter is used to neutralise that.

8. Limestone - $CaCO_3$,

Blue vitriol - $CuSO_4 \cdot 5H_2O$.

Washing soda - $Na_2CO_3 \cdot 10H_2O$,

Baking soda - $NaHCO_3$.

9. Aqueous solution of blue vitriol is acidic, so it turns blue litmus red.

10. X is sodium chloride.

11. Ant sting inject formic acid. It reacts with baking soda ($NaHCO_3$) of baking powder in following manner:

$$NaHCO_3 + HCOOH \longrightarrow HCOONa + H_2O + CO_2$$

12. Ammonia is basic, so washing soda, baking soda and lime water resemble with it.

13. Bleaching powder, baking soda and washing soda all have Na which is also present in common salt (NaCl).

Chlorine can be obtained by common salt but other methods are also available.

14. Salt contains two parts : cationic (positively charged, obtained from base) and anionic (negatively charged, obtained from acid). During the formation of salt, energy is released, so temperature of reaction mixture increases (because neutralisation is an exothermic process).

16.

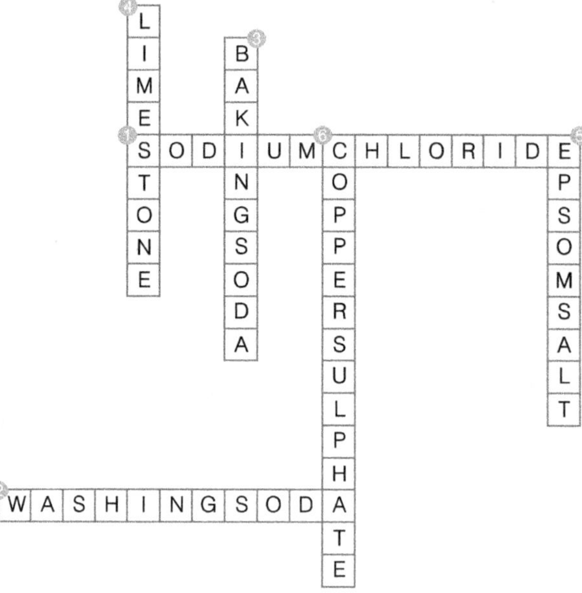

5 Physical and Chemical Changes

A Physical Changes

1. Shape, size and colour all may be change during a physical change but chemical composition remains the same. e.g. conversion of water into ice.

2. Since, melting, boiling and freezing come under the category of physical changes, so P must be expansion and Q must be physical changes.

3. Dissolution and crystallisation both are physical changes and hence, are reversible in nature.

5. Physical changes are reversible in nature. All other given statements are true.

6. Switching on a light bulb and ironing a damp T-shirt do not result in the change in composition, so these are the examples of physical changes.

7. During a physical change, no matter is lost or gained but colour may change.

8. Conversion of water into ice at very low temperature (0°C) is called freezing. Separation of crystals from a solution is called crystallisation.

In case of chemical change, change in composition is necessary.

10. When salt is dissolved in water, no change in composition takes place, i.e. it is a physical change and physical changes are generally temporary (i.e. reversible).

11. Because composition remains the same.

12. By freezing, water gets converted into ice, which is a solid form of water.

In case of solids, force of attraction are more due to which movement of particles decreases.

13. Rusting is not a crystallisation process, it results in the formation of a new substance, so it is a chemical change.

Others are the examples of crystallisation process.

14.

Down		Across	
1.	Melting	2.	Boiling
4.	Evaporation	3.	Sublimation
6.	Freezing	5.	Condensation

B Chemical Changes and Rusting

1. All the given may be observed during a chemical change.

3. P = Chemical, Q = Water, R = Air, S = Faster.

5. When iron turning are heated with sulphur powder, a new substance, called iron sulphide is formed, properties of which are quite different from the original one.

6. A chemical change may be reversible or irreversible but are generally irreversible in nature.

8. A chemical change is a permanent change. It always leads to the formation of new substances. However, it may occur with the evolution or absorption of heat.

Mixing of oil and water does not affect their chemical composition so, it is a physical change.

9. When magnesium is dissolved in hydrochloric acid, magnesium chloride, a new substance is formed.

Similarly, when copper carbonate is heated, it forms black coloured copper oxide, composition of which is quite different from the initial one.

So, these two processes are the examples of chemical change.

10. In physical change also the formed substance may differ from the initial one in shape, size and colour.

11. During cooking, respiration and photosynthesis all, chemical composition of the initial substance change.

13. Paint make the iron gate beautiful and rust free.

14. Burning of coal is a chemical change. Coal burns in air to give carbon dioxide and lot of heat is released during the process, i.e. the process is exothermic.

15. When chemical reactions take place in an electrical cell (electrochemical cell), it results in the generation of electricity.

16. Blue colour is of $CuSO_4$ (blue vitriol) and green is of $FeSO_4$ (green vitriol). The equation can be represented as

$$CuSO_4 + Fe \longrightarrow FeSO_4 + Cu$$

17. Hydrogen burns with 'pop' sound. So, R is hydrogen. Hydrogen is produced when metal (solid) reacts with some acid (liquid).

So, P = zinc and Q = hydrochloric acid.

18. Raining from clouds is a physical process.While others are chemical changes.

19. Plants synthesised their food (i.e. carbohydrates) like glucose ($C_6H_{12}O_6$) from carbon dioxide (CO_2). Because of the change in chemical composition, it is a chemical change. This process is called photosynthesis. A chemical change may be accompanied by evolution of a gas and change in colour, shape or smell.

20. $CO_2 + Ca(OH)_2$ X (Lime water) $\longrightarrow CaCO_3 + H_2O$ 'Y' (Water)

21. Because here the mass of oxygen supplied is less than that of magnesium.

(C) Physical as well as Chemical Changes

2. In I case, the composition of each wooden log remain the same but in II case, it changes, so I is a physical change while II is a chemical change.

3. Saltation increases the rusting, so treatment with salt cannot be used to overcome the problem. Others can be used.

4. The same change may be a physical as well as a chemical change. Further, a reversible change may be a physical change or a chemical change but all the physical changes are reversible.

6. I is a physical change as kerosene converts from its liquid state to vapour state but have the same chemical composition.

II is a chemical change due to the formation of new substances.

7. Crystallisation is a temporary change. Digestion and burning both are chemical changes due to the formation of new substances. Such changes are generally irreversible.

8. Iron being more reactive replaces copper from copper sulphate (blue vitriol) to give iron sulphate, colour of which is green. Reverse reaction is not possible due to less reactivity of copper as compared to iron. So, it is an irreversible chemical change.

Seema observed a reversible change because on cooling, the nail gets its original colour.

9. Dissolution and crystallisation both are physical changes.

6 Respiration in Organisms

1. While heavy exercising or physical activity like running, there is increased demand of energy in our body. Due to lack of oxygen, muscles respire anaerobically to fulfil the demand of energy and form lactic acid.

3. Q fragment of pie chart shows the composition of oxygen (21%).

The other components are P – Nitrogen (70%) R – Other gases (0.17%) and S – CO_2 (0.03%).

4. Respiration is the process of taking in air (oxygen from the environment and using it for releasing energy by oxidation of food, i.e. carbohydrates (glucose). It expel out wastes like carbon dioxide and water.

5. The exchange of gases in the lung take place across the membranes of small balloon-like structures called alveoli(A), attached to the branches of the bronchial passages.

11. Using limewater is the easiest way to test for the presence of carbon dioxide. The exhaled carbon dioxide produces a precipitate of calcium carbonate with limewater and thus, turn milky.

12. The figure labelled as A shows inhalation. It begins with the contraction of the muscles attached to the ribcage. Thus, causing an expansion in the chest cavity.

The figure labelled as B shows exhalation, in which intercoastal muscles between the ribs relax to reduce the space in the chest cavity.

14. The diaphragm is the dome-shaped sheet of muscle that separates the chest from the abdomen. It is also referred to as thoracic diaphragm.

17. Gas exchange between the air within the alveoli and the pulmonary capillaries occurs by diffusion. Thus, B part shows the capillaries.

18. Cutaneous respiration is the form of respiration in which gas exchange occurs across the skin or outer integument of an organism, e.g. earthworm.

Respiration through lungs is called pulmonary respiration, e.g. human.

The respiration that occurs through gills is called branchial respiration, e.g. fishes.

Respiration through trachea is called tracheal respiration, e.g. insects.

25. Anaerobic respiration does not involve oxygen. In this process, some amount of energy is released. Two of its types are:

$$Glucose \longrightarrow Lactic\ acid + Energy \uparrow$$
$$Glucose \longrightarrow Ethanol + CO_2 + Energy \uparrow$$

26. Test tubes A and C have least amount of carbon dioxide that's why it indicates red colour, whereas test tube have greater amount of CO_2 than (a) and (c), so it gives yellow colour. As, insects exchange CO_2 gas in the test tube.

29. The *(A)* trachea of the victim may have been injured.

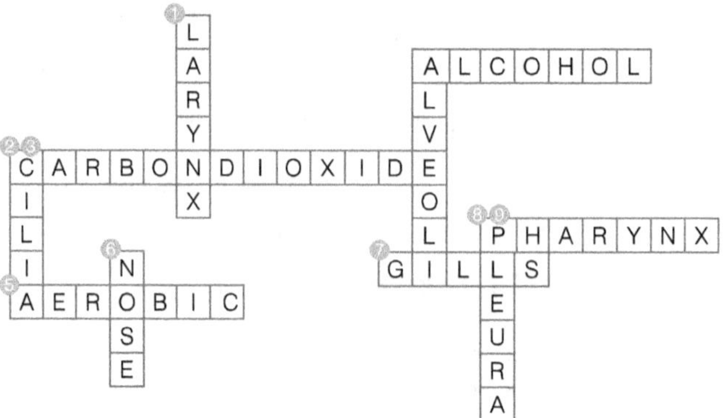

7 Transportation in Plants and Animals

3. The pulmonary artery carries deoxygenated blood from heart to the lungs. So, it has least amount of oxygen. Hence, *P* in pie chart shows the sample taken from the pulmonary artery.

4. Ammonia is produced as a result of catabolism of proteins, especially in aquatic animals. It is highly soluble in water and diffuses rapidly. These animals are ammonotelic, e.g. bony fishes, aquatic invertebrates.

6. Pulmonary vein carries oxygenated blood from the lungs and drain into left atrium of the heart.

   Inferior vena cava is a large vein that receives blood from lower extremities and transfer it to the right atrium of the heart.

   Pulmonary artery carries deoxygenated blood from the heart to lungs.

   Aorta is the main artery in the human body, that originate from the left ventricle of the heart and extends down to the abdomen.

8. Ureter is an important part of human excretory system. It is tube-like structure that passes urine from the kidney to urinary bladder

10. During transpiration plants losses water through stomata. The water moves outwards form of water vapours. Thus, when plant was covered with a glass covering, the vapours of water were seen inside the glass cover. It shows that transpiration is taking place.

11. **P** is aorta. It carries oxygenated blood from left ventricle to all tissues in the body.

    Q is pulmonary artery. It carries deoxygenated blood from the heart to lungs.

R is pulmonary vein. It carries oxygenated blood from the lungs to the left atrium.

S are valves. They separate the chambers of heart so that there is no mixing of blood.

16. **Q** is red blood cell. It is doughnut-shaped red cell with no nucleus.

    R is platelets. It plays a significant role in blood clotting.

    P is a phagocytic cell i.e. a type of white blood cell which can engulf bacteria.

    S shows plasma which is a colourless fluid part of blood.

18. Sphygmomanometer is an instrument clinically used for measuring blood pressure. The normal BP of a human being is 120 (systolic)/80 (diastolic).

25. Ureter is a tube-like structure that carry urine from kidney to urinary bladder.

32.

8 Reproduction in Plants

1. Many algae reproduces asexually by ordinary cell division or by fragmentation. They split into fragments and each fragment develops into mature, fully grown individuals that are clones or exact copy of the parent alga.

2. The eye of potato is like buds found on the margins of leaves of *Bryophyllum.* When they falls on moist soil, each bud can give rise to a new plant. Similarly, on planting the potato in soil, all the eyes (or buds) of potato start growing to produce new potato plants. These are vegetative propagules.

3. Sepals are collectively called as calyx, these forms the outer most whorl of flower.
   Together all the petals of a flower are called corolla. They are the modified leaves that surround the reproductive parts of flower.

6. Option (c) is correct because the flower can perform self pollination, as it has both stigma and anther.

7. The correct order of the processes in the life cycle of a flowering plant is dispersal → germination → pollination → fertilisation.
   (i) When the seeds are ready they begin to disperse, so that they have room to grow.
   (ii) The seed starts to grow into a new plant.
   (iii) Pollen is carried from one flower to another, so that plants can reproduce.
   (iv) Pollen travels down the style into ovary and fertilisation takes place.

8. Moss, fern and fungus, all of them reproduce through spore formation.

10. When the pollen falls onto the stigma in the same flower or a different flower on the same plant, the process is called self-pollination.

17. *P* shows the ovary of the gynoecium of a flower. It develops into fruit.

19. Bracket fungus fungi and bird's nest fern (a fern) reproduce by spores but *Mimosa* is a flowering plant. It reproduces by producing seeds.

23. Mosses like other land plants, are able to reproduce sexually and asexually. They can reproduce by spore formation. Modern moss have the tendency to photosynthesise, i.e. can make its own food.

29. The pollens are light and has a feathery structure to help it float longer in the air. It depends solely on the wind for dispersal. It is not dispersed by water as it does not have a waterproof covering.

   It is not dispersed by animals as it is neither fleshy nor has hooks to stick onto the fur of the animals.

   Lastly it is not dispersed by splitting as it does not have an explosive mechanism.

44. 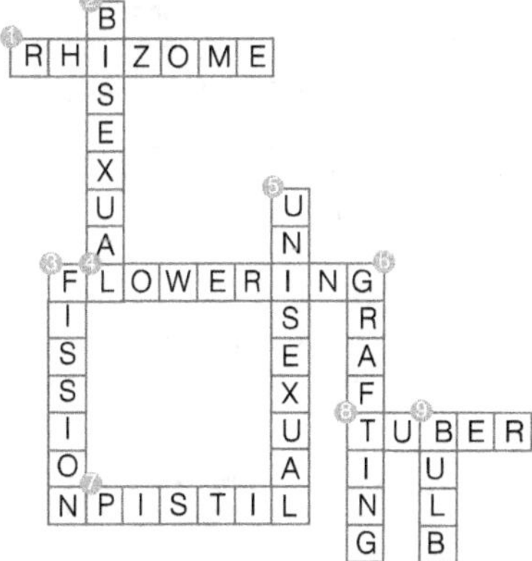

9 Motion and Time

(A) Motion, Its Time and Speed

1. Time taken to reach park $= \dfrac{\text{Distance}}{\text{Speed}} = \dfrac{0.5 \times 60}{2} = 15\,\text{min}$

   Time taken for jogging $= 30\,\text{min}$

   Time taken for back home journey $= \dfrac{0.5 \times 60}{1.5} = 20\,\text{min}$

   Total time taken $= (15 + 30 + 20)\,\text{min} = 65\,\text{min}$

   So, 6:30 pm + 65 min = 7 : 35 pm

2. Length of train = distance travelled by train while crossing Aman.
   $$= \text{Speed} \times \text{time} = 30 \times 3 = 90\,\text{m}$$

3. An object is said to be in motion if it changes its position with respect to its surrounding. An object is at rest is it does not change its position with respect to its surrounding.

4. Average speed $= \dfrac{\text{Total distance travelled}}{\text{Total time taken}}$

   $$= \dfrac{\substack{200 + 100 + 1000 + 50 + 50 \\ + 100 + 1000}}{(5 + 3 + 8 + 2 + 2 + 3 + 8) \times 60} = \dfrac{2500}{1860} = 1.34\,\text{m/s}$$

5. For Ist hour,
   $$t = 1\,\text{h}, s = 10\,\text{km/h}$$
   So, $d = s \times t = 10\,\text{km}$
   For IInd hour,
   $$t = 1\,\text{h}, s = 15\,\text{km/h}$$
   So, $d = s \times t = 15\,\text{km}$
   For IIIrd hour,
   $$t = 1\,\text{h}, s = 20\,\text{km/h}$$
   So, $d = s \times t = 20\,\text{km}$
   Total distance travelled
   $$= 10 + 15 + 20 = 45\,\text{km}$$

8. Distance travelled
   $$= \text{Speed} \times \text{time taken} = 44 \times 15 = 660\,\text{m}$$

10. Number of rotations
    $$= \dfrac{\text{Distance travelled}}{\text{Circumference}} = \dfrac{660}{2 \times \dfrac{22}{7} \times 3.5} = \dfrac{660}{22} = 30$$

11. Speed $= \dfrac{\text{Distance}}{\text{Time}} = \dfrac{800}{15} = 53.33\,\text{ms}^{-1}$

12. Time = 6 am – 5:20 am = 40 min

    Speed = 2 km/min

    Distance = $s \times t$ = 2 × 40 = 80 km

    Odometer reading

       = 234562 km + 80 km = 234642 km

13. I. speed   II. position   III. uniform   IV. ms^{-1}
V. rotational

19. Distance = $2\pi r$ (circumference)

    = 2 × 3.14 × 6371 = 40009.88 km = 40010 km

20. Speed = $\dfrac{\text{Distance}}{\text{Time}} = \dfrac{40010 \text{ km}}{24 \text{ h}}$ = 1667.083 km/h = 1667 km/h

(B) Distance-Time Graph, Time and Simple Pendulum

5. Distance travelled cannot be decreased with the change in time. It can be either increasing or zero. Hence, graph is not possible.

6. Graph I indicates the time is constant and distance is increasing which is not possible. Graph III indicates distance is decreasing with the change in time which is again not possible.

7. Average speed = $\dfrac{\text{Total distance}}{\text{Total time}} = \dfrac{20}{10}$ = 2 ms^{-1}

8. Since, clock A does not have second hand, so it cannot measure time below 1 min.

10. Time period of a pendulum depends upon its length and independent of the weight of bob. More the length of pendulum, higher will be its time period.

12. Time taken to complete one oscillation = $AO + OB + BO + OA$

    = 0.5 + 0.5 + 0.5 + 0.5 = 2 s

    Time taken to complete 10
oscillations = 2 × 10 = 20 s

13. I. speed   II. time-period   III. periodic   IV. time
V. non-uniform

18. Time taken for one oscillation = 2 s

    So, number of oscillations in 10 s = $\dfrac{10}{2}$ = 5

19. Frequency = $\dfrac{1}{\text{Time period}} = \dfrac{1}{2}$ = 0.5 Hz

21. Time taken to complete 20 oscillations

    = 20 × time period = 20 × 2 = 40 s

22.

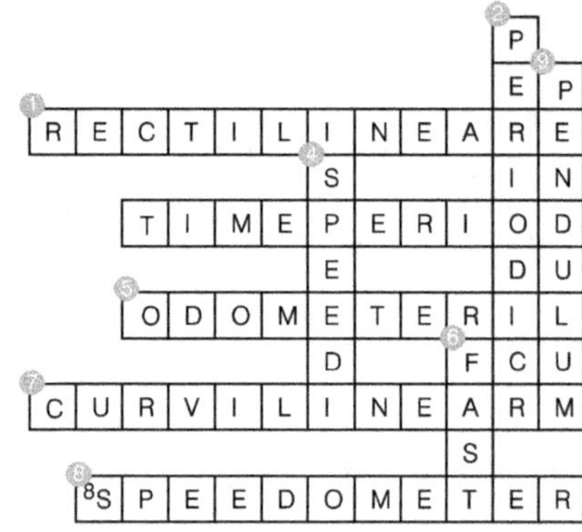

10   Electric Current and Its Effect

(A) Electric Current and Electric Circuit

1. A group of cells is a battery. A cell is represented by

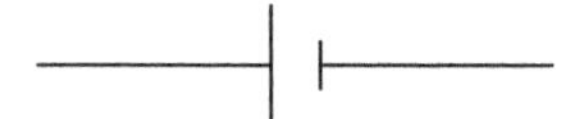

    A battery of two cells is given by

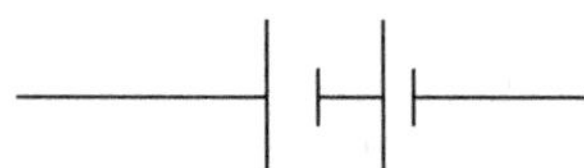

3. Using a variable resistance, box will help to control the brightness of the bulb in an electric circuit.

5. In option (a), the position of key is such that it does not affect the circuit.

6. The brightness of a bulb increases when connected parallel with the circuit. If only S_1 is closed, then the bulb will be in parallel with resistance R. If only S_2 is closed, then also the bulb will remain in parallel with the other resistance R.

7. Current passing through all the three bulbs is same. So, all the bulbs will glow with same brightness and at the same time.

8. Least count = $\dfrac{1}{20}$ = 0.05 mA

    So, the ammeter reading = 5 × 0.05 mA = 0.25 mA

9. An ammeter is always connected in series with the power supply whereas a voltmeter is always connected in parallel to the power supply.

10. Cotton is an insulator whereas all other are conductor of electricity.

11. Since, X is connected in series with the battery so it is an ammeter and is used to measure amount of current passing through the circuit. Also, Y is connected in parallel so, it is a voltmeter and is used to measure the voltage of the bulb.

12. Resistance, $R = \dfrac{V}{I} = \dfrac{Y}{X}$

14. When a switch is in OFF position, then the circuit is incomplete and hence current does not flow into the circuit.

15. (I) charges   (II) circuit   (III) negative   (IV) battery
(V) positive

21. Number of cells = $\dfrac{12}{1.56}$ = 7.6 ≈ 8 cells

23. The positive terminal of one cell should be connected to the negative terminal of the second cell to form a battery.

24. Circuit is incomplete for bulb Y so, it will not glow.

25. Component R is a bulb which consists of tungsten filament.

27. When switch 3 is closed, then circuit will be complete for bulbs P, R and T. Hence, P, R and T will glow.

B. Heating Effects of Electric Current

6. In parallel connection, current is divided and in series connection, current remains same throughout the circuit.

7. A fuse is used to protect the appliances from short circuiting and overloading.

8. For 4 hours, total energy used in kWh is given by

$$24 \times 0.001\,\text{kW} \times 4\,\text{h} = 0.096\,\text{kWh}$$

If cost of electricity = 20 p/unit

Then, total cost $= \dfrac{20}{100} \times 0.096 = ₹\ 0.0192$

12. If resistance increases in a wire, then heat produced in it also increases.

Heating element is made up of nichrome wire and tungsten wire is used in making filament of electric bulb.

14. During overloading or short circuiting, the fuse wire melts away and break the circuit.

15. (I) heat (II) element (III) melt (IV) tungsten (V) CFL

19. Unlike traditional electric bulbs CFL lamps do not have any filament and hence, it reduces loss of electric current in the form of heat.

23. Tungsten is a very ductile element and also it catches fire in presence of air when current is passed through it. Nichrome does not expand and can withstand high temperature. Moreover, it does not catch fire in presence of air when current is passed through it.

24. The higher expansion of X and Y than W and Z, respectively will bend the strips outside and contact will break.

C. Magnetic Effect of Electric Current

4. Iron does not detain magnetism when current is switched off, so it is the most suitable material to use as the core of an electromagnet.

5. Soft iron core is used in an electromagnet because it does not detain magnetism when current is switched off.

8. The north pole of the electromagnet should be towards negative terminal and the south pole of the magnet is towards the positive terminal of the electromagnet.

9. Iron, nickel and steel all are magnetic materials so the substances of container II and IV only can be separated using an electromagnet.

10. Unlike fuses, MCBs are automatic safety switches and need not be replaced. MCB serves the same purpose as fuse.

13. (I) magnetic field (II) electromagnet (III) solenoid (IV) electric bell (V) MCB

16. In an electric bell, electrical energy of supplied electric current is converted into magnetic energy of electromagnet which is further converted into kinetic energy of the gong. This kinetic energy is further converted into sound energy of the bell.

17. An electromagnet is a temporary magnet which remains magnetised only when electric current flows through the coil.

22. An electromagnet is operated only in DC power supply.

23.

1	2													
E	L	E	C	T	R	I	C	C	U	R	R	E	N	T
	C	L					M							
E	L	E	C	T	R	I	C	C	E	L	L			
	O	C		F			B	I						
	S	T		U				R						
	E	R		S				C						
	D	O	P	E	N			U						
		M						I						
		A						T						
		G												
C	O	N	S	T	A	N	T	A	N					
		E												
B	A	T	T	E	R	Y								

11 Light

A. Light, Reflection and Mirror

1. In case of a plane mirror, the object distance is equal to the image distance. So, initially the distance between Geeta and her image is

$$4 + 4 = 8\,\text{m}$$

When she moves 1m away, then her image will also move 1m away.

So, now the distance between her and her image is

$$8 + 1 \times 2 = 10\,\text{m}$$

2. The inner side of a spoon resembles concave mirror while the other side resembles convex mirror. A convex mirror always form virtual and erect images irrespective of the distance of object from the mirror.

5. In plane mirrors, image distance is always equal to the object distance.

So, the distance between object and image will be

$$(0.5 + 0.5)\,\text{m} = 1\,\text{m}$$

6. Images formed by a mirror are always virtual, erect and laterally inverted. In the given case, infinite virtual, erect and laterally inverted images will be formed.

7. Plane mirrors always form virtual, erect and same size images as that of object and convex mirrors always form virtual, erect and diminished images.

8. In case of a plane mirror, the object distance and image distance are always equal. Since, D is very far away from the mirror, so no image can be formed at D.

9. Correct statement of I is, the incident ray, reflected ray and normal ray always lie on the same plane. Correct statement of II is given in III.

11. Angle of incidence

$$= 90° - 50° = 40°$$

According to law of reflection,

Angle of incidence

$$= \text{Angle of reflection}$$

So, angle of reflection = 40°.

12. The light rays reflected from the ball will hit the mirror in the form of incident rays and reflect back to the person's eyes.

13. The image formed by a plane mirror will be virtual, erect and laterally inverted.

14. I. real   II. virtual   III. concave
IV. reflection   V. luminous

16. Laws of reflection are universal laws and are applicable to every object.

17. Convex mirrors are used as rear view mirror in vehicles as they form diminished image with a wide field of view.

20. Since, the mirrors are perpendicular to each other. So,

$$\theta = 90°$$

$$\text{Number of images formed} = \frac{360°}{90°} - 1 = 3$$

21. According to laws of reflection,

Angle of incidence = Angle of reflection

∴ The ray emerges at the same angle, i.e. 30°.

(B) Lens, Types of Lens and Dispersion

3. Splitting of white light into its constituent components is known as dispersion of light.

4. Concave lens always produces virtual, erect and diminished image.

6. The images formed by converging lens of distant objects are always real, inverted and diminished.

7. When light changes its medium, it bends towards the normal if medium is denser and away from the normal if medium is rarer.

9. Refractive index of glass is 1.5, water is 1.33 and air is 1.00.

So, speed of light will be least in glass and highest in air.

10. Since, ray YZ moves away from the normal. It indicates that medium Q is optically rarer than medium P. Hence, speed of light in medium Q will be higher.

13. Box A converges the rays of light incident on it, so the lens must be converging, i.e. convex lens. Box B diverges the rays of light incident on it, so, the lens must be diverging i.e. concave lens.

14. Refraction is the phenomenon of bending of light rays when they change their medium of propagation.

16. For a convex lens to act as a magnifying lens, which means the image should be virtual, erect and magnified, the object should be placed close to the convex lens with a distance less than focal length of the lens.

18. (b) Concave lens always forms virtual, erect and diminished images irrespective of the position of object in front of it.

20. (i) Convex   (ii) Converging   (iii) Dispersion   (iv) Seven
(v) Spectrum

29.

<table>
<tr><td></td><td></td><td>D</td><td>R</td><td>E</td><td>F</td><td>R</td><td>A</td><td>C</td><td>T</td><td>I</td><td>O</td><td>N</td></tr>
<tr><td></td><td></td><td>I</td><td></td><td></td><td></td><td>V</td><td></td><td>L</td><td></td><td></td><td></td><td></td></tr>
<tr><td>R</td><td></td><td>S</td><td></td><td></td><td></td><td>I</td><td></td><td>U</td><td></td><td></td><td></td><td></td></tr>
<tr><td>E</td><td>S</td><td>P</td><td>E</td><td>C</td><td>T</td><td>R</td><td>U</td><td>M</td><td>C</td><td></td><td></td><td></td></tr>
<tr><td>F</td><td></td><td>E</td><td></td><td></td><td></td><td>T</td><td></td><td>I</td><td>O</td><td></td><td></td><td></td></tr>
<tr><td>L</td><td></td><td>R</td><td>E</td><td>A</td><td>L</td><td>U</td><td></td><td>N</td><td>N</td><td></td><td></td><td></td></tr>
<tr><td>E</td><td></td><td>S</td><td></td><td></td><td></td><td>A</td><td></td><td>O</td><td>V</td><td></td><td></td><td></td></tr>
<tr><td>C</td><td>L</td><td>I</td><td>G</td><td>H</td><td>T</td><td>L</td><td></td><td>U</td><td>E</td><td></td><td></td><td></td></tr>
<tr><td>T</td><td>C</td><td>O</td><td>N</td><td>C</td><td>A</td><td>V</td><td>E</td><td>S</td><td>X</td><td></td><td></td><td></td></tr>
<tr><td>I</td><td></td><td>N</td><td></td><td></td><td></td><td></td><td></td><td></td><td></td><td></td><td></td><td></td></tr>
<tr><td>O</td><td></td><td></td><td></td><td></td><td></td><td></td><td></td><td></td><td></td><td></td><td></td><td></td></tr>
<tr><td>N</td><td>O</td><td>N</td><td>L</td><td>U</td><td>M</td><td>I</td><td>N</td><td>O</td><td>U</td><td>S</td><td></td><td></td></tr>
</table>